W9-BXT-802

Federalism and Environmental Policy

American Governance and Public Policy

A SERIES EDITED BY

Barry Rabe and John Tierney

This series examines a broad range of public policy issues and their relationship to all levels of government in the United States. The editors welcome serious scholarly studies and seek to publish books that appeal to both academic and professional audiences. The series showcases studies that illuminate the successes, as well as the problems, of policy formulation and implementation.

Federalism and Environmental Policy: Trust and the Politics of Implementation

Denise Scheberle

GEORGETOWN UNIVERSITY PRESS / WASHINGTON, D.C.

Georgetown University Press, Washington, D.C. 20007
© 1997 by Georgetown University Press. All rights reserved.

10   9   8   7   6   5   4   3   2   1   1997

Library of Congress Cataloging-in-Publication Data

Scheberle, Denise.
    Federalism and environmental policy: trust and the politics of
implementation / Denise Scheberle.
        p.   cm.
    Includes index.
    1. Environmental policy—United States.   2. Federal government—
United States.   3. Environmental protection—United States—Case
studies.   I. Title.
    HC110.A-Z.E5 IN PROCESS
    354.3'28'0973—dc21   97-6086
    ISBN 0-87840-655-7 (cloth)
    ISBN 0-87840-656-5 (pbk.)

To my father

Contents

Contents

Acknowledgments

Many people contributed to the completion of this book, and I am deeply grateful for their assistance. In particular, I would like to recognize the members of the American Political Science Association, without whose grant I would not have been able to conduct my research. I would also like to thank the University of Wisconsin–Green Bay, especially the Research Council members, who also financially supported my research.

I am also indebted to the many hard-working staff members located in the Environmental Protection Agency and Office of Surface Mining, state environmental agencies, and in EPA regional and OSM field offices. Many individuals donated their time to speak with me, or sent materials that allowed me to better understand the implementation of their program. Although many individuals come to mind, I would like to mention a few by name: Rita Bair, in Region 5 EPA, and Kevin McCormack, both of whom helped me immeasurably in understanding the wellhead program; Richard Miller and Bruce Frye from the OSM; Linda Martin and Susan McCannon from the state of Colorado; but most especially, Milton Lammering in Region 8 EPA—who is a storehouse of information, a keen intellect, an all-around supporter of desperate people trying to finish big projects!

My thanks also to Barry Rabe and John Samples who were very supportive of my study. Barry was especially helpful in recommending improvements to the book and encouraging me to go forward with the project. Finally, I appreciate my husband's willingness to forego weekend outings and put up with tense moments while I finished this work.

INTRODUCTION

Implementing Environmental Policies: Do Federal and State Working Relationships Matter?

In the 1990s, a collective light bulb has gone on in many federal agencies. The light bulb illuminates a simple premise: federal–state working relationships in environmental programs are at the heart of policy implementation. This suggests that when relationships between federal and state officials are positive, implementation of environmental programs is facilitated. To put it simply, federal and state officials in an ideal working relationship "pull together." Pulling together means that state and federal personnel involved in the implementation of a program work cooperatively, regarding each other with mutual trust and respect. Open communications and a sense of shared program goals also characterize the experience of "pulling together."

By the same token, poor working relationships among federal and state officials may inhibit progress in environmental programs. In these cases, relationships are "coming apart." State and federal officials may have little or no respect for each other, exhibit frustration, lack a common vision, and not fully trust the actions of officials from the other agency. Working relationships that have come apart contain hidden agendas, little or no effective communication, and, at worst, open hostility. It's easy to see how this kind of a working relationship could hinder the implementation of a public program.

Evidence of the light of understanding that positive intergovernmental relationships are important has taken several forms. At the national level, efforts are underway to understand, redirect, and rethink how federal–state relationships should be constructed. For example, the U.S. Environmental Protection Agency (EPA) established the State/EPA Capacity Steering Committee in 1993 to lead a federal–state dialog on creating and maintaining an environmental "partnership" between state and federal officials. As a result of this effort, EPA Administrator Carol Browner and several state officials signed a Joint Commitment to Reform Oversight and Create a National Environmental Performance

1

Partnership System on May 17, 1995.[1] Additionally, many of the media-specific programs within the EPA, such as the drinking water program, have made improving relationships with state officials a primary goal for the upcoming fiscal year.

Federal–state interactions in environmental programs have also been the focus of the U.S. Congress. At the request of the Committee on Governmental Affairs, the U.S. General Accounting Office (GAO) examined the quality of EPA–state relationships. In its April 1995 report, "EPA and the states: environmental challenges require a better working relationship," the GAO confirmed that working relationships were important and noted opportunities for improvement.[2]

According to the report, the largest obstacle to running environmental programs is the lack of sufficient resources. EPA and state officials agreed that federal funding has not kept pace with new environmental demands on state governments. However, other factors also contributed to less than stellar federal–state working relationships, including inconsistent EPA oversight across EPA regional offices, tendency of the EPA staff to micromanage state programs, lack of involvement of state staff in major EPA decisions affecting state programs, and the need for EPA to provide more technical support for increasingly complex environmental program requirements.[3]

A 1995 report by the National Academy of Public Administration suggested that a key part of a new direction for the EPA and for sustained progress in protecting the environment rests with the ability of the EPA and of Congress to hand more responsibility and decision-making authority to the states. According to the academy, "A new partnership needs to be formed, one based on 'accountable devolution' of national programs and on a reduction in EPA oversight when it is not needed."[4]

In a related effort, the Clinton Administration has indicated its commitment to reforming the federal bureaucracy to make it less top-heavy, more decentralized, and more committed to serving "customer" interests. President Clinton released the first report of the National Performance Review headed by Vice President Al Gore on September 7, 1993. Among the 384 major recommendations for improving performance were many recommendations for enhancing intergovernmental relationships and building federal–state partnerships.[5]

The administration's desire to enhance the cooperative nature of federal–state relationships in environmental programs is reflected in its recommendations for changing the focus of the EPA.[6] Central to the administration's strategy for the EPA is the need to "partner" with state, local, and tribal governments. To this end, the administration has asked the EPA to "vigorously pursue" Performance Partnership

Grants, which allow states increased flexibility in using environmental grant monies; consensus-based rule making that enlists the early participation of state and local governments in developing regulations; and a 25 percent reduction in paperwork, including reporting requirements for states.[7] The State/EPA Capacity Steering Committee, formed in 1993 to review federal oversight and improve the federal/state partnership in environmental programs, released the National Environmental Performance Partnership System plan in 1995. This plan works in tandem with Performance Partnership Grants by changing the way states are evaluated, increasing the use of environmental goals and indicators, and allowing states more input into the way oversight is conducted. States may opt into the National Environmental Performance Partnership System as early as 1997.[8] These actions illustrate the administration's desire to shift away from command–control orientations toward states and move toward more cooperative, "pulling together" approaches.

Even the Science Advisory Board (SAB), an independent group of scientists, engineers, and other professionals who most often provide technical advice to the EPA, recognizes the importance of agencies in enabling state and national governments to pull together. The SAB believes that EPA must "expand its current capabilities and look beyond near-term problems to long-term environmental protection."[9] However, the enormity of future environmental challenges suggests that the EPA cannot address them alone and, therefore, that intergovernmental cooperative efforts will be "even more important" in the future.[10]

Other federal agencies charged with implementing environmental programs have not ignored the charge to improve working relationships. The Office of Surface Mining Reclamation and Enforcement (OSM) is a case in point. In his testimony before Congress, Robert Uram, Director of the OSM, stated, ". . . the key to improving this program lies in building a positive working relationship among all who are interested in the national surface mining program. Over the last 18 months, everything we've done has been devoted to building that positive relationship [with primacy States and the Tribes]."[11]

While the idea of cooperative federal–state relationships is not new (after all, cooperative federalism as a way of running government has been around since the Great Depression), it appears that, at least for environmental programs, the dialog of intergovernmental cooperation, devolution of responsibility to state governments, and federal–state partnerships is underway in nearly every arena: the administration, executive agencies, Congress, state and local governmental associations, and various research institutions. Given that most environmental programs have been around for twenty years or more, why the recent crescendo of concern about federal–state relationships in environmental policy?

Perhaps one reason is that few policy areas place greater and more diverse demands on states than environmental programs. State governments are increasingly pressed to do more—from preserving wetlands to addressing non point-source water pollution, manning vehicle inspection programs, controlling pesticide applications, supplying safe drinking water to communities, controlling hazardous waste, encouraging recycling, and even testing schools and homes for radon.

Since 1970, which marks the beginning of the first significant involvement of the national government in environmental protection, Congress has designed most federal environmental programs so that they could be administered at the state and local levels. Congressional intent was to capitalize on the strengths of each governmental level: state and local governments would be the front-line delivery agents of environmental programs. Federal agencies, in turn, would set strong health- or technology-based environmental standards and monitor state performance within environmental programs.

Since then, cooperative agreements between state and federal governments have been established under the Clean Water Act, the Clean Air Act, the Resource Conservation and Recovery Act, and many other environmental laws. Legal relationships between state and federal agencies range from delegated relationships, where states are authorized to run an environmental program once their programs are approved by the federal agency, to cooperative agreements, whereby the federal government provides grants to support state nonregulatory environmental programs. Moreover, the tendency to rely on intergovernmental relationships to solve environmental problems is increasing, as environmental problems become more varied and more localized.

The recent national impetus for environmental action on the part of the state and local governments has sometimes occurred without sufficient (or any) funding. For example, the congressional call for states to protect ground water by protecting wellhead areas, part of the 1986 amendments to the Safe Drinking Water Act, authorized $35 million in federal funds to support state programs, but appropriated nothing. States were left to seek their own funding, or to pull funding from monies appropriated from the Clean Water Act. The combination of continuing demands on state governments coupled with unfunded or underfunded environmental mandates has put state and local governments in an implementation bind.

The Unfunded Mandates Reform Act, signed by President Clinton on March 22, 1995, signals that politicians recognize the concern of subnational governments about increasing national mandates, not only for environmental protection but also in other policy areas.[12] While some analysts believe that this may diminish the pace of national demands on state governments, it is not clear that this law will do much (if anything) to help the current situation of limited federal funding.[13] So, into the next century at least, state and local governments will continue to implement many environmental programs with limited or inadequate resources.

Also, federal environmental programs are increasingly challenged by state and local governments as unwarranted intrusions on what state and local officials view as the legitimate purview of subnational governments. The zeal to address environmental concerns from the national level may be viewed by state and local governments as "micromanaging" their programs, especially when those programs have long histories of what state officials view to be compliance with federal demands. Moreover, as citizens become more informed about environmental issues, they demand more environmental protection. Thus, state governments may feel squeezed from above and below with increasing requirements in national environmental programs and increasing pressure from citizens to ensure safe living and working environments.

Over the past two decades, state agencies have grown into their role as stewards of the environment. Many scholars have observed that states have enhanced their capacity to deal with environmental problems by enlarging staff, increasing the expertise and technical understanding of state-level implementors, and, for many states, adding state sources of funding.[14]

Finally, the increased focus on intergovernmental relationships coincides with reassessments of future directions for environmental protection. Many students of environmental policy agree that the third and fourth generation of environmental efforts will require new approaches if America wants to protect its ecosystems. Most notably, these new approaches include increased reliance on grassroots participation and less reliance on command–control regulation—or what DeWitt John refers to as "civic environmentalism."[15] Civic environmentalism is necessary because the unfinished business of environmental protection (restoration of ecosystem health, combatting non-point-source pollution, prompting individual behavioral change) requires the use of new tools and techniques. According to John, "The central idea animating civic environmentalism is that in some cases, communities and states will organize on their own to protect the environment, without being forced to do so by the federal government. . . . Civic environmentalism is fundamentally a bottom-up approach to environmental protection."[16]

In its 1996 report, the President's Council on Sustainable Development pointed to the need for sustainable communities and the involvement of citizens in environmental protection.[17] Sustainable communities are only possible when citizens make environmentally sensitive choices about land-use controls, protection of biodiversity, watershed management, and other important actions in the province of state or local control. Citizen actions, thus, are preventative in nature and value the natural resource in a way that cannot be accomplished by the federal government.

Given this kind of policy evolution, it is not surprising to witness increased concern about the nature and quality of intergovernmental relationships and the connection of those relationships to effective environmental protection programs. These programs are costly and proliferating; states are gaining expertise while at the same time experiencing increasing demands for environmental improvements from their citizens. Meanwhile, federal policy makers and officials within federal agencies recognize that all is not well in the implementation phases of many environmental efforts.

Since nearly everyone agrees that the web of federal–state interactions within environmental policy areas is becoming more complex, it is important to understand how well state and federal actors work together. Since the environmental decade of 1970, have federal–state relationships improved? Have they gotten worse? Were they ever bad? Most importantly, what facilitates cooperative relationships within programs that mandate certain levels of state performance?

Clearly, no "one size fits all" model exists that could be used for arranging (or rearranging) federal–state working relationships in environmental programs. To create a model with such an assumption would be akin to predicting the stock market—certainly tempting, but not likely to be foolproof. What is possible is to look at working relationships from the perspective of individuals in environmental programs and create a list of common observations of state and federal officials.

That is just what this book hopes to do—look at federal and state working relationships in five environmental programs in order to explore the interaction between those relationships and the implementation of policy. The first chapter is principally devoted to describing what implementation is all about, so that the reader knows that many other factors affect how (and if) a program succeeds. A conceptual framework for implementation is presented that provides an array of variables, of which intergovernmental relationships is one. Similarly, a typology of working relationships is offered as a starting point for reviewing existing federal–state relations.

Chapters Two, Three, and Four explore the implementation of five environmental programs and present the perceptions that state officials have about working relationships with their federal counterparts. Each of these chapters ends with a summary of what hinders or helps these programs to achieve desired policy goals. Chapter Five focuses on the role of the federal regional staff in environmental programs. This focus is important for at least two reasons. First, federal regional officials are the most frequent contacts of state officials in environmental programs. Second, these regional officers have unique perspectives for improving working relationships and policy implementation that is too often neglected. The last chapter offers some conclusions about environmental policy implementation and the nature of federal–state working relationships as seen in several environmental programs.

The astute reader may challenge the connection between effective programs and good intergovernmental working relationships, arguing that environmental laws were passed because state governments were reluctant to get into the business of environmental protection. Thus, without the strong arm of the federal government, America's environmental programs would not be as far along as they are today. Moreover, it could be argued that a continued federal presence, one that closely monitors the actions of state officials, is the only guarantee that environmental programs will be implemented. In other words, the danger in going too far down the road of harmonious federal–state interaction is that nothing will be accomplished. Regulatory provisions will fall by the wayside as federal officials try to provide maximum flexibility and autonomy to state implementors.

Clearly, the federal architecture of environmental laws reflects this concern. For example, federal overseers can reassume control of state programs if the state fails to live up to its end of the bargain. The Surface Mining Control and Reclamation Act is a case in point. The federal government has reassumed control over the operation of the surface mining program in two states. Under the Clean Air Act, the EPA is required to write a federal implementation plan for a state if the state fails to write an implementation plan that demonstrates reasonable progress toward reaching and maintaining national ambient air quality standards. Many environmental laws are dually enforceable by state and federal personnel, so that recalcitrant state inspectors or enforcement staff can be reminded of their obligations under the law. In short, Congress designed most environmental laws to recognize the need for the ultimate authority to rest with the national government.

As interesting as such a debate over which government should be in the driver's seat would be, it is not the focus of this book. This book is not about changing the line of command or dismantling the current arrangement of environmental laws. It takes as a given that, in the words of former EPA Administrator William Ruckelshaus, environmental programs need the "federal gorilla in the closet."[18]

Rather, it presents a simple story of how we might do better in implementing the current array of environmental programs. It assumes that intergovernmental implementation of environmental programs represents a philosophy of governance that is not likely to disappear. Finally, the study takes as a given that state and federal agency staff (not always the politicians, but the people with on-the-ground implementation responsibilities) have a common desire: to protect human health and the environment.

NOTES TO INTRODUCTION

1. U.S. Environmental Protection Agency, State/EPA Capacity Steering Committee, *Joint Commitment to Reform Oversight and Create a National Environmental Performance Partnership System* (Agreement signed May 17, 1995).

2. U.S. General Accounting Office, *EPA and the States: Environmental Challenges Require a Better Working Relationship* GAO/RCED-95-64 (Washington, D.C.: U.S. General Accounting Office, April 1995).

3. U.S. General Accounting Office, *EPA and the States: Environmental Challenges Require a Better Working Relationship*, p. 3.

4. National Academy of Public Administration, *Setting Priorities, Getting Results: A New Direction for the Environmental Protection Agency*, Report to Congress (Washington, D.C.: National Academy of Public Administration, April 1995), p. 2.

5. National Performance Review, *From Red Tape to Results: Creating a Government that Works Better and Costs Less* (Government Printing Office, 1993).

6. President Clinton, Vice President Al Gore, *Reinventing Environmental Regulation*, Report released on March 16, 1995.

7. President Clinton, *Reinventing Environmental Regulation*, pp. 10–11.

8. U.S. Environmental Protection Agency, "Joint Commitment to Reform Oversight and Create a National Environmental Performance Partnership System," policy statement released on May 17, 1995. The components of the system, as well as the rationale for its creation, can be found on-line through the EPA home page (www.epa.gov/docs/oversight/oversite.html).

9. U.S. Environmental Protection Agency, Science Advisory Board, *Beyond the Horizon: Using Foresight to Protect the Environmental Future*, EPA-SAB-EC-95-007, (Washington D.C.: U.S. EPA, January 1995), p. 18.

10. Science Advisory Board, *Beyond the Horizon*, p. 18.

11. Testimony of Robert J. Uram, Director of the Office of Surface Mining Reclamation and Enforcement, U.S. Department of the Interior, Before the Subcommittee on Energy and Mineral Resources, Committee on Resources, U.S. House of Representatives, June 27, 1995.

12. The law commissions the Advisory Commission on Intergovernmental Relations (ACIR) to review all existing mandates and evaluate whether or not they should continue. Additionally, the law requires the Congressional Budget Office to determine if a bill imposes a mandate on state and local governments costing $50 million or more annually. If such a determination is made, Congress would be forced to take a separate, majority vote to impose the mandate.

13. For concerns about the ability of the new law to halt environmental mandates from the perspective of local governments, see John Novinson, "Unfunded Mandates: A Closed Chapter?" *Public Management*, 77, no. 7 (July 1995):16–20.

14. For a discussion of state environmental programs, see James P. Lester, "A New Federalism? Environmental Policy in the States," in *Environmental Policy in the 1990s*, ed. Norman J. Vig and Michael E. Kraft (Washington, D.C.: Congressional Quarterly Press, 1990), p. 59–80.

15. DeWitt John, *Civic Environmentalism: Alternatives to Regulation in States and Communities* (Washington, D.C.: Congressional Quarterly Press, 1994).

16. John, *Civic Environmentalism*, p. 7.

17. The President's Council on Sustainable Development, *Sustainable America: A New Consensus for Prosperity, Opportunity and a Healthy Environment for the Future* (Washington, D.C.: U.S. Government Printing Office, February, 1996).

18. Quoted in John, *Civic Environmentalism*, p. 5.

1

Policy Implementation and Working Relationships: Strategies and Stories

INTRODUCTION

Suppose you were told to go from Maine to California in seven days and were offered a road atlas and a credit card. Suppose further that three other people would accompany you on the trip and share responsibility for a safe arrival. If fifty people were given this scenario, some would choose to rent a car; some would go by bus; others by train; some would fly. Even if the choices were further restricted—to require travel by car, for example—it is likely that not all fifty people would choose the same route, stay at the same motels, rent the same type of car, or arrive in California at the same time.

With this scenario, it's easy to see how each new decision (mode of travel, route of travel, places to stay, etc.) results in a different experience. (Did you stop at Yellowstone? the Grand Canyon? your mom's place?) These collective experiences define the trip. Every time someone makes a choice the story of the trip changes, and each trip, therefore, is unique.

The trip to California can be likened to the implementation of intergovernmental public policy. Congress decides through legislative fiat that a trip must be made (or a policy must be put into action). Congress, then, may define the parameters of the trip narrowly (in this case, requiring that a car be used) or more broadly (just get to California). Similarly, Congress may impose additional constraints such as the amount of fiscal resources available or the time allotted to achieve implementation results. Additional constraints outside the control of the implementors also affect implementation. Making the trip in June instead of January, for example, would most likely result in easier and faster travel.

The analogy also helps to explain why it is so hard to fully understand intergovernmental implementation. Congress cannot control every decision to be made in implementing a public program any more than someone might predict all of the ways in which this trip could be taken. Every policy contains the ability of implementors to make choices, and these choices are made by different people in any number of federal or state agencies. Moreover, this scenario also reinforces the importance of understanding what is happening to people who must undertake implementation responsibilities—because their willingness and ability to take on new activities affects the likelihood of policy success.

Now imagine that you have rented a car and the four of you have begun your journey. How do you decide who drives? How long do you travel each day? How many road stops do you make? What if you like listening to country music with the windows open, but the other travelers like rock and roll and air conditioning? How you handle the decisions inside the car will certainly affect your perception and enjoyment of the trip. In short, the quality of the trip is affected by the interaction of the travelers as much as by the choice of the vehicle, the route, or places to stay.

Envisioning what occurs inside a car during an extended road trip is one way of picturing how federal–state working relationships evolve. Certainly, the experience is prone to contention and conflict as the days get longer and the temperature (and tempers) inside the car get hotter. However, there is also the possibility that the trip will be pleasant and that by sharing driving responsibilities you'll arrive at your destination safely and in record time.

The point is that both the nature of the trip itself (choice of car, route, lodging, etc.)—representing implementation—and the interaction of the travelers inside the car (cooperative, contentious, or somewhere in-between)—representing working relationships—bring important insights to bear on the overall understanding of the implementation of any public policy. To ignore one or the other element is to potentially fail to get the whole implementation story.

This book examines five environmental programs in order to better understand two things: factors which facilitate or hinder progress in implementing environmental policy, and the nature of federal–state working relationships in environmental programs as perceived by federal and state officials involved in those programs. The premise of this book, just like the analogy of the road trip, is that implementation is a complex process and that working relationships make a difference in how implementation unfolds. Indeed, positive intergovernmental relationships can be central to effective policy implementation.

That is not to ignore the importance of very basic elements needed to implement public policy, including such things as adequate resources, necessary staff to support implementation, and sufficient authority to get things done. However, if good federal–state working relationships can facilitate policy implementation, then a deeper exploration into federal–state communication patterns, oversight postures, and the perceptions that state and federal officials have about their programs is also needed. This book seeks to do just that by examining a range of environmental programs through a conceptual framework of intergovernmental environmental policy implementation while also utilizing a typology of working relationships. When working relationships are included as part of the study of policy implementation, a clearer understanding of daily operation of various environmental programs is possible.

The chapter begins by discussing the concept of federalism and how other people have viewed intergovernmental relationships. A typology is then developed as a way of looking at federal–state working relationships. The third section develops the context of policy implementation, by reviewing some existing theories of policy implementation and then synthesizing key implementation elements into a new conceptual framework. The chapter concludes with a brief description of the study design and arrangement of the book.

CONCEPTS OF FEDERALISM AND WORKING RELATIONSHIPS

Federalism scholars have long recognized the need for collaborative approaches between federal and state officials in solving public problems.[1] The term "marble-cake federalism" was popularized by Morton Grodzins, who suggested that public responsibilities could not be precisely defined, but were shared by federal, state, and local officials. This functional sharing promoted patterns of cooperative and collaborative behavior.[2] Terry Sanford used a metaphor of a rowboat to describe the interdependency of federal, state, and local officials: "The governments are all in the same boat, tossed by the same waves and dependent upon each other's paddles. When any one fails to row, they all move more slowly, and the waves become more dangerous for all."[3]

Indeed, the proliferation of federal grants-in-aid beginning in the Great Depression and finding full flower in the Great Society programs of the Johnson Administration in the 1960s has compelled national and state governmental actors to work cooperatively to solve public problems.[4] Many laws passed by Congress rely on subnational governments (state and local governments) for implementation in exchange for federal assistance.

Federal–state relationships remain cooperative because joint efforts to implement programs may produce more satisfying results than any one level acting alone. Partnerships between governmental entities, then, provide reasonable solutions to achieving policy goals. Federal fiscal incentives act as the cement by which these relationships persist.

Certainly, this philosophy of federal–state collaboration resounds in the halls of the federal environmental and natural resource agencies in this study. In 1995 the EPA produced its interim guidance for "Performance Partnership Grants" for state and tribal governments, designed to create consolidated grants for state environmental programs.[5] As these grants are phased into environmental activities beginning in 1997, the EPA is prepared to offer states the option of combining program grants on a scale never before possible, all with the goal of increasing the federal–state "partnership."

Indeed, the language of partnership appears frequently on EPA documents and permeates its activities. As mentioned in the Introduction, working with state officials, the agency established a "national environmental performance partnership system" in 1995, with a goal to come to mutually agreed upon performance requirements and duties for state and federal partners in environmental programs.[6] The words "partnership" and "partner" appear often in EPA documents that describe customer satisfaction, where state governments are identified as EPA customers. As wryly put by one EPA official, "We're doing so much partnering these days, I don't know if I'm running an environmental program or going to a dance."

Formal Federal–State Arrangements

Most often when state and federal officials become partners, they do it within the context of a legal relationship. At least three types of federal–state legal relationships exist in environmental laws. First, when national laws preempt existing state activities, programmatic authority can be delegated back to state governments under a partial-preemption approach. States can choose to operate an environmental program, such as under the Surface Mining Control and Reclamation Act, and apply for delegated authority. (See Chapter Four for a larger discussion of this approach.) The federal oversight agency (in this case, the Office of Surface Mining) returns regulatory control to the state, but only after the state adopts enforcement programs that meet national standards. At this point, the state is said to have primacy, because it has the primary responsibility for operating the program. If subsequently a state fails to meet its enforcement obligations under the law, the federal oversight agency can reassume control of the program.

A second and less frequent way that states become involved in environmental laws is through a direct statutory order. In this case, congressional architects of environmental laws oblige the states to perform certain tasks. For example, Congress mandated that states implement wellhead protection programs under the Safe Drinking Water Act Amendments of 1986. Absent state activity, the federal agency would not assume responsibility for implementation. States can opt not to comply, but may face sanctions in other programs. Also, with no federal assumption of programmatic responsibilities (such as is provided for under the partial-preemption approach), states which ignore the mandate may be compelled under court order to perform their duties.

A third approach to federal–state interaction in environmental programs is to establish principally voluntary relationships and rely on grant monies as incentives for state participation. The Indoor Radon Abatement Act of 1988, for example, provided matching funds for states to conduct residential radon surveys. As is typical of this approach, federal grant awards are matched against state funds. As state programs get underway, the federal match may decrease in future grant years. Under the radon program, states had a 75 percent federal allotment the first year, a 60 percent match the second year, and a 50 percent match in subsequent grant years.[7]

Often one law contains multiple approaches. The direct order for states to create wellhead protection programs, for example, is part of a larger law that operates under a partial-preemption scheme, the Safe Drinking Water Act. Most importantly, many environmental programs provide some level of federal funding in order to facilitate state implementation.

These statutory relationships define one level of federal–state interaction. Equally important, however, are the ongoing working relationships that occur between federal and state officials. These working relationships include informal and formal contact that occurs between state and federal personnel in the operation of any intergovernmental program. To return to Sanford's rowboat metaphor, federal and state actors may be in the boat together, but they certainly may not agree about which direction to head.

The Complexity of Intergovernmental Interaction

Scholars have been exploring the nature of working relationships among federal and state officials for over twenty years. Martha Derthick was among the first scholars to identify the difficulties associated with getting new policies off the ground, especially those that relied on many levels of government.[8] Noting the "great difficulty of organizing cooperative activity on a large scale," she suggested that national implementation hopes were pinned to limited federal incentives offered to local implementors. In turn, local officials tried to manipulate federal incentives in their best interests. Thus, bargaining among intergovernmental actors is an inevitable part of the implementation process.[9]

Pressman and Wildavsky also described the "complexity of joint action" in intergovernmental implementation.[10] They identify multiple clearance points and interdependencies among implementation actors as potential obstacles to policy success. Their work offered an early suggestion that state actors don't march lockstep to the tune of the national government. Rather, national programs will be reshaped or even undermined by state or local officials. Eleven years later, Elazar agreed, ". . . only in rare situations have federal grant programs served to alter state administrative patterns in ways that did not coincide with already established state policies."[11]

Several scholars have looked specifically at environmental programs. William Lowry (1992) concluded that interstate competition for industry serves to dampen state enthusiasm for strong regulatory enforcement, while Evan Ringquist (1993) reviewed state air regulatory programs and found that strong federal regulatory requirements on states, coupled with adequate resources and enforcement, result in improvements in air quality.[12] David Hedge et al. (1990) suggest that the state political and economic milieu, as well as the orientation of state officials toward policy goals, play important roles in explaining implementation patterns and working relationships.[13] James Lester et al. (1983) argue that federal funding is essential to creating and maintaining effective state programs.[14]

A central thesis of these studies of comparative state environmental programs is the continued need for strong federal oversight and funding. Without the presence of the federal government, states' willingness to operate with environmental programs varies dramatically.

Role orientations of federal actors can also affect working relationships and implementation patterns. Much has been written about how vigorously federal overseers should "lean" on their state counterparts in order to secure compliance with federal goals. Gormley (1992) conceptualizes a range of possible approaches that federal implementation actors may choose to adopt when working with state officials.[15] Federal officials who employ "catalytic" controls in oversight encourage state agencies to resolve policy concerns and allow states considerable discretion. Hortatory controls, a middle-of-the-road approach, rely on political and other incentives to generate state compliance. In contrast, coercive controls leave state agencies virtually no room to maneuver as they respond to federal programmatic requirements. In this case, federal overseers adopt a strict "going-by-the-book" enforcement response toward state implementing agencies. In his study of working relationships between the U.S. Department of Agriculture and three southern states, Gormley concluded that the use of coercive controls was the least effective approach for federal officials to take in order to achieve policy results.

Federal approaches to intergovernmental policy implementation are also conditioned by the specific nature of the policy area. Programs with highly detailed, domain-specific knowledge may prompt the development of vertical working relationships that cut across governmental levels. This "picket fence" federalism, whereby state and federal actors share similar expertise and agreement on the nature of the policy issues and viable solutions, should foster collaborative problem solving.[16] If one takes the "picket fence" concept a bit further, it is quite possible that federal and state implementors may band together to shore up support for underfunded or unrecognized programs, especially when their program must compete with other activities for funding and staffing. In this situation, cooperative working relationships are enhanced even further by the desire of both sides of the relationship to maintain a viable program.

In sum, federalism is not only a constitutional principle—it strikes at the very core of policy implementation. Formal federal–state arrangements (such as granting a state primacy or providing federal funding for a state program through a cooperative agreement) represent one level of federal–state interactions. Regular interactions between federal and state personnel form the grist of federal–state working relationships. Failing to appreciate the complexities of federal–state working relationships is to miss an important element of implementation. Moreover, the potential range of relationships moves from confrontational (if federal implementors adopt unyielding role orientations toward their state counterparts) to strategic (when federal and state implementors come together to preserve a program).

A TYPOLOGY OF WORKING RELATIONSHIPS

Given that the nature of working relationships is important, is it possible to predict when working relationships are more likely to be positive among individuals responsible for making a program run? While many scholars have developed models of federalism (the marble cake, the rowboat, the picket fence, to name a few), few have looked specifically at the patterns of behavior that exist between federal and state officials within a particular program. Similarly, few models of implementation offer predictions about the factors that facilitate working relationships that "pull together," and most studies underemphasize the contribution that working relationships make to implementation performance. This section seeks to rectify these omissions by developing a typology of working relationships.

At the risk of oversimplifying the complexity of federal–state interactions, two characteristics of working relationships seem most critical to predicting whether or not federal and state officials will respond positively to each other. The first element essential to relationships is that of mutual trust. Individuals within a working relationship may vary in their belief that other participants are dedicated to effectively implementing the policy. High levels of trust are evident within a relationship when actors share goals, respect the actions of other actors, allow flexibility, and show support for individuals within the program. Accordingly, the typology illustrates two levels of trust among implementation actors, as shown on the left side of the typology. The typology suggests that federal staff members with implementation responsibilities may have either low or high levels of trust in the abilities, commitment and dedication of their state staff counterparts. Similarly, state officials with implementation responsibilities may have either low or high levels of trust in their federal counterparts regarding the same qualities. The result is either high or low levels of mutual trust.

A second element of working relationships is the extent of involvement by oversight personnel. The typology suggests that participants in different organizations (in this case, federal and state agencies) may have low or high levels of involvement in the program. Involvement may include formal or informal communication between federal and state staff, frequency and nature of oversight activities, provision of funding, sharing of resources, and personal and other contacts among actors.

Involvement, then, incorporates a wide range of possible interactions between federal and state officials. However, while trust is normative (more of it is better), involvement does not carry that connotation. In other words, high involvement among participants may not necessarily lead to positive working relationships. Federal staff involvement that is perceived by state officials to be nitpicking state programs or micromanaging state activities, for example, may be counterproductive to establishing the kind of working relationship that will facilitate implementation.

With the two characteristics of working relationships—trust and involvement—as the dimensions of the typology, four kinds of relationships are possible. What is life like for the actors in each cell in the typology? The next paragraphs provide some brief descriptions of the kinds of relationships that result when these two characteristics are considered.

Pulling Together: High Trust and High Involvement

When high levels of trust are coupled with high levels of involvement (shown in the upper right-hand corner of Figure 1-1), the strongest kind of working relationship results. The participants in the relationship are "pulling together" and the result is synergistic: the accomplishments of pulling together are greater than the sum of what each participant could do alone. Clearly, this is the cell of choice both for participants in the program and for observers of federal–state relationships.

Federal overseers recognize the abilities, the expertise, and the dedication of state agency staff. In turn, state staff accord the same

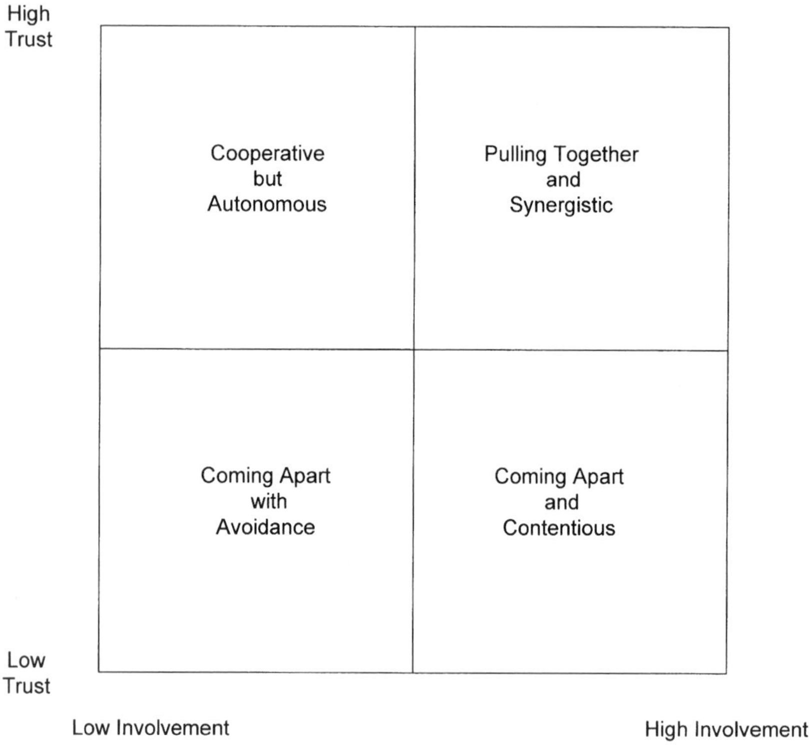

High
Trust

Cooperative but Autonomous	Pulling Together and Synergistic
Coming Apart with Avoidance	Coming Apart and Contentious

Low
Trust

Low Involvement			High Involvement

Figure 1-1 A Typology of Federal and State Working Relationships

level of respect to their federal counterparts. Moreover, federal agency officials exhibit concern about the success of the state implementation efforts—not because that's their job, but because they have a genuine desire to see state staff accomplish good things. The nature of the involvement, then, becomes one of assistance, with ample doses of technical assistance, consultation, and even logistical support, if possible, for on-the-ground implementation.

Skeptics may argue that high-trust, high-involvement relationships are nearly impossible to achieve and that seldom do federal and state officials "pull together." Indeed, the federal oversight role works against establishing high levels of trust, while the desire of state officials to act autonomously works against high levels of federal involvement. What is important is involvement based on a shared commitment to the policy objectives and a common recognition of the nature of the public problem to be solved. Interactions where knowledge is shared, advice and input is sought, and knee-jerk reactions to participant behaviors are avoided while positive activities are acknowledged, move federal and state participants toward the right kind of involvement and increased levels of trust.

On the other hand, some people may argue that, after all, cooperative federalism suggests that federal–state relationships are usually harmonious. Functional expertise among the participants suggests that federal, state, and local personnel within programs work very cooperatively together because maintaining bureaucratic control over public programs is the paramount value. When political actors threaten programs, state and federal actors quickly circle the wagons to protect their programmatic turf.

Assuming that state and federal bureaucrats naturally work together in harmony because of their shared interest in the program is to ignore the stronger elements of federal–state relationships and the distinct roles that federal staff and state staff play in policy implementation. For example, federal agency staff oversee the actions of state officials and promulgate national regulations, grant guidance documents, and state performance agreements; in turn, state officials run the inspection and enforcement programs, respond to public concerns and complaints, and promulgate state regulations and program requirements. Meanwhile, each actor has to please a different set of constituents and stakeholders. Bliss within federal–state relationships is unlikely, given these constraints and the different federal and state perspectives of the program. As Miles' Law suggests: "Where you stand depends on where you sit."[17]

In short, expect relationships that "pull together" to be few and far between. Pulling together happens not by chance, or even by design.

Pulling together is accomplished by the concerted efforts of both state and federal participants to achieve programmatic success. The book examines one program that has the attributes of pulling together—the radon program.

Cooperative But Autonomous:
High Trust with Low Involvement

When high levels of trust are coupled with low levels of involvement, the result is a relationship that is cooperative, but lonely. Here participants respect each other's roles, but lack sufficient interaction to create synergy in the relationship and fully "pull together." Participants have room to make their own decisions, but may be unaware of what other participants in the same program are doing. Programs operate in quasi-isolation and state agency officials often "go it alone"—without the ability to learn from their federal counterparts. In turn, federal officials lack sufficient knowledge of what is happening in the state and are unable to provide adequate support for state efforts.

Similarly, the federal oversight agency is likely to act without fully seeking the counsel and opinions of state officials. The result may be poorer program implementation because neither actor has the opportunity to understand the activities of the other one. Information infrequently disseminated slows down a program and impedes organizational learning. Programs operate sporadically and become very dependent upon state-level inducements and constraints, including the expertise of state staff. However, it is important to note that while federal–state contacts are infrequent and information channels are insufficiently used, communication when it does occur is aboveboard and open because both sets of actors trust each other.

Sometimes federal–state relationships gravitate to this cell because of fiscal and resource constraints placed on the federal oversight agency. Involvement is tough when resources are lacking. The wellhead protection program described in the next chapter is representative of this cell.

Coming Apart with Avoidance: Low Trust and Low Involvement

Low levels of trust result in suboptimal working relationships, as illustrated in the bottom half of the typology. Coming apart relationships can be further characterized as "coming apart with avoidance" or "coming apart and contentious," depending on levels of involvement.

As shown in the bottom-left quadrant, low involvement combined with low levels of trust characterize working relationships that are "coming apart with avoidance." Indeed, under these conditions, few reasons remain for federal and state officials in a program to work together, except for extrinsic statutory or legal obligations. These relationships are token, mandatory ones—with little expectation among the participants for positive outcomes or strong implementation performance. Neither side trusts the actions of the other, and communication among participants will likely be incomplete, confusing, or even dishonest.

Life for participants in this cell is like constructing a facade on a deteriorated building. From the outside the building looks solid, but on the inside the structure is crumbling. Residents of the building may be the only ones who know its true condition. Similarly, state and federal officials implementing a public program characterized by little involvement and low levels of mutual trust tend to avoid the obvious. That is, they seldom interact and, when they do, it is often to meet only the statutory requirements for contact. Thus, the facade is erected for the public to see, but little of substance is accomplished among the policy actors and the relationship, like the facade, is only skin deep.

The implications for the intergovernmental program are serious. Individual actors may feel so detached that they engage in "bare bones" operation of the program. Little reason exists to take risks and become a policy champion. Indeed, state officials who strongly embrace programmatic goals will find rapid, sure-fire implementation difficult at best, and probably impossible without large infusions of support from citizens or state administrators and/or legislators. By the same token, programs with this kind of working relationship are vulnerable during times of fiscal austerity at either state or federal levels, because policy professionals lack the necessary cohesion to present the need for continued political support. Thus, they are often unable to prevent the erosion of their program. The asbestos program, described in Chapter Three, is typical of this kind of relationship.

Coming Apart and Contentious:
Low Trust and High Involvement

Little mutual trust combined with high levels of involvement, shown on the bottom right quadrant of the typology, characterize working relationships that are also coming apart. Here, however, relationships are contentious. Participants are highly frustrated with what they view as unnecessary attention on the part of the other participants to administrative detail, program review, or organizational outputs. True, the participants are involved—but involved in the wrong way. Federal overseers are not inattentive to the actions of their state counterparts. Communication flows freely, but often does not produce satisfying results. Frequent expressions by participants that they are being "micromanaged" would be common in relationships in this cell.

Belowboard agendas are likely from both state and federal participants. State participants may comply with program requirements on paper, while running the program in the way they want to on the ground. Federal and state actors in this kind of coming-apart relationships hoard information that may be useful in operating the program. For example, state officials may shelter information about compliance rates of the target group under a regulatory program or the actions of state inspection staff. Federal overseers, in turn, may obscure discussions pertinent to program reviews, oversight inspections, or new program guidance documents.

End running may also be an outgrowth of this kind of relationship. State officials may "go around" federal regional staff to complain to federal staff in headquarters. Or they may seek a hearing in the political or judicial arena—playing their case to national politicians who have authority over the federal implementing agency. The arguments presented will go something like this: "We in the state of X are trying to run an effective enforcement program. The problem is that the federal oversight agency staff keeps getting in the way, by overstepping their authority, bogging us down in paperwork requirements, or engaging in countless bean-counting exercises while refusing to look at our accomplishments." End runs become increasingly commonplace as the frustration level among actors intensifies.

Not surprisingly, as state staff begin to end run the other participants in the working relationship, federal participants respond with their weapon of choice. They adopt the "gotcha syndrome"—where officials in the federal oversight agency look for ways to catch officials in the state implementing agency in violation of the dictates of the federal–state cooperative agreement or statutory mandates. State officials, in turn, begin to resent what they view as an unfair, unhelpful, and misdirected critique of their performance in the program. Hidden agendas and miscommunication become the hallmarks of this kind of relationship, and virtue and collaboration go out the window.

Breaking this vicious cycle of negative responses within a "coming apart with contention" relationship requires an almost herculean effort on the part of federal and state participants. Establishing trust is difficult after prolonged periods of obfuscation and control. Without dramatic intervention, this kind of relationship has its own force of gravity, destined to generate continued erosion of trust, resentment by all participants, and hypervigilance on the part of the overseer.

Equally vexing as symptomatic of this kind of working relationship is the fact that often participants have consensus about policy goals. The programmatic ends are not debated (state and federal staff want to reduce risks to public health or the environment); however, the means to that end are fiercely challenged. Ironically, this kind of relationship is prone to make participants lose sight of the bigger picture—the end goal which they share.

This unraveling of relationships is apparent in the surface mining program discussed in Chapter Four. Both federal and state officials in this coal mining regulatory program identify the poor quality of their working relationship as the largest obstacle to running the program. Only in 1996, nineteen years after the national coal mining law was passed, is there a possibility of moving to a more positive relationship.

In sum, four kinds of working relationships are possible, and relationships that have high levels of trust coupled with high levels of involvement are the most desirable. When this type of federal–state relationship is observed, it is also likely that the actors in the implementation story will feel positively about their program and the way the program is going. By the same token, state implementors who feel micromanaged by their federal counterparts will likely feel less comfortable with their intergovernmental programs.

The typology of working relationships suggests that, contrary to notions of cooperative, collaborative federalism, it is easier to have federal–state working relationships that are coming apart than those that are pulling together, at least by the definitions offered here. The implications for public policy and policy implementation studies are twofold: First, we must work harder to get the kind of relationship we want. Positive working relationships are not a given and must be sought. Second, absent sensitivity to fostering working relationships, federal–state relationships may actually work against effectively and efficiently implementing the program. Regardless, both positive and negative relationships will affect the outcomes of public policy.

Working relationships cannot be considered in a vacuum. Rather, they must be placed in the context of policy implementation. Policy implementation creates the environment in which federal–state working relationships are established. Implementation sets the parameters of the legal relationship, provides human and fiscal resources for working together, and creates a political, social, and economic arena for the program. To return to the California trip analogy, without implementation we would only be looking at what goes on inside the car without understanding the external factors such as the length and difficulty of the trip. The next section, then, looks at the larger picture of policy implementation, where the interactions of intergovernmental actors are part, but not all, of the reason for successful public programs.

DESCRIBING THE CONTEXT OF POLICY IMPLEMENTATION

Laws are usually passed because legislators believe that the current state of affairs needs changing. However, the mere act of passing legislation is no guarantee that real changes will occur. Legislation should be thought of as a first, rather than a last, step in the process of producing desired policy results. What occurs after a law is passed is called implementation, and it is in this phase that policy goals may—or may not—be achieved.

Intergovernmental policy implementation passes through several phases: the designation of the appropriate federal implementing agency and its subsequent promulgation of regulations; the corresponding designation of a state agency and the writing of state regulations; the accompanying enforcement actions of the state agency; the target group's reciprocating response (to comply, not comply, or somewhere in between); and, perhaps, ultimately a resolution to the policy problem that prompted the legislation in the first place. Revisions in state regulations, federal regulations, and the initial legislation prompt new implementation responses. Though most policy implementation passes through these phases, the least appropriate metaphor would be that of an assembly line, because implementation seldom occurs on schedule or as planned.

Defining and Measuring Implementation

In defining implementation in 1979, Carl Van Horn suggested that implementation "encompasses actions by public and private individuals or groups that affect the achievement of objectives set forth in prior policy decisions."[18] More than a decade later, Malcolm Goggin et al. (1990) defined the implementation of national policy by state governments as a "series of state decisions and actions directed toward putting an already-decided federal mandate into effect."[19] Both definitions contain the word "actions." Without action, there is no movement. However, along with actions are strategies of implementing officials about how much activity to undertake, what kind of activity to do, and whether or not implementation efforts are meaningful from their frame of reference.

Measuring implementation progress is a matter of asking "What happened after the policy was formulated?" and "Why did it happen this way?" One way of determining what happened is to measure the outputs of the agency charged with implementation. Progress, then, depends upon the generation of appropriate responses by agency officials and is measured by agency activities such as the number of enforcement actions taken against a target group, inspections made or permits processed, etc. However, measuring implementation "success" by agency activity doesn't always correspond to the attainment of legislative objectives. For example, a state agency may meet its inspection quota, but lots of inspections may not lead to a cleaner environment.

By the same token, agency staff charged with ultimate implementation responsibility make choices that determine if implementation proceeds toward the achievement of statutory goals. The inspection staff may conduct fewer inspections, but opt to be more thorough in considering each case. Thus, measures of agency output are only partially satisfying as surrogates for implementation performance and the need remains to ask, "Why did it happen this way?"

A second method of measuring implementation "success" is more demanding than the first. In addition to program performance or outputs, implementation also includes policy outcomes.[20] Implementation is considered complete only when policy objectives have been met.

However, outcomes in most public programs occur far into the future. For example, the "zero discharge" of pollutants into the water, the legislative goal of the Federal Water Pollution Control Act of 1972 (commonly known as the Clean Water Act), has yet to be met in 1997 and by most accounts will probably never be achieved. Since fully realized outcomes of policy may not be known, interim measures of statutory goals may be useful. So, in the case of the Clean Water Act, policy analysts may look to the number of water bodies that meet water quality standards or to other indicators of improving water quality. Complicating the ability to measure policy outcome is the lack of appropriate interim indicators of progress. Measuring improvements in water quality assumes that a state has sufficient data from which to make a judgment. Frequently data is lacking or policy analysts are unable to determine an appropriate surrogate outcome measure.

Some scholars have argued that evaluating implementation patterns is a function of the kind of program. Helen Ingram notes that: "The challenge presented to implementors depends very much on the problems passed along to them by policy formulators. Success in implementation must be evaluated within the context of particular problems, and critical factors affecting implementation will vary with what is being attempted."[21] She suggests that many environmental laws contain clear goals and highly prescriptive procedures for the implementing agency. Given that environmental policies also embrace scientific uncertainties about the extent of risk, the best technologies, necessary regulatory structures, and implementation of most environmental programs should be judged by the extent of policy learning that is acquired by key stakeholders.[22]

Whether one examines agency outputs, attempts to measure interim or final policy outcomes, or looks at the amount of policy learning that has occurred, understanding implementation is difficult. Seldom, if ever, does a policy analyst exclaim, "Eureka! Implementation is achieved." Nor is she likely to add, "I know how implementation works." If one general statement is common to studies of policy implementation, it is that the process seldom works as expected—on time and with satisfactory results.

Eugene Bardach suggests that three principle elements are common to the implementation of public policy: lack of achievement of stated objectives, delay, and excessive financial cost.[23] Why is that the case? Perhaps expectations for producing change are too high. Maybe an appreciation of the difficulties involved in implementing new policy is lacking, as policy implementors seek simple solutions to complex problems. More importantly, the same political dynamics that shape the often tortured path of policy formation (such as the competing roles of interest groups, differing values and orientations of lawmakers, and the interplay between federal and state officials) also shape implementation patterns.

IMPLEMENTATION: STRATEGIES AND STORIES

As indicated by the chapter title, the study of policy implementation and working relationships is a study of strategies and stories. "Strategies" because, for every program, different casts of actors adopt strategic approaches to the program based upon their role orientations, available resources, the extent of behavioral change required, and the prevailing political winds, among other reasons. "Stories" because each policy has its own legislative, administrative, and political legacy and current culture that determines, in large and small ways, the rate and progress of implementation. Central to the concept of stories is the notion that explaining implementation results is at least partially a function of policy formulation dynamics.

Strategies

Implementing officials employ strategies in order to win—where winning is often implicitly defined as conserving agency resources, deflecting criticism and legal attacks, and maintaining stature in the pertinent political community. Bardach states that, "Implementation games are also part of the larger game of politics and governance. Just as they draw their characteristic strategies and tactics from the game of politics, so too do they deliver their outcomes back to the larger game."[24]

One commonly identified place in the implementation process for strategies to emerge is where administrative actions of street-level bureaucrats intersect with private choices. Richard Elmore (1979), among other scholars, contends that this is the point where implementation results are most affected.[25] He examines the behaviors of the actors closest to the target group of the policy and then examines the delivery mechanisms of each successive level. Beginning with the last interaction (that between the street-level implementor and a receiver of the policy, such as a member of the regulated community), his "backward mapping" model moves upward, defining two characteristics for each subsequent set of actors: the ability of each level to affect the behavior of the target group and the lower-level bureaucratic agents; and the presence of resources sufficient for producing change in the target group. In this case, implementation depends upon the ability of actors at one level to influence actors at another, ultimately influencing the behavior of private groups or individuals.

Michael Lipsky writes that the decisions of "street-level bureaucrats, the routines that they establish, and the devices they invent to cope with uncertainties and work pressures effectively become the public policies they carry out."[26] Front-line implementors, for example, make choices regarding policy depending upon their attitudes, values, or local theories about the substantive issue at hand.[27] A state inspector may choose to comply with the dictates of the new policy and work toward substantive policy goals; he/she may elect to maintain existing behavioral patterns and ignore the new policy; the street-level bureaucrat may try to change the policy by voicing distaste for implementation procedures to the manager.[28] Really savvy street-level bureaucrats may simply go through the motions of what is required while not really changing anything.

Thus, two extreme strategies are possible, with a wide range of behaviors in the middle. On the one hand, street-level implementors may exhibit what Bardach describes as "massive resistance" in the implementation game—using discretionary powers to ignore procedural requirements and forgive target group performance.[29] On the other hand, these front-line implementors may also be the ones to rigorously pursue policy implementation, even in the face of political or administrative pressure to "back off" or "go easy" on the target group. In either case, the action of persons charged with on-the-ground performance is an important element in understanding implementation and may influence the nature of federal–state working relationships as well.

In sum, several issues are apparent about implementation strategies. First, the disposition of the bureaucrat and the agency culture should be compatible with the policy goals of the new legislation, so that goal displacement is minimized. Next, the extent of behavioral change required of the target group is often inversely related to achieving implementation, because it is likely to engender conflict between the front-line implementors, the agency, and the regulated industry. Finally, the role orientations of the enforcement personnel may influence the rate and nature of the implementation process, depending on whether a hard-line or negotiated regulatory posture is taken.

The emphasis on the strategic activities of the bureaucratic staff reveals two important assumptions about implementation. First, implementation power rests with the street-level bureaucrats, not legislative or administrative leaders. Policy makers, therefore, do not wield the only determinant influence over what happens in the implementation process. If this is the case, then explicit policy directives are probably not the most effective way of ensuring successful implementation. Other factors, such as informal working relationships between actors, symmetry in the dispositions of the staff and agency leaders toward policy goals, and the existence of countervailing external pressures from outside groups on the street-level bureaucrats are also key variables.[30]

Stories

A second element important to understanding implementation is to look for the legislative, administrative, and political stories that were part of the formulation of the policy and that remain part of the implementation process. Why use the metaphor of a story? As suggested by Peter Schwartz, "Stories are about meaning; they help explain why things could happen in a certain way. They give order and meaning to events—a crucial aspect of understanding future possibilities."[31] Moreover, stories provide an opportunity to describe how different characters see events (in this case, implementation events) and to cope with complexity.

Implementation "stories" have their origins in the legislative and political history of the law. To understand the story, you have to ask the right questions. For instance, what interest groups testified before the congressional committee? What was the level and scope of the presidential administration's interest in the law? What event (if any) propelled this policy onto the agenda of Congress? Understanding the political discussions that shaped the law helps to explain why the process of putting the law into practice is so difficult.

As argued by Deborah Stone, policy making is more than just a "production model" where the policy is formulated and then moves on to be implemented. Instead, Stone argues that "the essence of policy making in political communities is the struggle over ideas."[32] Causal stories, or the rationales for creating legislation, in turn influence the eventual law and thus influence the ability of administrators to implement public programs.

Parts of the story also include the availability of solutions to the policy problem and the capacity of implementing agencies to respond. Discovering these parts of the story means asking questions like: "How willing were the legislative architects to fund the program?" "What is the technical expertise of the agency?" "What is the scope and breadth of the problem?" The answers to these questions begin to tell the story of implementation.

The metaphor of a story is not used by many prominent implementation scholars, although their work has helped to identify important parts of the story. The approach of scholars such as Donald Van Meter and Carl Van Horn (1975) and Paul Sabatier and Daniel Mazmanian (1980) is to describe implementation success as hinging on variables that can best be manipulated from the top of the process.[33] Their "top-down" approach to understanding implementation contributes a comprehensive list of factors which influence public programs.

Sabatier and Mazmanian develop a model of implementation that places variables into three categories: statutory, nonstatutory, and technical (or problem tractability) variables. They choose to emphasize the story over the strategy. For example, they argue that the structure of the statute can have a powerful effect upon implementation, because the statute can delineate crucial elements such as the amount of fiscal and legal resources available to the implementing agency, the extent of the agency's authority over the target group, the number of veto points in the process, and the designation of the implementing agency itself.

A second element of the Sabatier and Mazmanian model looks at the nature of the problem. If the policy addresses a problem for which there are few technical solutions, poor causal theories, a highly-populated or hard-to-identify target group, or which requires substantial behavioral change, implementation will be impeded. A final model component addresses the influence of nonstatutory variables on implementation, such as public support, prevalence of interest groups, and the commitment of key legislators or executives. Thus, the structure of the statute, the nature of the problem, fiscal and staffing resources, and the ability of external actors to influence the process all change the character of implementation.

The assumptions of this and other "top-down" models that describe the elements of implementation are straightforward. First, they assume that policy makers can usually control organizational, political, and technical components of the implementation process through formal means. Thus, the intentions and carefully reasoned actions of policy makers at the top are more important than the dispositions of the bureaucrats at the bottom. A second assumption is that statutes or regulations, appropriated resources, and institutional relationships between agencies are the elements that should be manipulated to bring about successful policy implementation.

In sum, both strategies and stories are important to understanding why public programs get implemented. What is needed is a model that puts these pieces together in a conceptual package that can be used to evaluate implementation success. The next section develops such a model.

A FRAMEWORK FOR LOOKING AT ENVIRONMENTAL POLICY IMPLEMENTATION IN STATE AGENCIES

Figure 1-2 depicts a model of policy implementation that reflects the work of implementation scholars, integrates federal–state working relationships as a key factor in implementation, and employs strategies and stories as a way of understanding implementation variables. Specifically, the model portrays the implementation of environmental programs when state agencies are given primary responsibility for running the programs.

The framework offers a new conceptual approach to examining how and why public programs develop the way they do. This model takes as its starting point the concept of implementation "stories and strategies." Story components are generally considered as extrinsic factors, or those variables that are outside of the control of the state implementing agency. Strategic components, on the other hand, are intrinsic factors—those factors which are either within the agency's control or part of the constellation of forces unique to a particular state. By attempting to be parsimonious, the framework may exclude certain implementation variables. However, the overall framework should offer an opportunity for examining the major implementation factors associated with environmental programs.

Extrinsic Factors: Parts of the "Story"

As discussed earlier, implementation is best understood by examining the context which surrounded the policy formulation as well as the current political and institutional environment in which implementation proceeds. These elements include the extent of national-level political support, role orientations of the federal oversight agency personnel, the nature of the problem, resources allocated to states and

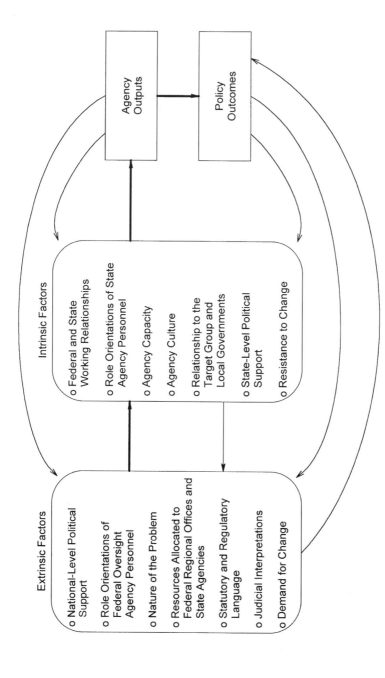

Figure 1-2 Extrinsic and Intrinsic Factors that Influence Policy Implementation in State Agencies

to federal regional offices, statutory and regulatory language, judicial interpretations, and the demand for change. Each will be described briefly in turn.

Under the general category of political arrangements are elements such as the support of national sovereigns, including the administration and the U.S. Congress. Much has been written about the ability of the administration to change the course of policy implementation. Most notable are the many changes to environmental programs, including staff and budget reductions and pro-business political appointees in federal environmental agencies that occurred during the Reagan Administration.[34] Similarly, the U.S. Congress, through its oversight activities and its ability to reauthorize or amend law, may significantly alter environmental efforts. (The recent attempts by the 104th Congress to reauthorize the Clean Water Act and change the Clean Air Act are cases in point.)

Also important in this category is the presence and intensity of interest group involvement. The growth of environmental groups which closely monitor the implementation of environmental programs through the use of citizen suits has frequently been effective at producing implementation performance on the part of the U.S. Environmental Protection Agency (EPA), other federal oversight agencies, or state agencies. Similarly, interest groups affect the way regulations are written as well as the shape of the new law.

Other political factors include the extent to which the public perceives the environmental problem as serious and the presence of a "fixer" to encourage implementation. As Bardach suggests, ". . . the character and degree of many implementation problems are inherently unpredictable. Even the most robust policy—one that is designed to survive the implementation process—will tend to go awry . . . someone or some group must be willing and able to set the policy back on course."[35] Thus, he looks to external monitoring of the process by a "fixer," a legislator or executive official who controls resources and may intervene when implementation falters.

Public support for the program may provide incentives to the agency to proceed with implementation, even in the face of resistance by the target group. The economic significance of the target group as well as the costs of compliance comprise potentially important elements of the political environment.[36]

Also important as extrinsic factors in implementation are the role orientations of federal oversight personnel. As discussed earlier in the context of working relationships, the type of oversight posture taken by the federal agency profoundly affects the quality of the working relationship between state and federal staff and may, in turn, change the way the state program is implemented.

The third extrinsic contextual element shaping policy implementation is the nature of the problem. Here, elements include the seriousness and pervasiveness of the public policy problem and the size and heterogeneity of the group being targeted for behavioral change. Many environmental problems are difficult to solve. Scientific uncertainty about causal relationships, difficulties in determining the extent of risk to ecological and human health from exposure to a contaminant, as well as the utility and availability of solutions to environmental problems, may constrain program development.[37]

The nature of the problem may also be defined by looking at the size and the characteristics of the members of the group targeted by the policy, as well as the extent of behavioral change required. For example, is the group homogeneous and about equally affected by compliance costs? When compliance burdens are disproportionately placed on members of the target group, one could expect that those members would resist rapid implementation of the program. Or look at programs that depend upon voluntary compliance for implementation. Here implementation success rests with the willingness of the target group, which may be as large as all American adults, to voluntarily change the way they do things—no small task.

Closely related to political support for the environmental program is the provision of adequate fiscal and human resources to operate state and federal regional programs. Virtually every implementation scholar includes resource allocation as an integral part of understanding the implementation of any program. Many environmental programs have been adopted with fewer federal resources appropriated than what is necessary to do the job—at least from the perspective of many people who regularly examine environmental efforts.

Another essential external factor in understanding the implementation of environmental programs by state agencies is the statutory language of the national law. Clear and unambiguous goals, realistic timetables for implementation, adequate appropriations of fiscal resources, and appropriate delegation of authority within the law are factors which alter the implementation of environmental policy.

In turn, a law which provides little guidance for policy implementors or is too prescriptive in how it allows implementors to proceed clearly has effects on how the program evolves. Additionally, environmental laws, the result of bargaining and compromise, reflect the prevailing political allegiances that were in power at the time. Thus environmental laws, like other laws, contain exemptions and exclusions for certain groups that will affect policy outcomes. Also important is the congruence of the national law with related state laws passed to complement the national law, to authorize the state agency to implement the program, or to supplement existing laws.

Also important to implementation is the way in which regulations are promulgated by federal agencies. Regulations can clarify statutory language and facilitate implementation. On the other hand, regulations can work to obfuscate statutory intentions and thereby impede implementation. Moreover, the development of regulations can proceed quickly, or at a glacial pace, which also affects the ability of state officials to launch an environmental program.

A fifth external factor in environmental policy implementation is the role of judicial interpretation. The courts interpret statutory language, as well as any promulgated regulations under the law. Court decisions may substantially affect the rate and nature of implementation. Environmental laws depend upon citizens' suits for enforcement. Citizens can sue to compel federal or state agencies to perform nondiscretionary duties; they can also enforce the law by bringing violators into compliance. Environmental programs that mandate performance by a target group frequently involve the courts through challenges to regulatory language. Nearly 80 percent of all EPA regulations are challenged; the Office of Surface Mining was a party in six cases challenging its decisions in 1995 alone.[38]

Finally, the demand for change is an important external force. This is really a subset of the other factors, in that the demand for a change in the status quo (or the life before the law was enacted) can come from any source: the federal oversight agency, the administration, interest groups, citizens, a "fixer," or policy entrepreneur. The tendency for many students of public policy is to view a problem as being solved once a law has passed. However, the model suggests that, absent countervailing tendencies toward inertia, implementation will proceed sluggishly simply as a function of human complacency.

Intrinsic Factors: Strategies

The second group of factors considered by the model are intrinsic factors, defined earlier either as those factors under the auspices of the implementing state agency or as those factors which are uniquely part of the state's political, economic, or institutional arenas. Here the major elements include federal–state working relationships; the role orientations of street-level implementors; agency capacity; agency culture; relationship to the target group or local governments; state-level political support; and resistance to change. Each of these factors will be described briefly.

The first factor, working relationships, isolates the role between federal and state agencies charged with implementation responsibilities. As described earlier, working relationships can be characterized as "pulling together" or "coming apart." Factors that affect federal–state cooperation include the presence of mutual trust and beneficial involvement. Trust and beneficial involvement are facilitated by effective communication between levels of government, shared goals among federal and state officials, the provision of fiscal and technical assistance by the federal oversight agency, and the effectiveness of chosen methods of program evaluation and oversight.[39]

A second intrinsic element identified in the implementation literature and subsequently in this model are the role orientations of agency personnel. Individuals given front-line implementation duties may have different perceptions about their enforcement roles than do state agency officials, federal agency officials, or other policy stakeholders. The strategies they employ, from resisting implementation through token enforcement to enthusiastic reception of their new responsibilities and zealous enforcement, affect the way implementation ultimately unfolds.

Agency capacity identifies elements within a state agency that affect how well an environmental program is run. Some agency capacity variables include adequate human and fiscal resources and the level of expertise among the agency staff. Capacity also relates to the amount of jurisdictional control and statutory authority given to the implementing agency, and the extent to which programs are fragmented between departments.[40]

The capacity of an agency to respond to a new program is also a function of the staff's willingness to take on this new task. This is agency culture, which may be loosely defined as the collected set of organizational values and attitudes and the extent to which those values are shared by all members of the implementation team. As Herbert Kaufman noted in his classic study of the U.S. Forest Service, agency culture can serve as a potent tool for maintaining the status quo and a level of homogeneity in staff perspective.[41] Thus, the degree to which administrators within the implementing state agency support the goals of the program, coupled with the congruence of legislative goals with existing agency culture, also may affect program implementation.

In addition to agency capacity, agency culture, and individual role orientations of front-line implementors, the existence of an individual or individuals to champion the program encourages implementation. Much like the policy entrepreneur helps to propel a potential policy onto the agenda, dedicated staff members or even a single individual can make a significant difference to whether or not the program gets off the ground.[42]

Three final factors complete the list of major intrinsic variables. The first, the nature of the target group, appears in this group for the same reason it is listed as an extrinsic variable. The target group within a state may be diffuse, numerous, heterogeneous, or politically powerful. To the extent that it is a powerful political player in the state, the target group may influence the way that the agency perceives its implementation roles. Moreover, the ability of the target group to respond varies among states because the target groups may be different. For example, small coal mining companies operating in the Appalachian coal region look very different from the large, financially well-heeled coal operations in the West.

Political support for the program at the state level is a significant factor in understanding how implementation proceeds. While national law may compel states to undertake environmental activities, the mere presence of a law is no guarantee that state administrators, top agency officials, state legislators, or the governor will be persuaded to implement it. Nor is it a guarantee that states will pass their own strong regulatory programs. Important to levels of political support is the extent of public concern, interest group and target group involvement, and the willingness of states to use own-source revenues if necessary to operate the program.[43]

Finally, the human tendency to resist change plays into the implementation of policy within a state. Just as there has to be a certain amount of momentum to push the implementation forward at the national level, state agencies may vary in their willingness to change their existing practices. This is especially true when organizations are asked to take on additional tasks or to go against standard operating procedures.

Dynamics of the Model

The framework suggests that both extrinsic and intrinsic factors affect the ability of the state implementing agency to implement environmental programs. Implementation produces both agency outputs (measures of agency activities, such as number of inspections conducted or violations cited in the case of regulatory programs) and policy outcomes, or measurable improvements in the environment. Note that the model allows for the independent ability of extrinsic variables to influence policy outcomes. For example, individuals within a target group may change their behavior in response to a new law or federal regulation before the state implementing agency requests such changes. Similarly, advances in scientific understanding or improvements in technology may prompt policy outcomes without the direct intervention of the state implementing agency.

The model also recognizes that each factor is closely related and may influence other factors (thus is in the same box). For example, political arrangements may affect resources available for federal oversight agencies or for states to use. The nature of the problem may affect the statutory language; internal variables such as agency culture and role orientations are often closely related. Or the political context of policy implementation (i.e., the support of sovereigns) may alter the state agency's capacity to implement the program.

Similarly, extrinsic factors influence intrinsic factors, as indicated by the large arrow in the model. The kind of law passed, federal court decisions, changing role orientations of federal oversight personnel, infusions of federal funding, a new president, or a congressional oversight committee will certainly affect working relationships, state political support, and agency capacity. To a lesser degree, intrinsic factors within a state may, in turn, affect extrinsic factors, as indicated by the smaller arrow between the boxes. For example, state agencies with little capacity to run the new environmental program may prompt Congress to allocate additional resources.

Finally, the model acknowledges that environmental policy implementation is an ongoing event. Feedback loops emanating from both the "agency outputs" and "policy outcomes" boxes suggest that changes in the implementation process may occur as decision makers become aware of implementation performance and on-the-ground results. In short, the rate and/or intensity of implementation activities may vary over time, depending upon changes in the external or internal factors, or in the repercussions from feedback into the process from agency output or policy outcome information.

CONCLUSIONS ABOUT IMPLEMENTATION

Implementation changes over time, being neither stable, forward-moving, nor guaranteed. Furthermore, every point in the process is subject to a unique set of implementation conditions and constellation of actors, employing various strategies to alter the course of implementation in order to maximize their position in the eventual outcome. Not only the course but the rate of implementation may change, depending upon the strength of political forces at any given time as the policy evolves. This, in part, is what makes implementation stories so interesting.

Moreover, actors enter the process at the point that holds the most promise for shaping policy outcomes. Thus, environmental interest groups use the courts to force the agency with implementation responsibility to write regulations or enforce the law.[44] By the same token, target groups facing the legislative "promise" of regulation may choose to try to influence the regulatory process, influence enforcement efforts after the regulations are promulgated, or pursue legal remedies challenging the appropriateness of regulatory requirements.

Finally, federal–state working relationships form an important subset of policy implementation. As programs mature, daily operations of federal and state agencies become paramount to policy success or failure. These regular interactions between personnel may greatly influence the eventual outcomes of a public program. Relationships, in turn, are based upon mutual trust and adequate levels of appropriate involvement, and vary among programs.

It is easy to see how each policy tells a different and unique implementation story. They are not as unique as fingerprints, perhaps, but nonetheless environmental programs have distinct problems to solve, political arenas in which to solve them, and state and federal officials who may have very different opinions about their new roles as policy implementors.

STUDY DESIGN AND RATIONALE

It is now time to travel to California, paying attention to the elements of the trip and the atmosphere inside the car. (That is to say, looking at both implementation and federal–state relationships.)

To that end, this book employs the working relationship typology (Figure 1–1) and the implementation framework (Figure 1–2) to examine five environmental programs: asbestos, coal mining, drinking water, radon, and wellhead protection. All of the programs depend upon the states for implementation. Beyond this common characteristic, each of these environmental programs was chosen as a representative case.

First, not all of the programs are regulatory. Three programs (asbestos, coal mining, and drinking water) are primarily regulatory in nature, but the other programs, radon and wellhead protection, are nonregulatory and rely primarily on the voluntary participation of state and local officials.

Second, working relationships vary by program. Radon and wellhead protection programs have positive federal–state interactions; the drinking water, asbestos, and surface mining programs are more adversarial.

Third, these programs vary in size. State drinking water programs and state coal mining programs are generally larger than state radon, wellhead protection, or asbestos programs. These two programs also tend to be better funded, although this may not be the case in some states.

Fourth, the five environmental programs have unique political and legislative histories. The asbestos program, for example, was established only after years of asbestos litigation and governmental apathy toward asbestos health risks. Wellhead protection, on the other hand, was passed almost as an afterthought to reauthorizing the Safe Drinking Water Act. As of this writing it remains an obscure program with tepid national or state political support.

This book takes a different approach to studying environmental policy implementation. The primary sources of information are the people who work in state and federal agencies charged with the responsibility of implementing the five environmental programs. Most of the data for this book comes from responses to surveys and interviews of state program directors and federal regional staff. Although reports and other "hard copy" data are used to support observations, the perceptions of individuals involved in each program are considered to be key to understanding what makes the program work. The Appendix has more information about the specifics of the research.

The perceptions of state program managers are the primary focus of this book. Their perceptions are reported in each of the substantive chapters. For example, primary data from state radon program directors appear after a discussion of the radon implementation story found in Chapter Three.

A second focal point is personnel in federal regional offices. Too little scholarly attention has been given to regional offices. Federal officials working in regional offices are closest to state implementors and may not perceive policy implementation or federal–state working relationships in the same way as their headquarters counterparts. Ongoing working relationships occur between federal regional personnel and state staff. Without looking at the regional office, it is impossible to understand the working relationships. Further, headquarters and regional officials are responding to different political and administrative environments, and thus may be constrained by different forces which, in turn, may alter their orientations toward policy implementation.

The book looks at federal–state relationships in two agencies: the U.S. Environmental Protection Agency (EPA) and the Office of Surface Mining Reclamation and Enforcement (OSM), housed within the U.S. Department of Interior. This provides the opportunity to compare the organizational cultures and role orientations between two federal agencies with different perspectives: the EPA aims to control pollution and protect human health and is responsible for a wide array of environmental programs; the OSM, as part of the Department of Interior, is a natural resource agency with the sole responsibility of implementing the surface mining law.

PLAN FOR THE BOOK

Chapter Two examines two programs created by one law: the regulatory drinking water program and the nonregulatory wellhead protection program. Chapter Three examines two programs concerned with the indoor environment. The first is the asbestos program, which requires states to control asbestos exposures in schools. The second is the indoor radon abatement program, which encourages states to alert their citizens to potential radon dangers in homes and schools. Chapter Four evaluates the surface mining program, the regulatory program for coal mining. Chapter Five examines federal–state working relationships and program implementation from the perspectives of EPA regional and OSM field office staff. Chapter Six offers some conclusions about the study, the utility of the implementation framework and working relationships typology, and whether state and federal officials are "pulling together" or "coming apart."

NOTES TO CHAPTER 1

1. Many scholars have noted the importance of state–federal relationships in policy implementation. For example, see Patricia Crotty, "The New Federalism Game: Primacy Implementation of Environmental Policy," *Publius* 17 (1987): 53–67; Martha Derthick, *New Towns In-Town* (Washington, D.C.: Urban Institute, 1972); William Gormley, "Intergovernmental Conflict and Environmental Policy: The Attitudinal Connection," *Western Political Quarterly* 40 (1987): 285–303; Deil S. Wright, *Understanding Intergovernmental Relations,* 3d ed. (Pacific Grove, Cal.: Brooks/Cole, 1988).

2. Morton Grodzins, *The American System* (Chicago: Rand McNally, 1966), p. 80; quoted in David H. Rosenbloom, *Public Administration: Understanding Management, Politics and Law in the Public Sector,* 3rd ed. (New York: McGraw-Hill, 1993), p. 123.

3. Terry Sanford, *Storm over the States* (New York: McGraw-Hill, 1967), quoted in *The Politics of Intergovernmental Relations,* ed. David C. Nice and Patricia Fredericksen (Chicago, Ill.: Nelson-Hall, 1995), p. 10.

4. For a discussion of the evolution of intergovernmental relationships, see Deil S. Wright, *Understanding Intergovernmental Relations,* 2nd ed. (Monterey, Calif.: Brooks/Cole, 1982), pp. 43–82.

5. U.S. Environmental Protection Agency, "Performance Partnership Grants for State and Tribal Environmental Programs: Interim Guidance," unpublished document (December 7, 1995).

6. U.S. Environmental Protection Agency, State/EPA Capacity Steering Committee, *Joint Committee to Reform Oversight and Create a National Environmental Partnership System* (Agreement signed May 17, 1995).

7. U.S. Environmental Protection Agency, Office of Indoor Air and Radiation, *Administrative Guidance for the State Indoor Radon Grants Program* (Washington, D.C.: U.S. EPA, 1992).

8. Martha Derthick, *New Towns In-Town* (Washington, D.C.: Urban Institute, 1972).

9. Martha Derthick, *New Towns In-Town*, p. 83.

10. Jeffrey L. Pressman and Aaron Wildavsky, *Implementation* (Berkeley, Calif.: University of California Press, 1973): p. 93.

11. Quoted in Jeffrey R. Henig, *Public Policy and Federalism: Issues in State and Local Politics* (New York: St. Martin's Press, 1985), p. 23.

12. William R. Lowry, *The Dimensions of Federalism: State Governments and Pollution Control Policies* (Durham, N.C.: Duke University Press, 1992); Evan J. Ringquist, "Does Regulation Matter?: Evaluating the Effects of State Air Pollution Control Programs," *Journal of Politics* 55, no. 4 (1993): 1022–45.

13. David M. Hedge, Donald C. Menzel, and George Williams, "Regulatory Attitudes and Behavior: The Case of Surface Mining Regulation," *Western Political Quarterly* 41 (1988): 323–40 and Denise Scheberle, "In the Eye of the Beholder: State and Federal Perceptions about the Surface Mining Control and Reclamation Act," in *Moving the Earth: Cooperative Federalism and the Implementation of the Surface Mining Act*, ed. Uday Desai (Westport, Conn.: Greenwood Press, 1993), pp. 184–97.

14. James P. Lester, James L. Franke, Ann O'M. Bowman, and Kenneth W. Kramer, "Hazardous Wastes, Politics and Public Policy: A Comparative State Analysis," *Western Political Quarterly* 36 (1983): 257–81.

15. William Gormley, "Food Fights: Regulatory Enforcement in a Federal System," *Public Administration Review* 52, no. 3 (1992): 271–80.

16. Deil S. Wright, *Understanding Intergovernmental Relations*, 3rd ed. (Pacific Grove, Calif.: Brooks/Cole, 1988).

17. Quoted in Deil S. Wright, *Understanding Intergovernmental Relations*, 2nd ed. (Monterey, Calif.: Brooks/Cole, 1982), p. 77.

18. Carl E. Van Horn, "Evaluating the New Federalism: National Goals and Local Implementors," *Public Administration Review* 39 (1979): 17–22, at 9.

19. Malcolm L. Goggin, Ann O'M. Bowman, James P. Lester, and Laurence J. O'Toole, Jr., *Implementation Theory and Practice: Toward a Third Generation* (Glenview, Ill.: Scott, Foresman and Co., 1990), p. 3.

20. For this perspective, see Paul A. Sabatier, "Top-down and Bottom-up Approaches to Implementation Research: A Critical Analysis and Suggested Synthesis," *Journal of Public Policy* 6 (1986): 21–48, and Richard F. Elmore, "Backward Mapping: Implementation Research and Policy Decisions," *Political Science Quarterly* 84, no. 4 (1979): 601–16.

21. Helen Ingram, "Implementation: A Review and Suggested Framework," In *Public Administration: The State of the Discipline*, ed. Naomi B. Lynn and Aaron Wildavsky (Chatham, N.J.: Chatham House Publishers, 1990), pp. 462–80, at 470.

22. Ingram, "Implementation: A Review and Suggested Framework," p. 477.

23. Eugene Bardach, *The Implementation Game: What Happens After a Bill Becomes Law* (Cambridge, Mass: MIT Press, 1977).

24. Bardach, *The Implementation Game*, p. 278.

25. Richard Elmore, "Backward Mapping: Implementation Research and Policy Decisions," *Political Science Quarterly* 84, no. 4 (1979): 601–16.

26. Michael Lipsky, *Street-Level Bureaucracy* (New York: Russell Sage, 1980), p. *xii*.

27. See Randall B. Ripley and Grace A. Franklin, *Bureaucracy and Policy Implementation* (Homewood, Ill.: Dorsey Press, 1982); Carl E. Van Horn and Donald S. Van Meter, "The Implementation of Intergovernmental Policy," *Public Policy in the Federal System*, ed. Donald S. Van Meter and Carl E. Van Horn (Lexington, Mass.: Lexington Books, 1976).

28. For a discussion of various regulatory styles, including a critique on overly zealous street-level bureaucrats, see Eugene Bardach and Robert A. Kagan, *Going by the Book: The Problem of Regulatory Unreasonableness* (Philadelphia, Penn.: Temple University Press, 1982).

29. Bardach, *The Implementation Game*, 1977.

30. Janice Love and Peter C. Sederberg, "Euphony and Cacophony in Policy Implementation: SCF and the Somali Refugee Problem," *Policy Studies Review* 7, no. 1 (1987): 155–73, and Goggin et al., *Implementation Theory and Practice: Toward a Third Generation*, p. 24.

31. Peter Schwartz, *The Art of the Long View: Planning for the Future in an Uncertain World* (New York, N.Y.: Bantam, 1991), p. 40.

32. Deborah A. Stone, *Policy Paradox and Political Reason* (New York, N.Y.: Harper Collins, 1988), p. 7.

33. Donald S. Van Meter and Carl E. Van Horn, "The Policy Implementation Process," *Administration and Society* 6, no. 4 (1975): 445–87; Paul A. Sabatier and Daniel Mazmanian, "Policy Implementation: A Framework for Analysis," *Policy Studies Journal* 8, no. 2 (1980): 538–60. For a fuller treatment of their framework, see Daniel Mazmanian and Paul Sabatier, *Implementation and Public Policy* (Glenview, Ill.: Scott Foresman and Co., 1983).

34. For a discussion of the influence of the Reagan administration on environmental programs, see Norman J. Vig and Michael E. Kraft, *Environmental Policy in the 1980s: Reagan's New Agenda* (Washington, D.C.: Congressional Quarterly Press, 1984).

35. Bardach, *The Implementation Game*, p. 5.

36. Denise Scheberle, *Scratching the Surface: State Implementation of the Surface Mining Control and Reclamation Act* (unpublished doctoral dissertation, Colorado State University, 1991).

37. See, for example, Michael S. Hamilton, "Introduction," in Michael S. Hamilton, ed., *Regulatory Federalism, Natural Resources and Environmental*

Management (Washington, D.C.: American Political Science Assn., 1990) and James L. Regens, "State Policy Responses to the Energy Issue: An Analysis of Innovation," *Social Science Quarterly* 61 (1980): 44–59.

38. U.S. Department of the Interior, Office of Surface Mining, *1995 Annual Report: Protecting the Natural Environmental, a Shared Commitment* (Washington, D.C.: Office of Surface Mining, 1996), p. 16.

39. Denise Scheberle, "Pesticides and Radon: State Perceptions of EPA and Administrative Support." (Paper presented at the Annual Meeting of the Midwest Political Science Association, Chicago, Illinois, 1994.)

40. For a discussion of the effect of fragmentation on effective management of environmental programs, see Barry G. Rabe, *Fragmentation and Integration in State Environmental Management* (Washington, D.C.: Conservation Foundation, 1986).

41. Herbert Kaufman, *The Forest Ranger: A Study in Administrative Behavior* (Baltimore: Johns Hopkins University Press, 1960).

42. See John W. Kingdon, *Agendas, Alternatives, and Public Policies* (Boston: Little, Brown, 1984) for a discussion of factors which put policies on the formal congressional agenda.

43. For a comparative study of state regulatory programs under the Clean Air Act, see Evan J. Ringquist, "Is Effective Regulation always Oxymoronic?: The States and Ambient Air Quality," *Social Science Quarterly* 76, no. 1 (1995): 69–87.

44. See, for example, R. Shep Melnick, *Regulation and the Courts: The Case of the Clean Air Act* (Washington, D.C.: The Brookings Institute, 1983).

2

Implementing the Safe Drinking Water Act: An Implementation Story of Two Programs

The provision of safe drinking water offers an opportunity to look at two environmental programs, one regulatory and one nonregulatory, created by the same law. Although they are vastly different in terms of scope, funding, size, and objectives, each program is deeply dependent upon state governments for implementation. Accordingly, this chapter is divided into two parts. The first section reviews the larger regulatory program that is implemented under the auspices of the Safe Drinking Water Act of 1974, hereafter referred to as the drinking water program. The second section looks at the wellhead protection program, a nonregulatory program that was created as part of the 1986 amendments to the Safe Drinking Water Act. Each section begins by highlighting important provisions of the program, then moves on to consider implementation constraints as identified by state and federal officials and by government and other documents. Perceptions of state program directors are provided on tables at the end of each section. The chapter ends with a summary of the implementation of these programs through the use of the conceptual framework developed in the previous chapter.

KEY ELEMENTS OF THE DRINKING WATER PROGRAM

The Safe Drinking Water Act (SDWA) enacted in 1974 significantly expanded the federal role in protecting public drinking water supplies.[1] Prior to 1974, state health departments had the primary responsibility for surveillance and regulation of public water systems. The federal role in monitoring the safety of drinking water was limited to the promulgation of drinking water standards by the U.S. Public Health Service in 1962. In 1969, the U.S. Public Health Service conducted a Community Water Supply Survey which indicated the need for additional protection of drinking water supplies. In the early 1970s, the EPA (which assumed responsibility for the federal role in drinking water after its creation in 1970) conducted evaluations of public water supply systems, identifying shortcomings in state drinking water programs. These studies helped to focus congressional attention on the need for a stronger national regulatory role in drinking water protection and resulted in the passage of the SDWA.[2]

After the passage of the SDWA, the federal role became one of overseer and standard-setter. Not unlike other environmental laws, SDWA required the EPA to set national standards which were protective of human health and then required public water suppliers to meet those standards. The Public Water Supply Supervision program established under SDWA became the base regulatory program protecting the nation's water supplies.

The federal drinking water program was designed to be delegated, with states having the authority to operate the program, including the inspection and enforcement components.[3] Some states, in turn, have delegated some regulatory responsibilities to counties or other local governments. States with primacy are required to have programs that include statutory and regulatory enforcement authority adequate to compel compliance; a system for conducting inspections of public water supply systems, called sanitary surveys; a process to certify laboratories which test for contaminants; and provisions for other management and oversight activities. SDWA authorizes the EPA to pay up to 75 percent of the costs of administering the drinking water program to primacy states. However, the actual EPA contribution since the early 1990s has been closer to 35 percent of the states' total program costs.[4] As of 1994, all states except Wyoming have primacy for managing their drinking water programs.[5]

Under SDWA, thousands of large and small public water systems are regulated. SDWA defines a public drinking water system (PWS) as any system that provides piped water to at least fifteen service connections (such as households, businesses, or schools) or regularly serves at least twenty-five people each day for at least sixty days per year.[6] PWSs can be community, nontransient noncommunity, or transient noncommunity systems. Community systems are subject to standards designed to protect people who may be exposed to drinking water contaminants year-round and therefore need a higher level of protection. As of August 31, 1993, about 240 million people were served by community water systems.[7]

Nontransient noncommunity water systems include schools, factories, and other large facilities that provide drinking water to their students or employees from their own water supplies. Historically, these systems were required to meet only those standards designed to prevent short-term health problems, such as standards for bacteria, nitrate, and turbidity.[8] After the 1986 amendments to the SDWA, however, these systems must meet the same standards as the community systems. Transient noncommunity systems serve transitory customers in areas such as campgrounds, motels, or gas stations. These systems are required to meet only those standards designed to prevent short-term, or acute, health effects.

In short, a wide array of public water suppliers, including some very small systems, fall under the jurisdiction of the SDWA. According to EPA estimates, of the nearly 200,000 public water systems, about 60,000 are community systems, 25,000 are nontransient noncommunity systems, and 115,000 are transient noncommunity systems.[9] Compounding the complex nature of the regulatory target group is the wide variation among community systems, as illustrated in Figure 2-1. While community water systems serve about 92 percent of the U.S. population, most of these water systems are very small. By looking at the first two categories of population size shown on Figure 2-1, one sees that 87 percent of the systems serve fewer than 3,300 customers, and together they serve about 10 percent of the U.S. population taking drinking water from public water supplies.[10] On the other hand, less than 6 percent of the community water systems serve 79 percent of U.S. citizens.[11]

With few exceptions, regardless of their size, the primary regulatory task for these public water suppliers under the SDWA is to control contaminants in the drinking water. Before that can occur, however, the EPA must identify contaminants, determine the public health risk posed by these contaminants, and then establish acceptable levels at which these contaminants may be present in public water supplies. The next section briefly describes the process of setting drinking water standards.

The SDWA requires the EPA to issue standards for any contaminant which may have an adverse effect on human health and which is known or anticipated to occur in public drinking water supplies. Thus, the EPA sets drinking water standards by first identifying a contaminant that is present or may be present in drinking water, and then conducting a risk assessment to determine whether to regulate the contaminant and what levels represent acceptable risk. A contaminant is defined as "any physical, chemical, biological, or radiological substance or matter in water."[12] Prior to 1986, the act required the EPA to propose and then promulgate a recommended maximum contaminant level (RMCL).[13] The RCML was then used as the basis for setting the maximum contaminant level (MCL).

As part of the 1986 amendments, Congress removed the RCML term and replaced it with the maximum contaminant level goal

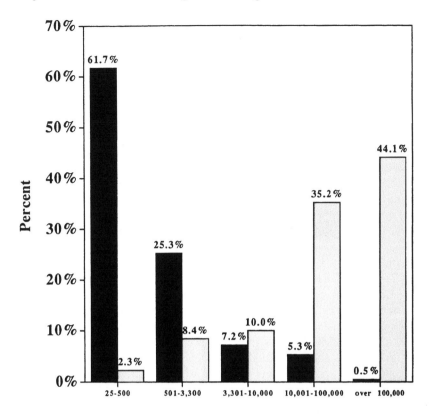

Population Size Category of System

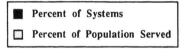

Figure 2-1   Distribution of Community Water Systems by Size

Source: U.S. Environmental Protection Agency, Office of Water, *Technical and Economic Capacity of States and Public Water Systems to Implement Drinking Water Regulations* (Washington, D.C.: U.S. EPA, September, 1993).

(MCLG). An MCLG is to be "set at the level at which no known or anticipated adverse effects on the health of persons occur and which allows for an adequate margin of safety."[14] Establishing a goal is a difficult process, which often involves animal toxicity studies, epidemiology studies, and exposure data to determine concentration thresholds for particular hazardous and toxic substances. The research often results in a no observable adverse effect level (NOAEL), or a dose quantity where no adverse health effect is seen. The EPA takes this information and applies various scaling and uncertainty factors, as well as assumptions regarding exposure to determine a reference dose. This reference dose then becomes the basis for the MCLG. Carcinogens, however, are assumed by the EPA to have no safe level of exposure. Therefore, the agency sets MCLGs of zero for carcinogenic contaminants.[15]

After the proposed MCLG is determined by the risk assessment process, the EPA sets primary and secondary standards for drinking water. Secondary standards are associated with aesthetic qualities of drinking water and are not enforceable by the EPA. Primary standards are enforceable by the EPA and are established either as maximum contaminant levels (MCLs) for individual contaminants or as general requirements for treatment techniques. These standards are reflected in the national primary drinking water regulations (NPDWRs). An MCL is set as close to the MCLG as "feasible."[16] Feasibility allows the EPA to consider technological limitations and costs of treatment, recognizing the difficulty of achieving in practice the MCLG. The MCL frequently translates into requiring the use of the best available technology. Once set, MCLs are enforceable standards which must be met by water supply systems defined by the act. Table 2-1 provides a sampling of national primary drinking water standards set by the EPA as of 1994.

When MCLs cannot be issued by the agency, the EPA administrator is authorized to promulgate a national primary drinking water standard that requires the use of a treatment technology (such as the use of granular activated carbon filters) in lieu of establishing an MCL. Variances from specific treatment techniques by public water suppliers may be granted by the administrator or the primacy state. Before granting a variance, a determination must be made that the MCL cannot be met even if the system uses the best technology, treatment techniques, or other means to control for contaminants, taking cost into consideration. Additionally, granting the variance must not result in an unreasonable health risk to the recipients of the drinking water.

If the public water system cannot meet an applicable MCL, for reasons other than its raw water supply or a regulation imposing the use of a treatment technology, the system may be granted an exemption. An exemption is granted for a period of three years, provided that no unreasonable risk to human health exists.

THE 1986 AMENDMENTS TO THE SAFE DRINKING WATER ACT

The SDWA was amended eight times between 1974 and 1995. The most significant amendments were passed in 1986.[17] In addition to the

TABLE 2-1   Some Primary Drinking Water Standards under the Safe Drinking Water Act (as of 1994)

Contaminant	MCLG (mg/L)	MCL (mg/L)
Volatile Organics		
Benzene	zero	0.005
Trichloroethylene	zero	0.005
Vinyl Chloride	zero	0.002
Coliform and Surface Water Treatment		
Giardia lambia	zero	technical treatment
Legionella	zero	technical treatment
Phase II: Inorganics		
Cadmium	0.005	0.005
Chromium	0.01	0.01
Xylenes (total)	10.00	10.00
Phase V: Inorganics		
Beryllium	0.004	0.004
Cyanide	0.20	0.20
Phase V: Organics		
Dioxin	zero	0.00000003
1,1,2-Trichloroethane	0.003	0.005
Proposed		
Radon	zero	300 picocuries/liter

MCLG = maximum contaminant level goal
MCL = maximum contaminant level
Source: U.S. Environmental Protection Agency, Office of Water, *National Primary Drinking Water Standards* (EPA 810-F-94-001A: February 1994).

changes identified in the overall review of the law in the preceding section, the 1986 amendments changed the implementation of the drinking water program in other important ways. First, the amendments sharply reduced the EPA's discretion both in choosing contaminants to regulate and in the pace by which primary standards are set. Section 1412 of the 1986 amendments required the EPA to establish standards for eighty-three contaminants by June 1989. This was no small task, especially considering that the agency had issued interim primary drinking water regulations for only twenty-three contaminants between 1975 and 1985.[18] Moreover, the list of contaminants was specified by Congress, with the EPA having the ability to substitute only seven contaminants.[19] The list of eighty-three included twenty-two of the twenty-three contaminants currently regulated, but that still meant that MCLGs and national primary drinking water regulations, including MCLs, must be set for sixty-one new contaminants.

Section 1412 also directs the administrator to publish a list of contaminants that may require regulation every three years, called the Drinking Water Priority List. The first list was published in the *Federal Register* in 1988 and an updated list was published three years later. To ensure the continued adoption of drinking water standards, the EPA must propose regulations for not less than twenty-five of these contaminants every three years, starting in January 1991.[20]

The EPA has divided the eighty-three compounds into groups and chosen to regulate each group in stages, based upon the availability of risk-assessment data and other studies which would aid the agency in establishing MCLGs and MCLs for each contaminant. Phase I regulated eight volatile organic chemicals (VOCs), three of which were shown in Table 2-1. Phase II regulated the concentrations of thirty-eight organic and inorganic compounds, including synthetic organic chemicals, other VOCs, and inorganic chemicals. The Surface Water Treatment Rule and Total Coliforms Rule, published in 1989, requires all public water systems using any surface water or groundwater under the direct influence of surface water to disinfect their water and control for the presence of pathogens such as *Giardia* and *Legionella.*

Among the more vexing of contaminants to regulate were radionuclides, particularly radon in water. The EPA first proposed a new radon in water standard in July 1991. Some EPA radon officials in the Office of Air and Radiation believed that the radon in drinking water standard was too restrictive, given the guidance level for radon in air and the relative costs associated with the regulation. Similarly, the American Water Works Association argued for a more reasonable standard, stating that the costs associated with the radon standard would exceed $2 billion per year.[21] Public Law 102-389, referred to as the Chafee–Lautenberg Amendment to the EPA's Appropriation Bill, was subsequently enacted in 1992 and required the EPA to report to Congress on the costs and benefits associated with the proposed drinking water standard. The EPA found that the costs associated with a 300 picocuries per liter (pCi/L) standard were $3.2 million per life saved, as compared with $700,000 per life saved under the radon in air guidance.[22] Under a court-ordered deadline, the EPA began promulgating final regulations for radon in drinking water in April 1993. The agency ceased after Congress refused to fund the EPA's promulgation of a radon standard as part of fiscal year 1994, 1995 and 1996 appropriations bills.

In addition to dramatically altering the standard-setting process of the SDWA, the 1986 amendments also established requirements for certain other types of treatment, such as disinfection and filtration, and required public water systems to monitor for unregulated contaminants.[23] The amendments further sought to protect drinking water taken from groundwater supplies by establishing the wellhead protection program (described in the next section) and requiring the EPA to promulgate monitoring regulations for hazardous waste underground injection operations. The amendments also provided funding for a sole-source aquifer demonstration program.

IMPLEMENTATION CHALLENGES FOR THE REGULATORY PROGRAM

As the brief overview of the provisions indicates, the Safe Drinking Water Act is a complex law presenting numerous implementation challenges. Using the framework developed in the previous chapter, implementation obstacles are described here by category.

Statutory and Regulatory Language

Clearly, the statutory language has complicated the progress of the SDWA. At the national level, the process of developing drinking water standards proved cumbersome and time-consuming for the EPA. As mentioned, frustration with the EPA's regulatory pace prompted the U.S. Congress to spur the agency into action by first creating a list of contaminants to be regulated (the list of eighty-three) and then requiring the EPA to set twenty-five new standards every three years. As of 1996, MCLs had been established for more than eighty contaminants, as well as proposed for radon, radium, and uranium.[24] Those standards have come with a political and economic price, as will be evident.

An additional problem related to the statutory and legal context is that all drinking water contaminants are treated as equally dangerous. In other words, with few exceptions, public water supply systems must monitor and control for contaminants in the drinking water, regardless of relative risk. In this sense, the 1986 amendments are creating additional implementation challenges. By the EPA's own admission, the need for public water suppliers to comply with all of the standards diverts federal, state, and local resources away from focusing on contaminants that may pose the greatest risk.[25] Worse yet, resources needed to address new or higher risk contaminants may not be available because of court-ordered compliance schedules.

One example of the failure to address the highest priority risks has been the agency's focus on toxic substances rather than on microbiological contaminants, such as *cryptosporidium*. In fiscal year 1992, the EPA estimated that roughly 79 percent of all MCL violations were violations of microbiological contaminant standards.[26]

Political Arrangements and the Nature of the Problem

While the pace of standard-setting may be troublesome to congressional representatives and environmental or public health groups, the cost of operating a monitoring program for contaminants has been overwhelming, especially for small public water systems. The problem of cost of compliance for small systems (which represent nearly 90 percent of community water suppliers) has been widely acknowledged and appears in several reports by the U.S. General Accounting Office (GAO) and the EPA.[27] The EPA estimated that the annual cost of compliance will be $1.4 billion by 1995, a figure which is likely to double with the addition of new drinking water standards and the upcoming disinfectants and disinfection by-products rule.[28]

Because small PWSs are subject to the same standards as larger systems, the proportional costs are much larger for smaller PWSs which do not enjoy economies of scale. In most instances, those costs are subsequently paid by households served by the PWS. According to GAO figures, on a per-household basis, the disparity between large and small systems can be dramatic. For example, the costs of bringing synthetic organic and/or inorganic contaminants to MCLs will cost households in large communities about $210 per year; per-household costs for residents of very small communities are likely to be over $1,500 per year.[29] EPA estimates that nearly 70 percent of the costs of compliance will be borne by small PWSs.[30]

One way for small systems to comply is to restructure, whereby groups of small systems share services or contract with private companies or large water systems for services such as operation and maintenance, meter reading and billing, or sample collection and analysis. As part of its review of the drinking water program, the EPA's Science Advisory Board has recommended that a "greater consolidation of small systems should occur" whenever it is necessary to provide monies to upgrade the treatment systems.[31] The EPA has also promoted restructuring through a brochure and manual on restructuring, but there are limits as to how effective restructuring can be at reducing the costs of SDWA compliance.[32] Small water systems may not want to consolidate with other systems for political or logistical reasons. In some cases, restructuring may not be feasible due to the ownership or location of the water supplier.

For example, not all of the very small or small water systems (classified by the EPA as serving fewer than 500 persons or between 500 and 3,300 persons) are public entities. Many are mobile home parks, investor-owned facilities, or homeowners' associations. Others are small clusters of homes in rural areas or suburban systems that lie within the U.S. Census Bureau's Standard Metropolitan Statistical Area. Indeed, a recent EPA study found that 60 percent of all small systems are privately owned and therefore not eligible for federal infrastructure grants, state grants, or other types of public funding.[33]

Regardless of the type of system, however, costs associated with compliance range in the billions of dollars and have stirred political debates about the appropriateness of the SDWA.

Perhaps most telling is the prominence of the costs of compliance in the drinking water program to the national political debate on un-funded mandates. The International City/County Management Association created an Environmental Mandates Task Force in 1992 to provide local governments with more opportunities to respond to federal and state environmental requirements. Not surprisingly, compliance costs associated with the drinking water programs occupied a major portion of the agenda at the kick-off meeting.[34]

As the concern over costly environmental mandates increased, four national local government groups—the National Association of Counties, the U.S. Conference of Mayors, the National League of Cities, and the International City/County Management Association—lobbied for regulatory relief. They held a "National Unfunded Mandates Day" on October 27, 1993, to show their support of federal mandates relief legislation that was then pending in Congress. (The unfunded mandates issue eventually resulted in legislation passed in 1995.)

Federal–State Relationships

The problem of small water systems complying with new drinking water standards not only presents a political dimension to implementation, it also illustrates intergovernmental tensions in implementation. Clearly, concern over the costs of compliance may increase the amount of animosity in relationships between federal, state, and local actors. Also troubling, however, is the tension in federal–state relationships that occurs when states are criticized for failing to enforce the requirements of the safe drinking water program.

Several GAO studies have identified ongoing deficiencies in state programs. In a 1990 report, the GAO noted that the six states it studied failed to take "timely and appropriate enforcement action against significant noncompliers."[35] A study by the EPA found that 28 percent of all community water suppliers (over 16,000 systems) were in violation of the SDWA.[36] State regulators, in turn, undertook formal enforcement action for less than 9 percent of these systems.[37] Troubling the issue of enforcement is the fact that the majority of significant noncompliers tend to be small systems. State officials are reluctant to adopt strong compliance postures toward systems that lack the ability to add new treatment technologies or monitoring staff. Thus, not only were PWSs failing to comply, states were failing to report these violations to the EPA or to take action to address the problem.

In 1992 the EPA initiated action for withdrawing the primacy status of three states: Alaska, Maine, and Washington.[38] Although these states ultimately retained primacy, it illustrates the tenuous nature of the federal–state relationship in the drinking water program.

As the federal funding share of state drinking water programs continues to erode, some states may opt to return authority for the drinking water program to the EPA. Connecticut and Massachusetts narrowly avoided returning the program after the funding for the state's share of the drinking water program was eliminated in each state's fiscal year 1993 budget. Ultimately, these states and others will find the drinking water program on precarious budgetary ground.[39]

By the EPA's own estimate, "no state, even after receiving a fee increase, has sufficient funding to meet all the requirements of the SDWA."[40] In 1992 the agency moved to allow states five additional years to comply with all aspects of the regulations. Meanwhile, many states have attempted to supplement federal funding with increased fees for water supply customers. However, between 1992 and 1994, only twenty-eight states successfully raised revenues within the state: twenty-one passed user fee increases; seven states added additional appropriations.[41]

PERCEPTIONS OF STATE DRINKING WATER OFFICIALS

While the foregoing discussion suggests a number of challenges confronting EPA and state officials faced with implementing the safe drinking water program, it is also important to identify the perceptions that state drinking water program directors have about their program. A series of interviews were conducted and a total of fifty-six surveys were mailed to state and territorial drinking water program directors in the summer of 1995. Forty-three surveys were returned, for a response rate of 77 percent. The following sections identify the range of perceptions that state officials have regarding the safe drinking water program.

Factors Which Facilitate or Hinder Implementation

When asked to identify factors that facilitate implementation of their state's drinking water program, state drinking water program directors ranked the technical expertise of their staff first, followed by adequate state funding, adequate staffing, and support of the department. (See Table 2-2.) Clearly, many state officials believe that their staff members are well-trained and possess adequate skills to conduct sanitary surveys. What is less helpful is the amount of technical assistance and support given to the states by the EPA. Only 2 percent of the state drinking water program coordinators believe that the technical expertise provided by the EPA facilitates the implementation of their programs.

TABLE 2-2 Factors Which Facilitate Implementation of the Drinking Water Program Directors (Percent of State Officials Ranking Factor as One of the Top Three)

Technical expertise of state staff	58
Adequate state funding	42
Adequate staffing	35
Support of the department	32
State laws regulating public water suppliers	26
Clear and consistent state program goals and requirements	23
Adequate federal funding	18
Support of local governments	14
Support of the EPA regional office	9
Clear and consistent EPA program goals and requirements	9
Available solutions to address contaminated drinking water	4
Citizen involvement and support	4
Technical assistance provided by the EPA	2

n = 43

When asked about factors that constrain the implementation of their programs, state drinking water program directors identify several factors, some of which were mentioned in the previous section. Echoing recent GAO investigations, only 29 percent of state drinking water program directors believe that they receive adequate funding to operate their programs. They also believe that many small public water suppliers lack the resources to mount the monitoring program and/or to update their facilities. (See Table 2-3.) Some drinking water program directors worry about the ability of small public water systems to perform their obligations under the SDWA, as illustrated by this comment:

> Monitoring for contaminants should be performed by the state regulatory agency (or our contractor) and not the water systems, so that we can truly determine the quality of the drinking water. Many systems do not

TABLE 2-3 Survey Questions About the Operation of State Drinking Water Programs and State-Level Implementation Variables (Responses of State Drinking Water Officials)

Survey Questions	% Agree	% Disagree	Other Programs % Agree*
Officials are concerned	77	7	53
Administrators are concerned	65	5	41
Program is effective	84	0	62
Program funding is adequate	29	45	37
Program is improving	72	19	63
Legislators are concerned	33	23	20
Citizens are concerned	42	12	44
Need a stronger state program	72	9	35
Need a stronger local program	41	27	47
Staff adequately trained	70	14	50

n = 43
*denotes the responses from 230 state directors for asbestos, coal, lead, radon, and wellhead protection programs (controlling for drinking water responses)

perform monitoring as required due to the costs involved, therefore we know little about their current water quality. Additionally, some systems do not use appropriate sampling protocols, thus making results questionable. The reality is that opportunities for fraud are great with a self-monitoring program.

Thus, resources at both the local and the state levels appear to be limited, according to the respondents in this study. Limited state resources hamper the ability of the state to conduct sanitary surveys; limited resources at the local level encourage noncompliance with monitoring requirements. However, most drinking water program directors believe that top-level officials in their state agency are concerned about protecting drinking water supplies (77 percent).

Political support outside the agency is somewhat mixed. While most directors agree that state administrators support their program (65 percent), they are less likely to agree that legislators or citizens are concerned about drinking water protection (33 percent and 42 percent, respectively). One state director commented that citizens assume that public drinking water supplies are safe and only pay attention to drinking water regulation after a highly publicized drinking water problem, such as the *cryptosporidium* scare in Milwaukee, Wisconsin, in 1993. However, perceived levels of political support of legislators, agency officials, and state administrators by state drinking water program directors are higher than the perceptions of directors of other environmental programs (33 percent to 20 percent; 77 percent to 53 percent; and 65 percent to 41 percent, respectively).

Perceptions About Working Relationships

Many state drinking water officials perceive a maze of federal regulations, inflexible and complicated EPA policies, and inappropriate program requirements. Indeed, state directors identified problems with the operation of the intergovernmental program as causing implementation problems more often than state-level funding or staffing constraints.

Only 2 percent of the state drinking water directors believe that the EPA drinking water program is effective (compared to 84 percent who perceive the state program to be effective). (See Table 2-4.) They are even less likely to believe that the EPA program is adequately funded than to perceive adequate funding for the state program (12 percent to 29 percent). They also are not very likely to perceive that the EPA staff members have a high level of expertise (only 19 percent

TABLE 2-4 Survey Questions About the Operation of the EPA Drinking Water Program and National-Level Implementation Variables (Responses of State Drinking Water Officials)

Survey Questions	% Agree	% Disagree	Other Programs % Agree*
EPA program is effective	2	54	24
EPA officials are concerned	67	14	59
EPA program is adequately funded	12	72	29
EPA staff have a high degree of technical expertise	19	47	16
Regional and headquarters staff view program similarly	0	85	29
Oversight needed to encourage program implementation	30	54	33
EPA sets reasonable MCLs	27	43	na

n = 43
*denotes the responses from 230 state directors for asbestos, coal, lead, radon, and wellhead protection programs (controlling for drinking water responses)

agree). As one state director commented, "EPA should provide more technical assistance to state programs, such as having staff epidemiologists and other experts we can turn to for help and advice. In our [EPA] region, they call on us for help in understanding their own regulations."

Perhaps most remarkable is the fact that no state drinking water director believes that the staff from the EPA regional offices and the staff from EPA headquarters view the state programs in the same way. Most of the state frustration with the intergovernmental implementation process is directed at actions which occur at the EPA headquarters level, as illustrated by these comments: "EPA resources should be shifted from enforcement of regulations to research and development. EPA's role should focus on developing scientifically sound standards which the states enforce." "EPA's responsibilities should be more focused on conducting necessary scientific research to establish appropriate MCLs and associated treatment technologies and states should be responsible for implementation of programs. Why spend so much [federal] money on enforcement when the EPA can't set reasonable standards?"

Another state director suggested that "those [EPA staff] in Washington, D.C., writing the rules should have field experience so they would understand what it takes to implement the rules and how those rules impact water suppliers, especially the small water suppliers." Another commented about the role orientation of the EPA headquarters staff: "EPA is legalistic and this must be changed. EPA should be a service to states, not the states a service to EPA. Regional EPA offices should have more autonomy from EPA headquarters because they have a better idea of what is going on." This dichotomy in state perceptions of EPA regional and headquarters staff is also supported by the data in Table 2-5. When asked whether the EPA regional staff are supportive of their program, 86 percent of state program directors agreed that they were, and the same number believe that they enjoy a positive working relationship with EPA project officers in the regional offices. However, only 30 percent of state drinking water program directors agree that EPA headquarters staff are supportive of state drinking water programs.

The data presented in Table 2-5 also suggest that the EPA has some room to improve the oversight activities associated with the implementation of the SDWA. Most notably, state directors express concern with unreasonable and inconsistent reporting requirements. Only 9 percent of state directors agree that their reporting requirements are reasonable; only 19 percent agree that they have sufficient flexibility to run the state program. Both of these percentages are much lower than those of state directors in other environmental programs (40 percent of

TABLE 2-5 Survey Questions About Federal–State Working Relationships (Responses of State Drinking Water Officials)

Survey Questions	% Agree	% Disagree	Other Programs % Agree*
EPA regional staff supportive	86	5	81
EPA headquarters supportive	30	26	42
Positive working relationship	86	5	81
State–EPA relationships have gotten worse	23	46	11
States have sufficient flexibility	19	63	61
Evaluations by EPA are fair	58	15	53
Reporting requirements are reasonable	9	56	40
Program requirements are consistent	23	28	33
EPA clearly communicates program requirements	21	43	32

n = 43
*denotes the responses from 230 state directors for asbestos, coal, lead, radon, and wellhead protection programs (controlling for drinking water responses)

whom agree that reporting requirements are reasonable and 61 percent of whom agree that they have sufficient flexibility). Finally, 43 percent of state drinking water program directors do not agree that the EPA clearly communicates program goals and requirements to them.

In part, the negative perceptions of the EPA headquarters activities come from the feeling that states have little significant input into the rule-making process. As one state director noted, "The EPA should include states right from the very beginning on rule development. States can provide better input on what the implementation problems will be because we live it every day. Right now, though, it seems like they ignore us."

Most troubling is the nearly unanimous concern voiced by state directors that the EPA tended to focus more on reporting requirements (state agency outputs) and less on what activities would achieve safer drinking water (policy outcomes). These comments are suggestive of a nearly universal mindset of state program directors toward the EPA: "Constantly changing and excessively complicated federal regulations, a 'one size fits all' enforcement approach by the federal government, ensures that we [the state agency] won't get to cleaner water. Moreover, this approach results in excessive costs for small [public water] systems, often with no or little impact on public health risk," and "New and changing requirements and priorities from EPA, some of which do not make a great deal of sense for our state, inhibit our ability to run an effective program."

Some of the frustrations of the state staff toward the EPA could more appropriately be directed toward Congress and the congressional instructions given to the agency in the 1986 amendments to the SDWA. As discussed in the earlier part of the chapter, the EPA is under both congressional directive and court order to promulgate new primary standards for eighty-three different contaminants and to add new standards every three years. This directive is far more conducive to a "command and control" regulatory style than to a cooperative approach geared toward sound science and regulatory negotiations. While some state officials seemed to believe that the standard-setting process could be controlled by the EPA, others noted the effect of the 1986 amendments. "Setting standards every three years seems to me to be a ludicrous policy. Why doesn't Congress acknowledge that one public water supply system may have a unique, but terribly important, contaminant that needs to be addressed from a public health point of view? We'd go farther [in protecting the public] with less money."

In sum, state drinking water program officials overwhelmingly feel that the drinking water program is effective and that it has improved in the last few years. When compared to other environmental program officials, they perceive higher amounts of state-level administrative and political support for maintaining their program. The most challenging extrinsic factor for implementing their programs is limited funding for small public water systems.

State drinking water officials agree that EPA regional drinking water staff members are supportive of state drinking water programs and that they enjoy positive federal–state working relationships. What concerns state drinking water officials as they implement their programs is the lack of technical expertise of EPA staff, cumbersome and unnecessary reporting requirements, a lack of communication with EPA headquarters staff, and a common sentiment that the EPA officials in Washington, D.C., are insufficiently interested and aware of the states' implementation obstacles and the challenges faced by public water supply systems.

Many state drinking water officials perceive EPA headquarters staff as being overly "top-down" and less interested in helping states run their programs than in developing ill-conceived and inflexible program requirements. While state directors agree that they have good working relationships with the EPA regional staff, they are less convinced that the EPA headquarters drinking water personnel are interested in helping them run a good state program that results in protecting the public from contaminants in drinking water.

RECENT RESPONSES BY THE EPA AND CONGRESS

The EPA has not been immune to the criticisms levied against the drinking water program. On March 29, 1995, EPA Administrator Carol Browner released the agency's "white paper" on the drinking water program titled, *"Strengthening the Safety of Our Drinking Water: A Report on Progress and Challenges and an Agenda for Action."*[42] The report highlighted five action items for the EPA: providing more public information about drinking water issues; focusing on the most serious health risks; providing technical assistance to protect source water and help small public water systems; reinventing federal–state partnerships to improve drinking water safety; and investing in community drinking water facilities to protect human health. The report represented the EPA's response to the president's environmental reinvention initiative, which had been issued on March 16, 1995.[43]

The initiative, part of the Clinton Administration's broader governmental reform effort under the auspices of the National Performance Review, identified twenty-five high-priority actions for the agency. Among them was a directive for the EPA to cut costs and increase flexibility for states and water suppliers by targeting regulations on substantial health risks, seeking a delay for court-ordered schedules for drinking water, and reducing monitoring burdens for chemical contaminants.[44]

The combined impetus of the EPA drinking water report and the president's initiative prompted the Office of Ground Water and Drinking Water to undertake a reassessment of the drinking water program and create a new approach toward federal–state relationships. This effort culminated in a draft *Drinking Water Program Redirection Proposal*, released for public comment on November 30, 1995.[45] The proposal has four objectives, each listed as equally important to the redirection effort: to engage in sound science with adequate data; to establish risk-based priorities for setting high-quality standards; to establish strong, flexible partnerships with state and local governments in implementation; and to have community-based effective source water protection. However, the draft proposal goes on to state that funding limitations prompt the redirection effort to "scale back" on the source water protection activities (most notably, wellhead protection).[46]

The proposed redirection of the drinking water program includes leveraging businesses and citizen groups to help protect source waters instead of focusing exclusively on state and local agencies; using regulatory negotiations to facilitate stakeholder involvement in rule development for disinfection and disinfection by-products; emphasizing voluntary efforts such as the Partnership for Safe Water program; and changing the emphasis of the agency's relationship with states to one of "compliance assistance" rather than "oversight."[47]

As shown on Table 2-6, the drinking water program transformation as identified in the proposal appears to be headed in the right direction, at least when the transformation is compared to the implementation challenges perceived by most state drinking water program directors. (See Tables 2-3, 2-4, and 2-5.) For example, the "new" oversight approach taken by the EPA will have fewer regulations, measure environmental results rather than state activities, and seek to empower state drinking water programs.

However, it is too soon to tell how (and if) these transformations will occur. Budget cuts proposed by the 104th Congress may jeopardize new initiatives. Equally important is the concern of EPA project officers in regional offices responsible for the wellhead protection program, who feel that the headquarters' proposed redirection is ill-conceived in two ways. First, even absent any budget cuts imposed by Congress,

---

TABLE 2-6   Drinking Water Program Transformation as Proposed by the EPA Office of Ground Water and Drinking Water

Old Approaches	New Approaches
Many new regulations (priorities based on risk)	Fewer new regulations
Measure activities	Measure environmental results
Source water protection and public water supply programs separate	Integrate prevention and implementation
Extensive oversight of regional/state programs	Empowerment/state partnerships
Rely on mandates	Balance mandates and voluntary approaches
"Do It" ourselves	Leverage stakeholders/energize communities
Intermittent coordination with stakeholders	Early, comprehensive stakeholder involvement
Detailed program reporting	Reporting simplified
Technical jargon	Plain English

Source: U.S. Environmental Protection Agency, Office of Water, *Drinking Water Program Redirection Proposal: A Public Comment Draft*, EPA-810-D-95-001 (Washington, D.C.: U.S. EPA, November 1995).

the redirection will reduce available funding and resources for well-head protection (headquarters staff will be reduced by nearly one-third).[48] Thus, the already struggling wellhead protection program is made more vulnerable by the redirection proposal for the regulatory program. Second, some regional staff feel that the proposal will redirect attention away from state implementation, giving more resources to community-based or large national water or health organizations.

The 104th Congress also took note of the gargantuan task it had placed on the EPA (in the form of setting standards) and the public water supply systems (in requiring all systems to comply with monitoring requirements) and amended the SDWA in 1996. P.L. 104-182, signed by President Clinton on August 2, revokes the requirement that the EPA regulate twenty-five contaminants every three years and allows the EPA to select new contaminants based on risk and occurrence in water supplies. Public water supply systems have up to three years to comply with new standards (with an additional two-year extension if approved by the EPA or state agency), instead of eighteen months under the 1986 amendments.

The 1996 amendments also give the EPA some latitude in setting standards based on relative risk. Most notably, the EPA may set a radon in drinking water standard that provides the same level of protectiveness for public health as does the radon in air standard. Also, the new law directs the agency to identify technologies that meet the MCLs and are affordable for small systems.

In a related effort, Congress appropriated $1.275 billion for the state revolving fund for drinking water projects. This amount includes the $725 million in fiscal 1996 that was lost when Congress failed to reauthorize the SDWA by a statutory deadline of August 1, 1996, and adds $550 million to be used by states in fiscal year 1997.[49]

In sum, both Congressional and EPA actions in 1996 create major changes to the way the federal government will respond to the implementation of a safe drinking water program. As of this writing, it is too soon to tell to what extent these statutory and administrative changes will shape implementation outcomes.

CONCLUSIONS ABOUT THE SAFE
DRINKING WATER PROGRAM

In light of the policy implementation framework (Figure 1-2), extrinsic factors seem to influence the implementation of this intergovernmental environmental program. Most influential are the statutory requirements and the fiscal challenges faced by small water systems. However, at least from the perspective of state drinking water staff, the role orientations of the EPA headquarters staff do not facilitate the implementation of state programs. Recently, however, internal efforts to redirect the drinking water program at the EPA and continued scrutiny by the GAO and other organizations seem to be moving the program in the right direction.

Intrinsic factors that help explain implementation include high levels of political support for strong drinking water programs and a state agency culture with high levels of empathy for community water systems. Empathy with small suppliers, however, has been associated with a reluctance on the part of the state to cite monitoring violations. Agency capacity, as viewed by survey respondents, is sufficient, but the capacity of the target group (public water suppliers) to comply with regulatory requirements varies, largely based on the size of the system. High costs associated with compliance to unnecessary monitoring and treatment requirements prompts local politicians to voice their opposition to the full implementation of the Safe Drinking Water Act and its 1986 amendments.

When the federal–state working relationship typology is considered, the relationship in the drinking water program seems to fall in the "coming apart and contentious" category. Even though working relationships are viewed by state program officials as positive, other measures of federal–state relationship indicate otherwise. For example, almost no one at the state level believes that the EPA is effective. (See Table 2-4.) Nor do the state respondents view reporting requirements as reasonable or consistent. Perhaps most telling is the perception of nearly one-fourth of state directors that state–EPA relationships have gotten worse in the past few years. (See Table 2-5.) These perceptions suggest that while the federal oversight agency is highly involved in the drinking water program, the nature of that involvement (providing more technical support, for example) could be improved. Finally, mutual trust seems to be low, as indicated by the comments of state and EPA staff.

However, this program is a regulatory program with stringent requirements on public water suppliers. What is needed is a comparison of the regulatory program under the SDWA to the nonregulatory wellhead protection program established in the 1986 SDWA amendments. The second half of the chapter deals with the wellhead program.

THE WELLHEAD PROTECTION PROGRAM: UNDERGROUND AND OUT OF VIEW

Section 1428 of the 1986 SDWA amendments established the first nationwide program to protect ground water resources used for public drinking water supplies, the Wellhead Protection Program (WHPP).

Termed the "jewel in the crown" of U.S. Environmental Protection Agency's groundwater protection efforts, the WHPP was thought to be a necessary, even critical, element to any comprehensive strategy to protect groundwater sources of drinking water.[50]

The statute gave responsibility for WHPP implementation to the states and required all states to submit WHP programs to the EPA for approval by 1989.[51] Thus, it is not a delegated program in the same sense as the much larger regulatory program for drinking water, in which states receive primacy upon approval. Rather, the statute requires direct action by the states. The EPA is required to review state programs, but has no authority to run a wellhead protection program in a state that chooses not to comply.

Compliance for states meant that they were required to delineate wellhead areas for protection, identify sources of contaminants within those delineated areas, and establish a management strategy to protect the groundwater resource. Two years after approval, states should make "every reasonable effort to implement the wellhead area protection program . . ." (Section 1428g). To help states implement the program, Congress authorized grants totaling $145 million for fiscal years 1987 through 1991.

As is the case with other environmental programs, the implementation reality bears little resemblance to the implementation goal in the statute. Nine years after the amendment was passed, fourteen states still had not submitted WHP programs for EPA approval. Moreover, only a handful of states with approved programs have finished delineating wellhead protection areas. Perhaps most importantly, federal grants to states to establish and maintain WHPPs never materialized. With the exception of a relatively few demonstration grants, the states never received any of the grant dollars authorized under Section 1428. Instead, states have relied primarily on grant dollars under Section 106 of the Clean Water Act and/or on their own-source revenues to protect wellhead areas. Thus, it is not surprising that many state and federal officials agree that, a decade after Congress mandated wellhead protection, state wellhead programs have a long way to go.

Further increasing the implementation challenge is the necessity of intergovernmental coordination. WHPPs require extensive cooperation among all levels of government, including local governments and public water suppliers. The EPA lacks a regulatory ratchet like it has under the larger drinking water program and relies instead on a more conciliatory approach to encourage state implementation. States, in turn, must rely on the willingness of local governments to enact land-use controls that sufficiently protect ground water resources. Local governments may be reluctant to protect drinking water supplies if such protection means interrupting the activities of local businesses, particularly in the absence of convincing evidence regarding existing or potential sources of contamination.

Even so, the protection of ground water is an important public health activity. Approximately half of America's drinking water is supplied through ground water resources.[52] Moreover, the ability to restore contaminated ground water may be limited. Thus, it is prudent to protect ground water and prevent contamination from occurring in the first place. Yet, while ground water protection continues to be discussed in Congress, in the EPA, and in state forums, WHPPs receive little national attention and are generally omitted from larger discussions about protecting drinking water. As discussed in the previous section, recent efforts by the EPA to redirect the drinking water program may actually work to further dilute the level of attention and resources paid to wellhead protection.[53]

Thus, the wellhead protection program, established as part of the 1986 amendments to the Safe Drinking Water Act, is considerably different from the larger program. WHPPs are often funded from monies taken from the Clean Water program (not the SDWA) because no federal grants were appropriated (although grant money was authorized for the establishment of WHPPs). The tenuous nature of available federal funding for the program has worked to increase the cooperative nature of federal–state relationships and reduce the urgency for states to have EPA-approved programs. Finally, absent state mandates on local governments, WHPPs rely on the interest of local communities in protecting groundwater supplies. The next section reviews specific requirements for state WHPPs.

KEY PROVISIONS OF THE WELLHEAD PROTECTION PROGRAM

Under the 1986 amendments, state WHP programs are first to be approved by the EPA. According to statutory language, approved state WHPPs must include seven elements: a description of the roles and duties of state and local agencies; the delineation of wellhead protection areas (WHPAs), including the selection of criteria for delineation; the identification of all anthropogenic sources of contaminants within the wellhead protection area; the development of a management plan for controlling contaminant sources and protecting groundwater resources; a contingency plan for the location and provision of alternate drinking water supplies; a provision for protecting new wells; and opportunities for public participation and education.[54]

A major activity is to delineate the wellhead area needing protection. The SDWA defines a wellhead protection area (WHPA) as "the surface and subsurface area surrounding a water well or wellfield supplying a public water system, through which contaminants are reasonably likely to move toward and reach such water well or well-field." Section 1428(a)(2) of the SDWA requires that delineations be based on "all reasonably available hydrogeologic information on groundwater flow, recharge and discharge, and other information the State deems necessary to determine the wellhead protection area."

Although the EPA provides delineation guidelines, the process of delineation is a complex technical task requiring specialized expertise.[55] WHPAs can vary in size, depending on their geology, pumping rates, and well construction. Under the SDWA, delineations of WHPAs must be based on "all reasonably available hydrogeologic information."[56] However, states may "phase in" more sophisticated delineation techniques by moving from a fixed-radius method of delineation to more advanced modeling techniques. (The simplest delineation, fixed radius, protects the area around the wellhead without regard for hydrogeologic information by drawing a circle around the wellhead. To apply this method, all that is needed is a determination of the distance of the radius [say 100 feet] and a compass to draw the circle on a map.)

Many states use the fixed-radius delineation as a baseline for more protective delineations. For example, Idaho identifies four major zones within a WHPA, with a fixed radius of 50 feet for wells used for the first zone (Zone IA), a two-year time of travel for groundwater flows based on hydrogeologic mapping and modeling for the second zone (Zone IB), increasing the time of travel to five years for the third zone (Zone II), and then establishing the WHPA at the known recharge areas and flow boundaries (Zone III).[57] When the final phase is completed, the zone of contribution for potential contaminants to the groundwater is reasonably understood.[58]

State programs submitted to EPA must contain the rationale for the selected WHPA delineation method, as well as a plan for refining the original delineation. States opting for an arbitrary fixed-radius de-lineation technique are encouraged to move to more hydrogeologic-based methods as soon as possible.[59]

Once the WHPA is delineated, sources of contamination must be identified. Subsection 1428(a)(3) of the SDWA requires states to "iden-tify all anthropogenic sources of contaminants which may have any adverse effect on the health of persons." Human activities that can potentially contaminate groundwater include releases from landfills or surface impoundments, leaking underground storage tanks, industrial facilities, or other point sources, as well as nonpoint sources such as the application of agricultural chemicals or releases from areas contain-ing septic tanks. In developing their WHPP, states must describe the process by which they will systematically identify source categories (such as landfills) and then individual sources within each category located in the WHPA.

Once the delineation and source identification phases have begun, states must develop a management program that contains provisions of technical and financial assistance to local governments and the process of implementing control measures for the WHPA. Control measures could include permit requirements for siting or operating facilities, spill prevention control, agricultural best management practices, and various types of land-use restrictions.

While the process seems relatively straightforward, the ability to record a state's progress in wellhead protection program implementation is difficult. EPA guidance documents for state WHPPs, including both the initial 1987 guidance and the 1995 biennial report guidance, assume that state WHPPs will move in a linear fashion, beginning with an approved program, proceeding to delineating WHP areas, and ending with effective management of those areas by local officials.[60] Thus, the agency assumes that wellhead delineations precede management of the wellhead areas; by this logic, states with "better" programs have completed more wellhead delineations. Some states, such as Illinois, have opted to move first to manage source water and then to delineate the precise area to be protected.[61]

Another challenge in assessing the implementation of the wellhead protection program has been the difficulty in establishing a viable set of reporting criteria for states to report their progress. For example, is a state which chooses to do the less expensive and faster fixed-radius delineation making more progress than a state which selects a more accurate, but also more difficult to complete, delineation based on hydrogeologic data? The first state completes more delineations; the second state completes more accurate ones. Or, as is the case in Illinois, are states that seek to manage areas around wellheads before delineations are completed working backwards and, therefore, less effectively?

The EPA wrestled with this problem of establishing meaningful biennial reporting requirements for nearly eight years, releasing new guidance in 1995.[62] Under the new guidance, states will report the status of public water systems according to what each system has accomplished. Systems can be classified as "tier 1," meaning that they have taken no action to protect wellhead areas; "tier 2," if they have notified the state that they intend to develop a WHPP; "tier 3," if delineations have been completed and potential sources of contamination identified; and "tier 4," if the public water system has adopted management and contingency plans. Management plans vary by state and may include either nonregulatory approaches, such as voluntary modifications of activities within a WHPA, or regulatory approaches, such as land-use controls and prohibitions of certain activities within WHPA, or elements of both approaches. Additionally, states must report this information for community water systems served by groundwater by system size (noncommunity water systems are not required to be reported).

One implication from this discussion of statutory requirements for state WHPPs is that the process is neither easy nor straightforward. One would expect that state and EPA officials responsible for getting the program underway would be very cooperative, given the complexity of the task involved and the need to work together to understand the issues associated with wellhead protection. The next section highlights the perceptions that state and EPA staff have about the implementation of the program.

PERCEPTIONS OF STATE WELLHEAD PROTECTION OFFICIALS

As with the drinking water regulatory program, surveys were sent in 1995 to all state and territorial wellhead program directors, asking them to identify implementation constraints. They were also asked to assess the progress of their program and the quality of their working relationships with EPA regional and headquarters staff, as well as with local governmental officials. A total of fifty-three surveys were sent, forty-seven were returned for a response rate of 89 percent.

Following the survey, telephone interviews were conducted with state wellhead protection program coordinators, the project officers responsible for overseeing the state WHPP program in three EPA regional offices, EPA headquarters personnel charged with implementing the WHPP provisions of the Safe Drinking Water Act, and regional or local governmental officials who were identified by state or EPA staff as being actively involved in wellhead protection programs. In all, twenty-eight interviews occurred between January 1, 1995, and January 31, 1996.

Factors Which Facilitate or Hinder Implementation

Tables 2-7 through 2-10 provide a summary of the survey results. Table 2-7 provides the ranking by state officials of factors which facilitate WHPP implementation. Tables 2-8, 2-9, and 2-10 present the perceptions of state wellhead program directors about state-level and federal-level implementation elements, including their perceptions about their working relationships with EPA staff.

Table 2-7 suggests that state officials view the willingness of local officials to support the state WHPP as the single largest factor facilitat-

TABLE 2-7 Factors Which Facilitate Implementation of the Well-head Protection Program (Percent of the State Officials Ranking Factor As One of the Top Three)

Technical expertise of state staff	15
Adequate state funding	17
Adequate staffing	42
Support of the department	15
State laws mandating wellhead protection programs	6
Clear and consistent state program goals and requirements	25
Adequate federal funding	38
Support of local governments	57
Support of the EPA Regional office	2
Clear and consistent EPA program goals and requirements	2
Available solutions to address ground water contamination	15
Support of regional planning and other organizations	17
Citizen involvement and support	42

n = 47

ing implementation, followed closely by citizen involvement and support, adequate state staffing, and federal resources. This ranking is supported by comments during interviews. When asked to identify the biggest constraint to implementing a WHPP, most state officials identified the lack of federal funding as the largest obstacle. The link to federal funding is especially critical for WHPPs, since thirty-nine state officials report that they rely on federal grants to fund most of their program. Most state wellhead programs operate through the much larger state water programs created in response to the Clean Water Act and are closely linked to other state efforts to protect ground-water resources. A few state wellhead programs, however, are tied to their states' drinking water program (not surprising, given their common statutory basis in the 1986 SDWA amendments).

The feeling of state wellhead coordinators that their program is dwarfed by the larger water programs is apparent in the survey responses. The following comment was typical of most state WHPP directors interviewed:

"Our program is run with insufficient funds and manpower. This is ridiculous when wellhead protection is the keystone of groundwater protection in this state. Why do we [the state] keep funding pollution control of surface water and ignore source water protection?"

Closely related to the lack of funding is the perception that state staffing levels are grossly inadequate to run an effective WHPP. Seventeen states do not have the luxury of more than a single full-time equivalent (FTE) staff members dedicated to WHPP; only three states have more than ten FTE. State WHPPs are new programs, too. In 1995, 36 percent of the programs were less than three years old. In short, state wellhead protection programs are likely to be manned by one or two people and to be fledgling programs operating through much larger drinking water or clean water programs.

The willingness of municipalities to take responsibility for wellhead protection, especially when such responsibility may require changes in land use, is often elusive, according to state officials. Local governments are reluctant to confront a political climate that may resist land-control ordinances. This is especially true when the expense of local wellhead protection programs is borne by communities (which may also be paying for monitoring and control of contaminants under the drinking water regulatory program). One official estimated the cost of delineation of the wellhead area in his community to be between $15,000 and $40,000. More troubling, however, is the potential cost of removing possible sources of groundwater contamination (such as underground storage tanks), which could range from ten to twenty times the cost of delineation.

Local communities also worry about "legally defensible" delineations. Fixed-radius and other arbitrary delineations may open up the possibility of charges of unfairness by business owners and others who find their activities around a wellhead restrained. More sophisticated approaches, however, are also more expensive and may be beyond the expertise of local communities. Thus, local governments look to other governmental levels for technical expertise.

According to some state and local officials, local communities aren't unwilling so much as they are apathetic or lack knowledge about the benefits of wellhead protection. In these instances, the need for education and technical assistance is paramount. These observations of interviewees are instructive:

"A mandatory program [for local governments] is all nice and good, but without the buy-in of local officials for the program, where does it get you? Once you educate a community about the benefits of protecting the groundwater, such as asking them how much it would cost to replace their public well, they get enthused about WHPP."

"WHPP is a hard sell to local communities. Sure, it's a good idea, but small [public water] systems using part time or voluntary staff have trouble making it happen."

"Local officials need more guidance, more tools, more technical assistance if we are ever going to make the [WHP] program effective."

Despite these obstacles, many local communities are beginning to implement WHP activities. The willingness of local officials to undertake groundwater protection is perhaps nowhere more apparent than in New York, where the Long Island Regional Planning Board petitioned the state legislature for special protection from groundwater contamination, allowing no new development on Long Island. Planning Board officials were driven by the need to maintain groundwater quality and quantity, particularly since residents are completely dependent upon groundwater resources for drinking water supplies. Not many communities, however, have the ability to declare development off-limits absent compelling data illustrating the imminent contamination of groundwater.

In sum, the support of local governments is the most important facilitating agent for implementing state WHPPs, with adequate funding and staffing, citizen involvement, and support also important. Many state officials point to the need for education and public outreach that captures the attention and interest of local communities as essential to program implementation. State-level constraints on implementation are reviewed in the next section.

Perceptions About Program Success and State-level Variables

Survey and interview research suggests that state program officials feel that state-level implementation variables affect their ability to operate a program. Perhaps the most striking observation to be made from these data is that less than half of the state WHPP coordinators (45 percent) believe that their program is effective, compared to 71 percent of state officials in other environmental programs (see Table 2-8). One obvious obstacle is funding. Mirroring the concern over federal funding, only 15 percent of responding state officials believe that state funding is adequate. Moreover, a paltry 8 percent of the state officials believe that state legislators are concerned about wellhead protection (compared to 26 percent of the respondents directing other environmental programs and 33 percent of the state drinking water program directors).

Only 38 percent of state WHPP directors believe that top-level administrators of their agencies support wellhead protection programs. On the other hand, state directors of the drinking water program are much more likely to perceive support (65 percent), as are about half of the directors in other programs (52 percent). The lack of programmatic support sometimes comes as a trade-off between the regulatory program established under the SDWA and the wellhead program, as illustrated by this comment:

"Wellhead protection is only one of very many issues. It is often not the 'issue of the month,' so it doesn't get the attention it deserves in the state legislature. What's worse is the perception of administrators [in this agency] and others that the Safe Drinking Water program protects people, so why focus on source water?"

TABLE 2-8   Survey Questions About the Operation of State Wellhead Protection Programs and State-Level Implementation Variables (Responses of State Wellhead Protection Program Officials)

Survey Questions	% Agree	% Disagree	Other Programs % Agree*
Officials are concerned	70	9	55
Administrators are concerned	38	13	52
Program is effective	45	21	71
Program funding is adequate	15	76	30
Program is improving	79	8	61
Legislators are concerned	8	41	26
Citizens are concerned	49	11	42
Need a stronger state program	36	33	44
Need a stronger local program	76	13	38
Having an EPA-approved program is important	45	32	na

n = 47
*denotes the responses from 230 state directors for asbestos, coal, lead, radon, and drinking water programs (controlling for wellhead program responses)

Many WHPP officials believe that their programs often take a back seat to other environmental programs. The comment quoted illustrates the tension between the WHP and regulatory drinking water programs, but other environmental programs also interfere with WHPP implementation. One WHPP official noted that the "huge water program [under the Clean Water Act] just dwarfs anything we try to do—they've got the money and there's little coordination between our program and theirs." Another official suggested that other environmental programs should shape their program around wellhead protection, with "priority given to potential problems in wellhead areas."

When asked whether having an EPA-approved program was important, state officials had mixed reactions. While 45 percent agreed that EPA approval was important, many officials felt that it was important because it provided a funding opportunity through the Clean Water program or, in some cases, added status to the program. Few officials felt that WHP programs approved by the EPA were necessarily better programs. The EPA designation helped to get funding for a program with little political or executive support at the state level or even within the agency.

Thus, the perceptions of state WHPP officials suggest that agency capacity variables (staffing and funding), political variables (legislative, executive, and citizen support) and inter- and intra-agency relationships all contribute to the implementation of WHPP.

Perceptions About Federal-State Relationships and the EPA Program

If state WHPP coordinators view the funding for their programs as inadequate, they are even more likely to believe that wellhead protection program funding for the EPA is inadequate. (See Table 2-9.) Only 7 percent of the state WHPP directors agree that the EPA has enough money to run a program, compared to 31 percent of the directors in other state environmental programs and 12 percent of state drinking water officials. (See Table 2-4.) Not surprisingly, few state WHPP officials believe that the EPA program is effective (26 percent), although this is higher than in other programs (17 percent) and much higher than in the drinking water regulatory program (2 percent).

TABLE 2-9 Survey Questions About the Operation of the EPA Wellhead Protection Program and National-Level Implementation Variables (Responses from State Wellhead Protection Program Officials)

Survey Questions	% Agree	% Disagree	Other Programs % Agree*
EPA program is effective	26	17	17
EPA officials are concerned	70	15	58
EPA program is adequately funded	7	74	31
Regional office and headquarters view program similarly	24	44	24
Oversight needed to encourage program implementation	43	43	30

n = 47
*denotes the responses from 230 state directors for asbestos, coal, lead, radon, and drinking water programs (controlling for wellhead protection program responses)

These sentiments, however, must be considered carefully. While state WHPP officials do not believe that the wellhead protection efforts of the EPA are adequately funded or that the national program is particularly effective, they support the operations of the EPA regional staff.

State WHPP directors overwhelmingly view their working relationships with EPA regional staff as positive (94 percent), and 89 percent believe that EPA regional staff are supportive of the state program. (See Table 2-10.) State perceptions of EPA headquarters, however, are not as positive. Only 30 percent of responding state officials believe that EPA headquarters staff supports the state program; only 24 percent believe that EPA headquarters staff views the state program in the same way as does EPA regional staff. (However, no state official in the regulatory drinking water program believes that EPA headquarters and regional staff share the same view of their program.)

TABLE 2-10 Survey Questions About Federal-State Working Relationships (Responses of State Wellhead Protection Program Officials)

Survey Questions	% Agree	% Disagree	Other Programs % Agree*
EPA regional staff supportive	89	4	80
EPA headquarters supportive	30	13	32
Positive working relationship	94	2	79
State-EPA relationships have gotten worse	9	77	14
States have sufficient flexibility	68	6	49
Evaluations by EPA are fair	57	9	53
Reporting requirements are reasonable	26	41	37
Program requirements are consistent	35	29	31
EPA clearly communicates program requirements	35	20	28

n = 47
*denotes the responses from 230 state directors for asbestos, coal, lead, radon, and drinking water programs (controlling for wellhead protection program responses)

When asked what one thing they would change to improve the federal–state relationship in implementing the WHPP, state officials most often sought to reduce the role of EPA headquarters. The clear message from most state WHPP coordinators is that they prefer working with EPA regional staff, as illustrated by these comments:

"Get the [EPA] headquarters out of overseeing state WHPPs. They have no concept of reality in the Western states from their 'ivory tower' vantage point in Washington, D.C."

"[EPA] headquarters has a very unrealistic opinion of what wellhead protection is—it would be better if they had a limited role."

While most comments regarding the EPA regional–state relationship were positive, state officials noted some opportunities for improvement. On the wish list of many state program directors was increased technical support, coupled with better communication of program goals and a better understanding of implementation constraints at the state level. Also important is continued streamlining of the reporting requirements under the program. As shown in Table 2-10, less than half of the responding state officials believe that reporting requirements are reasonable or consistent (26 and 35 percent, respectively). However, the EPA receives higher marks for providing program flexibility (68 percent) and fairly evaluating state programs (57 percent). Finally, state officials wished for more input into the development of national WHPP goals and activities.

When asked what he would change about the EPA's approach to state WHPPs, one respondent suggested:

"Change the focus on numbers in the reporting format. The quality of protection and the measures states are actually adopting are more important than the number of delineations. Management activities should be recognized. While some standard reporting requirements may be needed to make comparisons [between states] and to evaluate progress, [EPA] headquarters seems to be far too interested in quantity over quality."

CONCLUSIONS ABOUT THE WELLHEAD PROTECTION PROGRAM

The data reported in this section of the chapter suggest some extrinsic and intrinsic implementation factors that are influencing the implementation of the wellhead protection program. First, agency capacity at both the state and federal level is constrained by lack of funding and, consequently, lack of staffing. Capacity is also constrained by reliance on the support of county, municipal, and community officials for program implementation, as well as by the shared delegation of responsibility between state agencies (most often between health and environmental departments).

Also important are national, state, and local levels of political support for WHP programs. The resistance, or apathy, of local communities constrains implementation as local public water suppliers address the politically unpalatable prospect of changing land-use patterns or initiating land-use controls.

However, the study suggests that local communities do not necessarily dig in their collective heels when it comes to protecting groundwater. Several local initiatives illustrate quite the opposite point. Some communities, such as Long Island, New York, are protecting their groundwater in the absence of mandated state programs.

Local communities can facilitate WHPP implementation by using existing staff, processes, and tools to address groundwater contamination. For example, zoning authority, land-use ordinances, provisions under the Community Right to Know law, floodplain planning, and even building inspections are at the disposal of local communities. The challenge, then, is to develop an entrepreneurial spirit among private and public organizations with the ability to leverage current local activities in new ways to protect groundwater. When applied to the framework, this supports the independent effect that contextual variables (i.e., local governments initiating behavioral change) can exhibit in program implementation.

Recent regulations promulgated by the EPA provide further incentives for local WHP planning. Public water supply systems that can demonstrate that their groundwater supplies are not vulnerable to contamination from synthetic organic chemicals may seek a monitoring waiver for those chemicals under the SDWA, thus reducing the costs of compliance with SDWA requirements. Communities with state-approved WHPPs are able to demonstrate that they have sufficiently protected groundwater drinking supplies.

The nature of the problem addressed by WHPP is also a factor. Delineations require specialized understanding and expertise that may not readily be available to local communities. Moreover, state legislators and administrators have not viewed wellhead protection as a high-priority activity, by virtue of staff allotments and own-source funding.

Closely linked to this constraint is the fact that aquifers typically transcend political boundaries. It does little good for one community (or one state) to initiate an aggressive program if other communities using the groundwater resource do little to prevent contamination. The multijurisdictional dimension of the problem complicates the ability of governmental unilateral response to produce desired policy outcomes.

WHPPs are at once constrained and supported by state efforts at developing comprehensive groundwater strategies. When EPA released its final guidance for comprehensive state groundwater protection, the guidance recognized wellhead protection as a "required and integral part" of state groundwater plans, to be "afforded extra management focus" across all programs in the groundwater framework.[63] Coordinating the programs at the state level to achieve an integrated groundwater focus, however, has proved a daunting task for many states, especially when programs are allocated among different agencies and authorities are under different laws (the Clean Water Act and SDWA). In the short term, some state officials suggest that creating a comprehensive groundwater strategy has actually impeded wellhead protection activity.

Intergovernmental relationships appear especially important. Although most officials report accommodative working relationships with EPA regional staff, it appears that not all (local, state, and federal) actors share program goals and that most state officials appear dissatisfied with EPA headquarters activities, although not with the same tenor as state drinking water officials.

Continued and even enhanced effort at outreach and education are needed to garner support of local communities to protect wellheads. Local initiatives are important. Both states with approved programs and states without approved programs rely on voluntary local wellhead protection efforts (although some state officials recommend mandatory wellhead protection programs for local governments). Much of the WHPP activity falls to municipal governments as local communities face the consequences of contaminated groundwater. Thus, the recognized seriousness of the problem seems much more dependent upon local officials' perceptions of the possibility of groundwater contamination than on state agency officials' perceptions.

The framework's separation of policy outcomes from agency outputs seems useful. While no conclusions are offered about which state WHP programs are most effective, it is clear that the output measure (program status) is not an appropriate surrogate for state performance, nor is it likely to point to desired policy outcomes (protection of groundwater). Most EPA regional staff interviewed indicated that program approval status was not an appropriate indicator of successful state programs. One EPA project officer observed that one of the earliest states to submit a program plan had accomplished virtually nothing to date. His comment was that after approval, the plan just "sat on the shelf gathering dust . . . nothing is going forward."

Finally, statutory constraints are also a factor. The SDWA mandated that states adopt a wellhead protection program, then authorized (but failed to appropriate) grant monies. The result was a program that looked good on paper, but largely failed in reality. Recent revisions to the SDWA proposed in 1994 and 1995 conveniently delete the wellhead protection language from the act, while maintaining the focus of the program.[64] The regrettable result of the snail's pace of wellhead program implementation is that opportunities to be proactive, to prevent pollution before it damages groundwater drinking supplies, have been missed.

When the working relationship typology is considered, the wellhead protection program seems most appropriately placed in the category of "cooperative but autonomous." The reasons for this placement are straightforward. First, extremely small state and EPA regional staff sizes and sparse budgets prevent the frequent contact that would help provide synergy to the federal–state relationship. EPA staff have been hard-pressed to provide appropriate guidance for state programs; information dissemination and knowledge sharing often occurs informally and through associations such as the state groundwater protection council rather than through state–federal communication.

High levels of mutual trust are evident, however, despite limited federal patterns of involvement. When EPA officials were asked to reflect upon the nature of their working relationships with state officials, project officers interviewed rated their working relationship with their state counterparts as "excellent." They attributed this positive relationship to the nature of the program. Absent any regulatory ratchet and any specifically appropriated wellhead protection monies, many EPA regional officials adopted a cooperative, nonthreatening approach.

One project officer commented: "It's a delicate arrangement. We've bared our souls to them [state officials] and told them that protecting citizens is our mission. Some states told us [EPA] to 'take a hike' and were suspicious of EPA's rhetoric. Now, states are beginning to believe that we have no hidden agenda. Which is a good thing, because we don't."

Another reason offered by EPA project officers for the positive relationship between state and EPA wellhead personnel was the high degree of flexibility and latitude accorded to state officials. No project officer mentioned pressuring states to submit wellhead protection programs for approval. Rather, the activity was seen as a desirable, but not necessary, state output. Coupled with this latitude is an apparent unwillingness to compare state programs or force one particular program model on states. Several project officers noted the wide variation in wellhead protection programs among states in the region, but were unwilling to draw conclusions about relative state program effectiveness.

In short, while EPA involvement in state programs is lower than in the drinking water program, like survivors on a lifeboat, EPA regional and state wellhead staff cling on to their program, hoping for increased levels of recognition by political sovereigns or even within their own agencies. High levels of trust are easier to maintain in this kind of underfunded, relatively obscure program, if only to maintain programmatic survival. However, the interviews indicate that EPA and state staff share the goal (almost fervently in some cases) that protecting groundwater makes good policy sense. Issues of how to delineate wellhead areas become secondary to the larger argument of how to persuade national, state, and local stakeholders of the value of the WHPP.

CONCLUSIONS ABOUT BOTH PROGRAMS

Comparisons between the long-established regulatory drinking water program and the wellhead protection program reveal similarities and differences in perceived implementation obstacles. While both programs identify funding as a major constraint, drinking water officials were more than twice as likely to believe they had adequate funding as their counterparts in the wellhead program. The regulatory program also benefits from stronger state-level support, at least as perceived by officials from both programs. Drinking water officials overwhelmingly view their program as effective (84 percent) and perceive greater levels of support from administrators and officials within their agencies than do wellhead protection program directors.

When perceptions about federal–state relationships are compared, wellhead protection program officials are more likely to see the EPA efforts as effective (26 percent to 2 percent). State drinking water officials do not believe that they have sufficient flexibility to run their programs; most wellhead protection directors perceive adequate flexibility. Directors of the regulatory program are also less likely than their counterparts in the wellhead program to agree that reporting requirements are reasonable (9 percent to 26 percent, respectively).

Perhaps most interesting are the perceptions that are common to both programs. For example, both drinking water and wellhead protection directors agree that the EPA regional staff is supportive of the state program (86 percent and 89 percent, respectively) and that working relationships are positive (86 percent and 94 percent). Also, state officials from both programs are likely to have less positive views of EPA headquarters. Only 30 percent of the respondents from each of the programs believe that the EPA headquarters staff are supportive, and few state officials believe that the EPA regional and headquarters staff view the state program in the same way. Finally, officials from both programs wish for better communication by the EPA of program goals and objectives, and consistency in program requirements.

Thus, the conclusions from this research suggest that different forces shape the implementation process of these programs. Some of these forces, such as the statutory deadlines for MCLs, compel a fixed route of march for the agency that incurs the wrath of states, local governments, and public water suppliers. Other external forces complicate the implementation process, including political support for the program and the complexity of the problem. For the drinking water program, most of the public water supply systems are very small and lack the technical and economic capacity to comply. Similarly, in the wellhead protection program, local communities must bear the brunt of the responsibility for implementing the program.

Other forces are at work that run contrary to the criticisms levied against the implementation process. State officials from both programs consider their working relationships with the EPA regional staff to be positive, despite concerns about reporting requirements and sufficient flexibility. Finally, the lingering impression left from the research on the attitudes of state officials is that the EPA headquarters staff are too far removed from the issues at hand to understand on-the-ground implementation problems. These observations about implementation, however, need to be explored in other programs. The next chapter looks at two environmental programs designed to protect people from indoor environmental hazards: radon and asbestos.

NOTES TO CHAPTER 2

1. Pub. L. 93-523, December 16, 1974.

2. U.S. Environmental Protection Agency, Office of Water, *Technical and Economic Capacity of States and Public Water Systems to Implement Drinking Water Regulations: Report to Congress*, EPA-810-R-93-001 (Washington, D.C.: U.S. EPA, September 1993), p. 3.

3. Stephen E. Williams, "Safe Drinking Water Act," in *Environmental Law Handbook* (13th ed), ed. Thomas F. P. Sullivan (Rockville, MD: Government Institutes, 1995), pp. 203–24.

4. U.S. General Accounting Office, *Drinking Water Program: States Face Increased Difficulties in Meeting Basic Requirements*, GAO/RCED-93-144 (Washington, D.C.: U.S. GAO, June 1993), p. 3.

5. U.S. General Accounting Office, *Drinking Water: Combination of Strategies Needed to Bring Program Costs in Line with Resources* GAO/T-RCED-94-152 (Washington, D.C.: U.S. GAO, March 14, 1994), p. 2.

6. SDWA Sec. 1401(4), 42 U.S. C. Sec. 300f(4); U.S. Environmental Protection Agency, *The Safe Drinking Water Act: A Pocket Guide to the Requirements for the Operators of Small Water Systems* (San Francisco, Calif.: U.S. EPA, Region 9), p. 4.

7. Office of Water, *Technical and Economic Capacity of States and Public Water Systems to Implement Drinking Water Regulations*, p. 6.

8. Office of Water, *Technical and Economic Capacity of States and Public Water Systems to Implement Drinking Water Regulations*, p. 4.

9. Office of Water, *Technical and Economic Capacity of States and Public Water Systems to Implement Drinking Water Regulations*, p. 4.

10. U.S. General Accounting Office, *Drinking Water: Key Quality Assurance Program Is Flawed and Underfunded*, GAO/RCED-93-97 (Washington, D.C.: U.S. General Accounting Office, April 1993), p. 8.

11. These figures appear in the EPA report, U.S. Environmental Protection Agency, Office of Water, *Technical and Economic Capacity of States and Public Water Systems to Implement Drinking Water Regulations* (Washington, D.C.: U.S. EPA, September 1993), p. 7. However, the large number of small public water supply systems is widely reported as an implementation obstacle. See, for example, U.S. General Accounting Office, *Drinking Water: Key Quality Assurance Program Is Flawed and Underfunded*, p. 9.

12. SDWA Section 1401(6), 42 USC Section 300f(6).

13. Williams, "Safe Drinking Water Act," p. 204.

14. SDWA Sec. 1401(3), 42 U.S.C. Sec. 300f(3).

15. U.S. Environmental Protection Agency, *The Safe Drinking Water Act: A Pocket Guide*, p. 8.

16. SDWA Sec. 1412(b)(5), 42 U.S.C. Sec. 300g–1(b)(5).

17. The Safe Drinking Water Act Amendments of 1986 are contained in P.L. No. 99–339.

18. Office of Water, *Technical and Economic Capacity of States and Public Water Systems*, p. 26.

19. Lawrence Jensen, "Safe Drinking Water Act," in *Environmental Law Handbook* (12th ed), ed. Thomas F. P. Sullivan (Rockville, MD: Government Institutes, 1993), p. 253.

20. Office of Water, *Technical and Economic Capacity of States and Public Water Systems*, p. 26.

21. U.S. Environmental Protection Agency, Office of Water, *Report to the United States Congress on Radon in Drinking Water: Multimedia Risk and Cost Assessment of Radon*, EPA 811-R-94-001, (Washington, D.C.: U.S. EPA, March 1994), p. *viii*.

22. U.S. Environmental Protection Agency, Office of Water, *Report to the United States Congress on Radon in Drinking Water: Multimedia Risk and Cost Assessment of Radon*, EPA 811-R-94-001, (Washington, D.C.: U.S. EPA, March 1994), p. *viii*.

23. Williams, "Safe Drinking Water Act," p. 205.

24. U.S. Environmental Protection Agency, Office of Water, *National Primary Drinking Water Standards* (Washington, D.C.: U.S. Environmental Protection Agency, February 1994).

25. U.S. Environmental Protection Agency, Office of Water, *Strengthening the Safety of Our Drinking Water: A Report on Progress and Challenges and an Agenda for Action*, EPA 810-R-95-001 (Washington, D.C.: U.S. EPA, March 1995), p. 11.

26. Office of Water, *Technical and Economic Capacity of States and Public Water Systems*, p. 117.

27. For example, see the following reports: *Drinking Water: Key Quality Assurance Program Is Flawed and Underfunded*, GAO/RCED-93-97 (Washington, D.C.: U.S. General Accounting Office, April 1993); *Drinking Water Program: States Face Increased Difficulties in Meeting Basic Requirements*, GAO/RCED-93-144 (Washington, D.C.: U.S. General Accounting Office, June 1993); *Drinking Water: Combination of Strategies Needed to Bring Program Costs in Line with Resources*, GAO/T-RCED-94-152 (Washington, D.C.: U.S. General Accounting Office, March 1994); U.S. Environmental Protection Agency, Office of Water, *Technical and Economic Capacity of States and Public Water Systems to Implement Drinking Water Regulations*, EPA 810-93-001 (Washington, D.C.: U.S. EPA Office of Water, September 1993).

28. U.S. General Accounting Office, *Drinking Water: Combination of Strategies Needed to Bring Program Costs in Line with Resources*, p. 7.

29. U.S. General Accounting Office, *Drinking Water: Combination of Strategies Needed to Bring Program Costs in Line with Resources*, p. 7.

30. U.S. General Accounting Office, *Drinking Water: Combination of Strategies Needed to Bring Program Costs in Line with Resources*, p. 7.

31. U.S. Environmental Protection Agency, Science Advisory Board, *An*

SAB Report: Safe Drinking Water, Future Trends and Challenges, EPA-SAB-DWC-95-002 (Washington, D.C.: U.S. EPA, March 1995), p. 13.

32. U.S. Environmental Protection Agency, Office of Water, *Helping Small Systems Comply with the Safe Drinking Water Act: The Role of Restructuring*, EPA/812-K-92-001 (Washington, D.C.: U.S. EPA, September 1992).

33. Office of Water, *Technical and Economic Capacity of States and Public Water Systems*, p. 81.

34. International City/County Management Association, *Environmental Mandates Task Force: Policy and Legislative Strategy Meeting*, proceeds from the first meeting on December 8–9, 1992 (Washington, D.C.: ICMA, 1992).

35. U.S. General Accounting Office, *Drinking Water: Compliance Problems Undermine EPA Program as New Challenges Emerge*, GAO/RCED-90-127 (Washington, D.C.: U.S. GAO, June 1990), p. 3.

36. Office of Water, *Technical and Economic Capacity of the States and Public Water Systems*, p. 113.

37. Office of Water, *Technical and Economic Capacity of States and Public Water Systems*, p. 121.

38. U.S. General Accounting Office, *Drinking Water Program: States Face Increased Difficulties in Meeting Basic Program Requirements*, p. 4.

39. U.S. General Accounting Office, *Drinking Water: Widening Gap Between Needs and Available Resources Threatens Vital EPA Program*, GAO/RCED-92-184, (Washington, D.C.: U.S. GAO), p. 7.

40. Office of Water, *Technical and Economic Capacity of States and Public Water Systems*, p. 110.

41. Office of Water, *Technical and Economic Capacity of the States and Public Water Systems*, p. 109.

42. U.S. Environmental Protection Agency, Office of the Administrator, *Strengthening the Safety of Our Drinking Water: A Report on Progress and Challenges and An Agenda for Action*, (March 29, 1995).

43. President Bill Clinton and Vice President Al Gore, *Reinventing Environmental Regulation*, report issued by the White House on March 16, 1995.

44. *Reinventing Environmental Regulation*, p. 21.

45. U.S. Environmental Protection Agency, Office of Water, *Drinking Water Program Redirection Proposal: A Public Comment Draft*, unpublished document (EPA-810-D-95-001, November 1995).

46. Office of Water, *Drinking Water Program Redirection Proposal*, p. ii.

47. Office of Water, *Drinking Water Program Redirection Proposal*, p. 7.

48. Office of Water, *Drinking Water Program Redirection Proposal*, p. 10.

49. Patrick Crow, "EPA Working on Guidance for SRF Distribution," *Water World* 12, no. 9 (November/December 1996), p. 6.

50. U.S. Environmental Protection Agency, Office of Water, *Why Do Wellhead Protection? Issues and Answers in Protecting Public Drinking Water Supply Systems*, EPA 570/9-91-014 (Washington, D.C.: U.S. EPA, September 1993).

51. Section 1428, 42 U.S.C. 300 h-7.

52. U.S. General Accounting Office, *Groundwater Quality: State Activities Guard Against Contaminants*, GAO/PEMD-88-5 (Washington, D.C.: GPO, February 1988).

53. U.S. Environmental Protection Agency, Office of Water, *A Drinking*

Water Program Redirection Proposal, draft for public comment, EPA 810-D-95-001, unpublished document (November 1995), p. *iii*.

54. U.S. Environmental Protection Agency, Office of Water, *Guidance for Applicants for State Wellhead Protection Program Assistance Funds Under the Safe Drinking Water Act*, EPA 440/6-87-011 (Washington, D.C.: U.S. EPA, June 1987), p. 1.

55. U.S. Environmental Protection Agency, Office of Research and Development, *Handbook: Ground Water and Wellhead Protection*, EPA 625/R-94/001 (Washington, D.C.: U.S. EPA, September 1994).

56. U.S. Environmental Protection Agency, Office of Ground Water Protection, *Guidance for Applicants for State Wellhead Protection Program Assistance Funds Under the Safe Drinking Water Act*, EPA 440/6-87-011 (Washington, D.C.: U.S. EPA, June 1987), p. 19.

57. Office of Research and Development, *Handbook: Ground Water and Wellhead Protection*, p. 147.

58. While sophisticated techniques clearly improve upon arbitrary methods of establishing wellhead protection areas, some uncertainty as to the precise area for delineation will always be present.

59. U.S. Environmental Protection Agency, Office of Water, *Guidance for Applicants for State Wellhead Protection Program Assistance Funds under the Safe Drinking Water Act*, p. 17.

60. U.S. Environmental Protection Agency, Office of Water, *Wellhead Protection Program Biennial Report Guidance, October 1993 through September 1995*, unpublished document released March 6, 1995.

61. Telephone conversation with wellhead protection coordinator in March 1995.

62. U.S. Environmental Protection Agency, Office of Water, "Wellhead Protection Program Biennial Report Guidance," (unpublished document dated March 1995).

63. U.S. Environmental Protection Agency, Office of Water, *Final Comprehensive State Groundwater Protection Program Guidance*, EPA-100-R-93-001 (Washington, D.C.: U.S. EPA, 1992), pp. 1–3.

64. See U.S. Senate, *Safe Drinking Water Amendments of 1994*, report of the Committee on Environment and Public Works, 103rd Congr., 2nd sess.

3

Radon and Asbestos: Two Indoor Environmental Programs

Chapter Two explored two environmental programs designed to protect drinking water: the drinking water regulatory program and the wellhead protection program. This chapter reviews two programs designed to protect people from indoor environmental contaminants: radon and asbestos. Both programs are authorized under separate titles of the Toxic Substances Control Act of 1976 (TSCA). The asbestos program, created under the Asbestos Hazard and Emergency Response Act of 1986 (AHERA) as Title II of TSCA, is designed to protect children from exposure to asbestos in schools. AHERA requires officials to inspect schools for asbestos-containing materials (ACMs) and, if found, limit asbestos exposure through proper management.

The radon program, operating under the Indoor Radon Abatement Act of 1988 (IRAA) as Title III of TSCA, on the other hand, is designed primarily as a voluntary public information program and risk-characterization program. As such, it has no regulatory target, and states are encouraged to be partners with the EPA in sounding the public alarm about the health risks of radon.

The chapter begins by providing an overview of the asbestos program, followed by the results of survey and interview research. The radon program is considered in the second section in the same way, and the chapter concludes by discussing the implementation patterns evident in each program, as well as the nature of the federal–state working relationships.

THE ASBESTOS PROGRAM

Asbestos is a naturally occurring mineral that was widely used in the 1940s through the 1960s in a large number of building products intended for insulation, fireproofing, or acoustical soundproofing. Although once hailed as the "miracle fiber" because of these beneficial properties, asbestos has long been associated with cancer and lung disease. Asbestos fibers may become released into the air and inhaled.

Once inhaled, these fibers may penetrate into the lungs and be associated with causing asbestosis (a scarring of the lung tissue), lung cancer, and mesothelioma (a cancer of the mesothelium or pleural linings of the lungs). Despite these adverse and even fatal health effects, the federal government was a major consumer of asbestos during World War II and continued to support the asbestos industry during the 1950s and 1960s. Thus the government supported an industry that was producing a wide range of products containing a carcinogen and made little effort to alert the public. The long history of policy avoidance, while not the major focus of this study, is still important to understanding the implementation of AHERA.

In some sense, AHERA can be characterized as the product of a prolonged process of federal asbestos policy formulation and public attention to asbestos as a health risk. As the following brief description suggests, media attention to the negative health effects associated with asbestos exposure was absent during the time of greatest occupational exposure. It was only after the long latency period between exposure to asbestos and observable health effects had expired that the media took asbestos up as an issue and the public demanded governmental action.

It is also useful to note that asbestos exposure is regulated under several different laws, including the Clean Air Act, the Toxic Substances Control Act, and the Occupational Safety and Health Act. Many state regulations go beyond what is required under federal law to regulate occupational exposures or exposures in public or commercial buildings. What follows is a brief summary of the evolution of public awareness of asbestos and the eventual public policies that emerged.

Although the health risks associated with high levels of asbestos exposure were long known to health care professionals, and articles documenting the dangers of occupational exposure to asbestos were published in medical journals as early as 1947, the mass media, the public, and the federal government paid little attention to asbestos until the 1970s [1] By the 1970s the long latency period between asbestos exposure and cancer incidence had expired; thousands of shipyard workers exposed to high levels of asbestos during World War II provided ample case studies of mesothelioma and lung cancer.[2] Professional medical journals featured articles on asbestos-related diseases, several of which were written by Irving L. Selikoff, Director of Environmental Health for Mount Sinai Medical Center.[3] Selikoff sounded the public alarm, warning people to protect themselves from the "third wave" of asbestos-related diseases: the first wave included asbestos miners and mill workers; the second wave included occupational exposures of insulation installers such as the shipyard workers; the third wave would include school janitors, building maintenance workers, and members of the public (including children) who had nonoccupational exposures to asbestos fibers.

With mounting epidemiological evidence, asbestos lawsuits proliferated. By 1982, some 30,000 lawsuits had been filed by asbestos victims or their heirs against asbestos companies. Almost half of the lawsuits were brought by people exposed by direct action of the government.[4] The leading supplier of asbestos insulation for ships and airplanes during World War II, Johns-Mansville, Inc., filed for bankruptcy protection in 1982. On April 1, 1996, the company disappeared altogether after paying more than 94,000 asbestos-injury claims and over $1.5 billion in settlements.[5]

The feeding frenzy of asbestos lawsuits stirred the interest of the media. For example, in 1983 the Public Broadcast System aired a special titled, "Asbestos: the lethal legacy," which highlighted the failure of government to protect the public from occupational exposures to asbestos. Consumer advocates including Ralph Nader and Paul Brodeur also became involved in warning the public about asbestos.

Most importantly from the perspective of the AHERA program, states became embroiled in local conflicts about asbestos in schools. School districts in several states closed schools temporarily because of concerns about unsafe asbestos levels, and groups such as the National Education Association called for a national presence in regulating asbestos in schools.[6]

One could speculate that by the mid-1980s the general public understood that asbestos was dangerous and that the government had failed to protect them. AHERA was crafted in this climate of public fear and mistrust of government.

DEVELOPMENT OF ASBESTOS LAW BY CONGRESS

After decades of avoiding dealing with asbestos, Congress moved in the 1980s to protect children from asbestos exposure in schools. The Asbestos in Schools Act, passed in 1982, required schools to inspect for friable asbestos containing materials (ACMs). In 1984 Congress authorized a federal grant and loan program to assist schools in asbestos management under the Asbestos School Hazard Abatement Act. That act authorized expenditures of $50 million for the program in 1985 and $100 million per year for each of the next five years to assist schools with financing asbestos removal or control, mostly in the form of noninterest loans.[7]

AHERA was passed in 1986 as Title II of TSCA in order to strengthen the federal directive to control asbestos exposure in schools.[8]

While the Asbestos School Hazard Abatement Act authorized nearly $600 million in grants and loans to schools to address asbestos hazards, it did not require school officials to manage asbestos once they had found it. AHERA went beyond the grant and loan provisions to require that public and private schools be inspected for asbestos, that the public be notified if asbestos was found, and that schools initiate appropriate asbestos management plans. AHERA also called for certification of asbestos contractors that work in schools and required the EPA to issue model accreditation plans (MAPs) for training and accreditation through state or EPA training courses. It further required the EPA to conduct a study of asbestos risk in public buildings, creating the potential for a program like AHERA to regulate asbestos management in buildings.

AHERA mandated action on the part of the EPA, by requiring the agency to write regulations for the management of asbestos, inspect schools for compliance, and conduct studies of asbestos exposures in public buildings. Local Education Associations (LEAs) were required to establish asbestos management programs for their school buildings and to inspect for asbestos. The role of states was determined through their participation in the enforcement of AHERA and their decision to participate in the EPA's model accreditation plan for training and certifying asbestos contractors and inspectors. States that chose to do neither one of these activities had an implementation role limited to approving school management plans.[9] However, the EPA could delegate AHERA responsibilities to state governments (but not to local governments) by approving the state program. States with an approved enforcement program received "waivers," which allowed state officials to monitor LEAs.[10] Nowhere in AHERA, however, was removal of asbestos from schools required.

In developing AHERA, Congress seemed ready to champion protection of children at all costs. AHERA explicitly states that asbestos control must protect human health, regardless of the cost of the action. Even the title of the law, which includes the words "emergency response," suggests that Congress viewed asbestos in schools as a serious problem in need of immediate attention. AHERA demanded rapid implementation. It required EPA regulations governing asbestos in schools to be in place by 1987, and school management plans were to be submitted to state agencies the following year. Only when Congress realized that the timetable was unworkable and that asbestos removal contractors were in short supply, did it amend AHERA to extend the deadline for local education agencies (LEAs) to comply to May 9, 1989.[11]

In a 1991 public hearing concerning asbestos, Senator Malcolm Wallop (R-WY) summarized the collective congressional mindset regarding AHERA: "Five years ago the Congress reacted to the growing national phobia about asbestos by enacting AHERA, conveying all of the proper terminology, to alarm the public about the latest threat to their health while reassuring them that Congress would take care of the problem. The bill passed the Senate with little debate and no dissent. We were all anxious to ensure that our schools posed no threat to the health of our children."[12]

Congressional architects of AHERA were also eager to get EPA to address asbestos in schools and spotlight the EPA as the culpable party. During 1987 hearings on asbestos, U.S. Representative Mike Synar stated, "EPA has a responsibility to enforce the law of this country. In the last decade, they have not done it. I am hopeful that we have jogged them into recognizing that Congress is going to do ... the type of tough oversight until we get the type of response that we demand and that the American public demands."[13] When the EPA released its 1988 report to Congress suggesting that asbestos in commercial buildings posed little risk to the public, several congressmen, including Frank Lautenberg (New Jersey) challenged the EPA for its lack of concern for America's health.[14]

In short, the role of Congress was to move decisively to protect children (without fully comprehending the extent of the health risks associated with ACMs) and to make certain that the EPA responded quickly to the dictates of AHERA. It fell to the EPA, and the states, to make the asbestos control program under AHERA a reality.

DEVELOPMENT OF ASBESTOS REGULATION BY THE EPA

Federal regulatory action to control asbestos preceded the passage of AHERA. The EPA had responded to concerns about asbestos under different statutory authorities. In 1971, the EPA first listed asbestos as a hazardous air pollutant as part of its new authority under Section 112, the National Emission Standards for Hazardous Air Pollutants (NESHAPs) provisions of the Clean Air Act. In 1973 the EPA promulgated final asbestos NESHAP rules to control exposure to asbestos. The standard included "no visible emissions" for milling and manufacturing of asbestos products and during demolition of buildings; the EPA also prohibited the spray application for most uses of friable asbestos (asbestos that crumbles under hand pressure when dry).[15] Further additions to the EPA's Asbestos NESHAP regulations were made in 1974 and 1975, when the EPA created specific requirements for the removal of friable ACMs from commercial or institutional buildings, including schools, undertaking major renovation projects.[16]

The NESHAP rule, however, affected buildings where physical alterations were planned, either through outright demolition or renovation. It was silent about asbestos-containing materials (ACMs) in existing buildings that were not undergoing major remodeling, which included most schools. How, then, did schools get involved in asbestos removal, both before AHERA and as part of responding to AHERA?

Clues to how the federal government may have promoted the idea that removal of asbestos was a prudent practice for schools can be found in the EPA's earliest guidance documents and in its "Asbestos-Containing Materials in Schools" rule (40 CFR Part 763). In 1979 the EPA produced a guidance document for asbestos management in schools and buildings, referred to as the Orange Book. The Orange Book, and a subsequent guidance document published three years later, the Blue Book, did little to discourage removal of asbestos. Indeed, the Blue Book suggested that removal was "always appropriate, never inappropriate."[17] In 1982, four years before AHERA was passed, the EPA published the first Asbestos-in-Schools Rule, which required schools to test for friable asbestos and inform the community if ACMs were found.[18]

By the mid-1980s, the EPA had somewhat modified its position on the appropriateness of asbestos removal. In 1985 the EPA officially put management of asbestos in place ahead of removal when it issued a third guidance document, referred to as the Purple Book.[19] However, in its final rule published in 1987, the EPA left the choice of removal of asbestos or management in place up to the local education associations (LEAs): "Nothing in this rule shall be construed to prohibit removal of asbestos containing building materials from a school building at any time, should removal be the preferred response action of the LEA."[20] Elsewhere in the final rule, the EPA offers conflicting advice, first stating that, "EPA disagrees that removal is the only appropriate response in all cases of significantly damaged ACM," then stating that, "EPA agrees that, particularly with regard to significantly damaged friable miscellaneous and surfacing ACM, isolation of the functional space and removal is often the most appropriate and possibly, only acceptable, response."

Later guidance documents, such as the Green Book, offer LEAs a range of management strategies.[21] These documents emphasize management of asbestos through encapsulation or enclosure, or monitoring as part of an operations and maintenance program. In 1990 the agency went so far as to say that, "removal is often not a school district's best course of action to reduce asbestos exposure" and that "improper removal can create a dangerous situation where none previously existed."[22] Later that year, EPA administrator William Reilly declared that removal of asbestos by schools was an unintended consequence of EPA asbestos regulations and that "a considerable gap has opened up between what EPA has been trying to say about asbestos and what the public has been hearing."[23] However, given the earlier EPA language found in the first guidance documents and final rule, it is easy to see how the message of asbestos removal was what was heard by school officials.

Yet another EPA action under different authority occurred in 1989, when the EPA issued a rule under the Toxic Substance Control Act to ban all asbestos products. When issuing the rule, the EPA stated, ". . . it is well recognized that asbestos is a human carcinogen and is one of the most hazardous substances to which humans are exposed in both occupational and nonoccupational settings."[24] The ban on all asbestos products was later overturned by the U.S. Court of Appeals for the Fifth Circuit in 1991 for being overly broad and creating an unreasonably expensive prohibition.[25]

In sum, EPA regulatory actions regarding asbestos have occurred in several areas and generated a number of mixed signals for policy implementors. The NESHAP standards have been directed at asbestos removal in commercial buildings, but have also been applied to renovating schools. Early guidance for schools to manage asbestos suggested that asbestos removal was prudent, although later guidance suggested otherwise. In 1989, the EPA sought to ban outright the production of this "most hazardous substance." Thus, it seems easy to understand how state officials, school officials, and the public might interpret the posture of the agency to favor asbestos removal, even though current agency guidance documents and the recent rhetoric of EPA administrators suggest a more tempered response.

THE CURRENT STATE OF ASBESTOS POLICY IMPLEMENTATION

The years following AHERA were turbulent ones for asbestos policy, as scholars and medical professionals began to criticize what they saw as unnecessary asbestos removal in schools. From this point of view, the federal government had come full circle. For years it had refused to develop a reasoned asbestos policy; now it had gone too far and, as a result, school officials were needlessly yanking out asbestos-containing ceiling tiles, floor tiles, and insulation.

In late 1989 and early 1990, two articles written by prominent U.S. and international health professionals published in the *New England Journal of Medicine* and *Science* proved to be watershed events in focusing attention on this new unintended consequence.[26] In subsequent years, popular media have reported on the negative implications of removing asbestos at any cost. Since 1992, articles criticizing the frequent removal of asbestos in schools have appeared in major news magazines like *Time* and *U.S. News and World Report*. Articles in medical journals and safety magazines have also pointed to the needless exposure of school custodians.[27] A recent General Accounting Office (GAO) report on the condition of American schools suggested that schools continue to spend more money on asbestos management than on any other environmental pollutant: 57 percent of school districts studied had incurred asbestos-related expenses (compared to 25 percent that had incurred expenses for dealing with lead-based paint or lead in the water and only 18 percent that reported radon-related expenses).[28] Moreover, the GAO estimated that $11 billion was needed to remove or correct asbestos, lead in water or paint, or radon, in schools and that most of the cost was attributable to asbestos.[29]

While Congress passed the Asbestos Hazard Abatement Act in order to provide federal funding to assist schools in asbestos management, the funding has never been sufficient to cover the number of requests. From 1988 to 1991, the EPA received 1,746 qualified applications with requests from LEAs for financial assistance totaling nearly $600 million, but awarded only $157 million to the 586 school districts with the "worst" asbestos problems.[30] LEAs, in turn, must seek other sources of funding (most often from school operation and maintenance budgets) to manage asbestos-containing materials in school buildings.

Meanwhile, asbestos litigation continues, with untold costs to the national economy. In 1994, *USA Today* reported that over $20 billion had been spent in settling asbestos claims and predicted that the smaller asbestos companies may be forced out of business, in the same way that the largest suppliers of asbestos (such as Johns-Manville) have been.[31]

In this decade, evidence suggests that asbestos exposure has increased because school officials have sometimes chosen to remove asbestos.[32] They have been caught in the cross fire between intense public reaction against asbestos, a stiff Congressional posture to protect children "at all costs," and changing guidance on asbestos management from the EPA. Thus, they have responded in an understandable fashion: why risk lawsuits or even community backlash by just managing asbestos? Senator Wallop, after relating a story of Kelly Walsh High School, a Wyoming school that closed for a year because ACMs were found, stated, "I have talked to school superintendents who feel that they have no choice, that if they allow it there [asbestos in schools], they will soon be on trial for irresponsibility and liability for not having removed it regardless of what the law says."[33]

In sum, the legacy of governmental neglect of the health dangers associated with asbestos exposures prompted, at least in part, a burgeoning number of class-action lawsuits by people with occupational exposures to asbestos or asbestos-containing materials. It also prompted the EPA first to proclaim "just say no" to any asbestos found in school buildings and then to move to the current policy of management of asbestos-containing materials in place. State officials and school district supervisors were thus placed in a difficult position: remove asbestos now or deal with it forever, as part of an asbestos management program. This set the stage for political conflicts and resistance by LEAs.

Complicating this already confusing array of issues surrounding AHERA implementation is the recent pullback from the program by the EPA, which is evident by the availability of federal funding. Since 1994, state asbestos programs, like the wellhead protection programs described in Chapter Two, rely on federal funding not specifically dedicated to their program. (Wellhead protection program funds were authorized, but never appropriated by Congress under the Safe Drinking Water Act.) State AHERA programs receive federal money appropriated for general TSCA enforcement, which means those funds are also available for enforcing other efforts under TSCA, most notably polychlorinated biphenyls (PCB) control programs.

EPA regional offices receive TSCA funds for cooperative agreements for states from EPA headquarters and make their own determinations of how much the states should receive. For fiscal year 1995, the administration budget submitted to Congress included a disinvestment in TSCA state grant programs of over $1.4 million.[34] The proposed divestiture was realized. In fiscal year 1995, EPA headquarters distributed nearly $3.7 million in TSCA funding as follows: Region 1, $701,606; Region 2, $258,487; Region 3, $295,413; Region 4, $406,193; Region 5 $738,533; Region 6, $332,340; Region 7, $443,119; Regions 8 and 9, $258,487 each.[35] Region 10 received no pass-through money for asbestos because no state in the region wanted to enter into a cooperative agreement with the EPA.[36]

States receiving federal funding must engage in enforcement activities under AHERA, including conducting a required number of inspections, providing EPA regional offices with inspection reports and copies of warning letters to schools not in compliance, developing and implementing a Neutral Administrative Inspection Scheme, and detailing staff and travel expenditures.[37] TSCA grant guidance requires that states provide at least 25 percent matching funds for the program.[38] The administration of these grants is conducted at the EPA regional level, and states with waivers or partial waivers to operate the enforcement program receive priority consideration for federal grants.

The divestiture by the agency in AHERA enforcement is also evident by the reduction in staff. In the regional offices, most of the AHERA inspector positions are filled under contract with the National Council of Senior Citizens.[39] These positions have been cut in half in many regions. For example, EPA Region 2, which serves the states of New York and New Jersey as well as Puerto Rico and the Virgin Islands, recently reduced the number of AHERA inspection staff from six to two.[40] Each inspector may budget for no more than one inspection per month, which would total twenty-four school inspections for the year. Likewise, in response to EPA headquarters' efforts to consolidate enforcement of many regulatory programs, enforcement activities have been shifted into one division in many EPA regional offices. Thus, AHERA coordinators located in EPA regions may not run the compliance program.

This overview of the asbestos program, however, provides only the backdrop for understanding AHERA implementation and an appreciation for changes in EPA policy and commitment to asbestos. To gain a better understanding of the states' role in AHERA, we need to examine the perspective of state asbestos officials.

STATE ASBESTOS OFFICIALS' PERCEPTIONS ABOUT AHERA

This section describes the perceptions that state asbestos program officials have about the implementation of their programs. Information about the programs was collected from responses to mailed surveys and from interviews with state program directors. Fifty surveys were sent to state officials responsible for asbestos programs; thirty-seven were returned, for a response rate of 74 percent. Ten interviews were conducted with asbestos directors in 1996.

Many state officials directing asbestos programs wear two or more hats: they enforce the NESHAP provision for asbestos under the Clean Air Act, they certify and license asbestos contractors, they provide or supervise training in asbestos management, and they operate the AHERA program. Other states give the responsibility for AHERA to staff who are also running the state occupational safety and health program. Thus, for many state officials, implementing AHERA is only part of what they do. About half of the state officials responsible for running the asbestos program are located in state departments of environmental quality; the rest are equally likely to be located in state departments of public health or of labor.

Finally, some states, such as New York, divide asbestos duties between departments. New York assigns responsibility for oversight of licensing of asbestos abatement projects to the Department of Labor and for accrediting asbestos training programs to the Department of Health.

Some state asbestos programs predate the passage of AHERA in 1986. Only 8 percent of the asbestos officials responding to the survey stated that their programs were less than five years old; 73 percent are between six and ten years old; but 19 percent of state programs were more than ten years old in 1995, thus predating AHERA. Of state officials, 49 percent identified the passage of AHERA as the reason for establishing their state programs; 42 percent believe that state laws governing asbestos were more fundamental to creating the program.

State asbestos programs tend to be small, with 56 percent of the respondents saying their program operates with a staff of five or fewer full-time equivalent personnel. Only 5 percent of the state asbestos programs have more than twenty-five full-time equivalent staff.

The paucity of federal resources available for AHERA implementation, as described in earlier sections, compels many state officials to rely on state funding. Of state officials, 32 percent stated that they receive no federal funding at all for their asbestos programs, and another 35 percent stated that less than half of the funding for their programs came from the EPA. Only six states listed federal funding as the primary source of funding.

Factors That Facilitate or Hinder Implementation

It is not surprising, then, that over half (51 percent) of state asbestos program directors identify adequate state funding as the most important element to successful implementation, as shown on Table 3-1. Also,

TABLE 3-1 Factors Which Facilitate Implementation of the Asbestos Program (Percent of State Officials Ranking Factor As One of the Top Three)

Adequate state funding	51
State laws mandating asbestos control	43
Adequate staffing	43
Adequate federal funding	35
Support of the department	32
Technical expertise of state staff	27
Support of the EPA regional office	26
Clear and consistent state program goals and requirements	22
Clear and consistent EPA program goals and requirements	11
Support of school district staff	5
Citizen involvement and support	5
Available solutions to address asbestos exposure	3
Support of local governments	0

n = 37

43 percent identify state laws mandating asbestos control and adequate staffing as being important to program implementation. Factors which are not facilitating AHERA implementation from the perspective of state asbestos program staff include the support of local governments, the support of school districts, and clear and consistent EPA program goals and requirements.

State asbestos officials overwhelmingly believe that their staff is adequately trained to run the asbestos program. (See Table 3-2.) Of state asbestos staff responding to the survey, 81 percent believe that the state program is effective and 73 percent feel that the program is better now than it was three years ago. Asbestos officials perceive very little support from state legislators (19 percent), but most believe that citizens are concerned about asbestos control and are very supportive of their efforts (51 percent). State asbestos officials are more likely than the state managers of the other environmental programs to agree that funding for their program is adequate (54 percent to 32 percent, respectively). However, they are not likely to perceive that LEAs have adequate resources to manage asbestos.

When asked what they would change about their states' asbestos programs, responses were varied. Among the most frequent response was a desire for more state inspection and enforcement staff. As one state official put it, "To have an effective program, you must maintain a presence in the field. Currently, only one individual is responsible

---

TABLE 3-2 Survey Questions About the Operation of State Asbestos Programs and State-Level Implementation Variables (Responses of State Asbestos Program Officials)

Survey Questions	% Agree	% Disagree	Other Programs % Agree*
Officials are concerned	61	19	56
Administrators are concerned	59	19	48
Program is effective	81	8	63
Program funding is adequate	54	35	32
Program is improving	73	19	63
Legislators are concerned	19	27	23
Citizens are concerned	51	3	44
Need a stronger state program	38	32	46
Need a stronger local program	23	37	62
Staff adequately trained	89	3	75

n = 37

*denotes the responses from 230 state directors for radon, coal, lead, drinking water, and wellhead protection programs (controlling for asbestos responses) for field inspections for the entire state." A similar comment from a different state official suggested that too few inspections were conducted. "You must perform frequent inspections in order to have a viable asbestos program. If the state presence is not maintained, contractors become lax in following work practice requirements."

Other state officials felt that local jurisdictions should be more involved and interested in implementing AHERA. Only 5 percent of state asbestos officials noted that local school districts are supportive of the AHERA program. One official commented, "We [the state department staff] developed the management plans for 456 schools. We continue to do so, and look forward to the day when more local people get on the band wagon and develop their own plans."

For some school officials, however, involvement in the asbestos program is synonymous with spending significant resources for asbestos management in their buildings. In an era of tightening school budgets, spending money for asbestos management or removing asbestos may come at the expense of other school programs, as mentioned in the previous section. As one state official put it, "Schools do not have any financial support for asbestos management from either the state or the federal government. Is it any surprise, then, that a lot of small, private schools have problems complying with AHERA?"

Yet another area for improvement recognized by state asbestos staff was to consolidate asbestos activities into one department. "We need better coordination among various state agencies; we also need to reduce overlapping responsibilities." Or, as another official commented, "In our state, controlling asbestos exposures is divided among three departments. We have close communications and working relationships, but this division sometimes makes it difficult to coordinate activities."

Finally, some state officials noted the political backlash that asbestos abatement actions have received. "Our program is susceptible to continual changes in the political atmosphere—not only in Washington [D.C.], but in our state legislature." Another hoped that his state would "bring back the policy makers who recognize the potential hazards of asbestos and who will promote commonsense, level-headed approaches to preventing problems and controlling hazards."

In short, the unintended consequence of LEAs interpreting AHERA to mean asbestos removal rather than management in place has negative consequences in some states, with state officials feeling that asbestos programs are political targets of state legislatures and executive administrations. Six of the ten persons interviewed declared that their state legislature didn't want the AHERA program to continue. One official observed that while asbestos was a concern for the public, it was an economic nightmare for school districts. School officials, after paying millions to remove asbestos, were beginning to get the attention of state legislators. "Believe me, there's some people in the state who would like to see the end of AHERA."

Other state officials offer a different perspective. They believe that asbestos exposure in schools remains a serious problem that needs to be monitored. The recent reduction in EPA funding and availability of EPA inspection personnel jeopardizes AHERA implementation. "Most of our schools are in compliance now. They've got approved management plans and conduct periodic inspections. It doesn't mean they're going to stay that way [in compliance], especially since they know that no EPA person or state inspector is going to come knocking at their door."

The EPA Asbestos Program and Working Relationships

Concerns that state officials have about their programs, however, seem small when compared to the perceptions they have about EPA efforts in overseeing AHERA. Only 28 percent of state officials responding to the survey believe that the EPA asbestos program is effective. (See Table 3-3.) This compares to 81 percent who believe the state asbestos program is effective. Similarly, state asbestos officials are much less likely to believe that the federal asbestos program is adequately funded (25 percent) than believe their own programs are adequately funded (54 percent).

State asbestos program coordinators also do not feel the need for a federal overseer in order to run an effective state program. Only 16 percent agree, and 59 percent disagree, with the statement that without the EPA presence their program would not be as effective. Perhaps most telling, only about one-third of state officials responding to the survey (36 percent) believe that EPA officials are very concerned about protecting the public from asbestos (compared to 68 percent of state directors of other programs).

More than half of the respondents agreed that early efforts by the EPA relied too much on removing asbestos, rather than managing it in place (58 percent), and about the same number feel that the recent EPA efforts to de-emphasize the asbestos program is not a positive action on the part of the agency.

When asked what they would change about federal efforts to implement the asbestos program, state officials made several recommendations. Foremost among the recommendations was to increase, or at least continue, funding of state programs. "EPA should partner with

TABLE 3-3 Survey Questions About the Operation of the EPA Asbestos Program and National-Level Implementation Variables (Responses of State Asbestos Program Officials)

Survey Questions	% Agree	% Disagree	Other Programs % Agree*
EPA program is effective	28	33	19
EPA officials are concerned	36	36	68
EPA program is adequately funded	25	47	27
Regional and headquarters view program similarly	28	45	25
Oversight needed to encourage program implementation	16	59	37
Early efforts relied too much on removal	58	17	na
De-emphasizing asbestos at the EPA is a good thing	33	50	na

n = 37
*denotes the responses from 230 state directors for radon, coal, lead, drinking water, and wellhead protection programs (controlling for asbestos responses)

the states, particularly financially. States basically do the work, but the money is drying up and the asbestos program will cease to exist in many areas," commented one official.

Several other state officials echoed concerns about the EPA pulling out of the asbestos program, as is evident in these comments:

"Most states have functioning asbestos programs. However, the EPA is taking on fewer asbestos activities, assuming that the states are handling everything. This isn't true. The states need continued funds and support from the EPA."

"The de-emphasis of the asbestos program within EPA only leaves the state programs more vulnerable. Our program is in jeopardy because our state legislators are all too willing to bow out of AHERA implementation. There's still a lot of asbestos to be dealt with, so I hope something changes."

In addition to more federal funding and increased federal commitment to the asbestos program, several state officials perceived opportunities to improve EPA management of the program. Some states simply wanted the EPA to stay out of the state program. Others pointed to inconsistent implementation among EPA regions. As one official noted,

"EPA should coordinate more efficiently between the [EPA] regions. Regional offices interpret the Federal Register in different ways—our [EPA] regional office is far more restrictive than other regions."

Yet other state asbestos officials felt that the reporting burden under the cooperative grant program is too onerous. One state official said that they refuse EPA grants because the grants are small and don't justify the paperwork involved. Several officials pointed to what they perceived as a lack of EPA staff knowledge of field conditions, or what implementation would be like for small, fiscally stressed school districts. For example, some state officials believed that the EPA engaged in rule-making activities without bringing them into the process and without understanding what effect the new policies would have in the states.

"Before implementing AHERA, EPA should check and see if there are enough expert inspectors and management planners in the workforce. Most of the asbestos management plans done by schools in our state were poorly done, because we did not have enough trained consultants and contractors to help school officials." Finally, several state officials noted a lack of agency trust of the state program to accomplish implementation. As one official suggested, "EPA should either respect the way our [state] program is run, or give us some money to help run it."

Despite these concerns, however, 86 percent of state asbestos program coordinators believe they have a positive working relationship with their EPA regional counterparts, and the same number believe that the EPA regional office supports the state asbestos program. (See Table 3-4.) Only 13 percent of state officials believe that the state–EPA relationship has gotten worse in the past few years. However, just 39 percent of state asbestos directors responding to the survey believe that the EPA headquarters staff is supportive of their program.

What accounts for this discrepancy? Why do state officials perceive the support of EPA regional staff, but not of EPA headquarters staff? One reason rests with the feeling of some state officials that the EPA has done a poor job of communicating its program requirements. Only 19 percent of state asbestos officials agree that EPA has clearly communicated its program to states. One official pointed to the Model Accreditation Program provisions as being too inflexible; another simply stated that the EPA should spend more time with state program managers prior to issuing policies and regulations. When referring to the EPA headquarters, one state official commented, "They never really envisioned how the asbestos program would work from the ground up. They should partner with us both philosophically as well as financially."

TABLE 3-4 Survey Questions About Federal–State Working Relationships (Responses of State Asbestos Program Officials)

Survey Questions	% Agree	% Disagree	Other Programs % Agree*
EPA regional staff supportive	86	3	85
EPA headquarters supportive	39	19	42
Positive working relationship	86	5	85
State–EPA relationships have gotten worse	13	62	14
States have sufficient flexibility	69	9	54
Evaluations by EPA are fair	71	6	56
Reporting requirements are reasonable	56	3	33
Program requirements are consistent	32	27	33
EPA clearly communicates program requirements	19	47	33
EPA stays in frequent contact with me	57	14	71

n = 37

*denotes the responses from 230 state directors for radon, coal, lead, drinking water, and wellhead protection programs (controlling for asbestos responses)

This comment identified the feeling of other state program coordinators that they were left out of the picture. "EPA should provide states with advance copies of pending legislation and EPA guidance documents. We should have more say in interpreting the guidance. Even better, the EPA should provide clarification materials and more written correspondence so we know what is going to happen."

CONCLUSIONS ABOUT THE ASBESTOS PROGRAM

Using the working relationship typology from Chapter One, interview and survey data suggest that the intergovernmental asbestos program is best categorized as having low levels of mutual trust and low levels of involvement—or, in the language of the typology, "coming apart with avoidance." State asbestos officials feel that the federal program is important to the extent that it provides leverage in their state for these officials to continue the asbestos programs. However, state officials believe that the EPA is not very concerned about public health risks associated with asbestos in schools, nor is the agency particularly effective at implementing AHERA. Some of this ineffectiveness is clearly linked to a lack of funding, but some ineffectiveness is associated with less than stellar program management, at least from the perspective of state officials. An improved asbestos program would include more federal–state interaction, more continuity among EPA regional offices, and a more consistent federal posture toward asbestos.

When the implementation framework is reviewed, several extrinsic and intrinsic factors seem to be influencing asbestos policy implementation. This case reveals the poignancy of the policy history: delay on the part of the U.S. Congress to deal with asbestos health risks in turn allowed a larger population to be exposed to asbestos-containing materials. Subsequent passage of AHERA directed political attention at the schools, which were ill-equipped to deal with what was now labeled the "asbestos scare." In turn, the EPA vacillated on its guidance to states and to school districts, prompting confusion on the part of the target group (schools) about how to comply. Within both the EPA and state agencies, agency culture militates against a wholesale embracing of AHERA enforcement. It's expensive and often leads school districts down the path of asbestos removal, which may not be the optimal policy choice. Asbestos as a policy issue, then, lacks the support of many state-level stakeholders; national political arrangements are such that Congress acts to "protect all children," while at the same time allowing the EPA asbestos efforts to be greatly reduced. Finally, the public demand for change has brought about the demise of the asbestos industry and has reduced the amount of asbestos exposure, independent from a strong enforcement of AHERA.

THE RADON PROGRAM

Radon policy, like asbestos policy, presents an interesting policy formulation canvas on which to tell the implementation story. Like asbestos, the negative health effects of exposure to radon have been known for decades. However, indoor radon as a policy issue rose from virtual obscurity to widespread public attention in 1985 not because of lawsuits (as in the case of asbestos), but because of a local human interest event. This event captured the attention of the media and, for a while, publicizing radon as a health risk became a popular thing to do.

Before 1985, few people had heard of radon; within the year the EPA created an indoor radon program; in 1988, federal radon legislation was in place. Ten years after radon became widely recognized as a public health risk, state and EPA radon programs are up and running, but radon stories are no longer the darling of the media. Many state radon programs, established primarily through the "carrot" of federal grant money, are now relatively obscure as public and media interest in radon has waned.

The following sections present the implementation story of this policy that rose like a phoenix from the depths of public and governmental inattention and may now be struggling to retain its place in the sun.

FORMALIZING A FEDERAL-STATE RADON PROGRAM

Radon is an invisible, odorless, radioactive gas that occurs naturally because of the decay of uranium. Since uranium is common in the earth's crust, radon is a part of outdoor air. Exposure to radon becomes dangerous when radon gas is concentrated inside homes and buildings as it is drawn inside through pathways such as cracks in the foundation or openings around sump pumps.

The EPA now considers radon a "Class A," or known, human carcinogen and the second leading cause of lung cancer, next to smoking, in America.[41] EPA estimates that exposure to radon causes between 7,000 and 30,000 lung cancer deaths each year, making it one of the most dangerous environmental pollutants in terms of human health risk of all pollutants the EPA seeks to control.[42]

An understanding of the health risks associated with radon developed over several decades. International and domestic epidemiological studies of underground miners in the 1940s first revealed correlations between levels of radon exposure and incidence of lung cancer.[43] Between 1963 and 1988, twenty major epidemiological studies of various groups of underground miners led to the conclusion that radon can cause lung cancer.[44] Health professionals began to link radon's health risk to residential settings when even low levels of radon in occupational exposures were associated with increased incidence of lung cancer. Federal officials associated nonoccupational radon exposures with lung cancer in 1979, in an EPA report that attributed 10 to 20 percent of the U.S. incidence of lung cancer to radon.[45] However, radon exposure data in private homes was limited, and federal officials did not generally view radon exposure in nonoccupational settings as dangerous.[46]

Not surprisingly, few federal–state cooperative efforts to reduce radon levels in private homes existed before 1980. Joint state–federal efforts prior to 1985 consisted of mitigating radon levels in homes in a few well-defined geographic areas where radioactive materials had been used as part of the aggregate in home foundations or where homes had been built on disturbed mining lands, such as in Grand Junction, Colorado.[47]

That changed, however, in 1984 when a home in Pennsylvania was found to have radon levels that exceeded any previously measured in a private residence. Stanley Watras, a construction worker at the Limerick Nuclear Generating Station near Philadelphia, repeatedly triggered the plant's radiation alarms when he entered the building. This was puzzling, especially since the plant was not yet generating fission products. Subsequently, health physicists from the utility and their consultant performed a radiation survey in the Watras home.[48] Technicians from Philadelphia Electric Company measured a radiation concentration so high that the senior health physicist immediately notified the Pennsylvania Department of Environmental Resources (DER).[49]

After verifying test results of 2,600 picocuries per liter (pCi/L), the DER hand-delivered a recommendation that the Watras family immediately evacuate their home. The home's radioactivity levels exceeded by 100 times the level of radiation dose permitted for uranium miners, and the lung cancer risk to the Watras family was estimated by some scientists to be equivalent to smoking 135 packs of cigarettes a day.[50] (The current EPA guidance is 4 pCi/L; ambient outdoor air concentrations of radon throughout the country range from 0.10 to 1.5 pCi/L.) A DER literature review of radon concentrations in residential structures revealed that the Watras' radon level was the highest level ever recorded for a private residence.[51]

Largely in response to the Watras event, the EPA established a Radon Action Program in 1985. State input was solicited by the newly formed Radon Action Committee, but no systematic intergovernmental program was developed. Through the Superfund Amendment and Reauthorization Act in 1986, Congress endorsed an intergovernmental response to addressing radon, but did not authorize a comprehensive grant program for the states.

THE INDOOR RADON ABATEMENT ACT (1988)

The first formal intergovernmental effort to address radon exposure came with the passage of Public Law 100–551, the Indoor Radon Abatement Act (IRAA), on October 28, 1988. Like AHERA, which established a goal of protecting children from asbestos regardless of costs, IRAA had an ambitious objective. Congressional architects declared that "the national long-term goal . . . is that the air within buildings in the United States should be as free of radon as the ambient air outside of buildings."[52] However, Congress provided few tools to the EPA or to states to meet this goal.

Under IRAA, the EPA was given authority to implement a radon public information program and to determine the extent of public exposure to radon. The agency was required to publish an updated version of its *Citizen's Guide to Radon* by June 1, 1989.[53] (Amid controversy over radon testing protocols, an updated document was not published until May 1992.) The guidance document was to include both testing protocols for homeowners and "action levels" for radon exposure.

More importantly for this purpose, Sections 305 and 306 of the IRAA established a federal–state program to encourage testing of homes and schools, as well as perform public information campaigns. A key element of the initial federal–state program was the EPA–state radon screening survey. In conjunction with the EPA, states were encouraged to participate in a survey of randomly selected homes to be tested for radon. Radon measurements were taken using short-term (3–7 days) testing devices placed in the lowest livable area of the home. From 1985 to 1990, thirty-four states agreed to participate.[54] By 1992, forty-two states had participated in joint EPA–state radon surveys, six states preferred to conduct their own surveys (in order to use long-term testing devices or for other reasons), and two chose not to participate due to funding or other constraints.[55]

A second nationwide study by the EPA was conducted in 1992. The results of the National Residential Survey indicate that about 6 percent of U.S. homes have average radon levels greater than 4 pCi/L.[56] However, wide variations in residential radon exposure exist among states, depending upon geological features and housing stock, as confirmed by the state–EPA screening surveys and other data. For example, the eight states with the highest estimated radon concentrations in the livable spaces of homes account for about half of the U.S. homes with exposures greater than 20 pCi/L.[57]

IRAA encouraged state participation in alerting the public to the dangers of radon by establishing a three-year State Indoor Radon Grants (SIRG) program. The SIRG program divided federal funding among participating states according to criteria established by the EPA.[58] States would match federal funding each year on a sliding scale: 25 percent in the first year; 40 percent the second year; and 50 percent the third year. States were expected to operate self-funded programs after the third year.

In the first year, states received SIRG funds to establish and maintain basic radon programs.[59] States enjoyed considerable latitude in establishing a basic program. Many states established toll-free radon hotlines, developed public information materials, and offered radon training for contractors, school officials, and real estate agents.[60] States also began evaluating home radon exposure through participating in the EPA survey program, or by making radon test kits available to the public by other means.

Beginning in 1993, the EPA added performance criteria designed to measure environmental results. In addition to a qualitative assessment of program adequacy, states would be evaluated according to the increased number of homes that have been tested for radon; the number of homes with high levels of radon that have mitigated; and the extent to which residents know about radon.

Radiation program branch staff in the ten EPA regional offices were given responsibility for soliciting and approving SIRG applications and overseeing state programs. Each regional office designated a SIRG contact to coordinate state radon programs and regional outreach efforts. Regional SIRG contacts were to serve as information conduits between the states and EPA Radon Division.

The Radon Division staff in the Office of Air and Radiation (recently reconfigured as the Office of Radiation and Indoor Air) at EPA headquarters retained responsibility for coordinating the public information campaign, including developing the *Citizen's Guide to Radon* and other outreach materials. The Radon Division, while not making individual state grant decisions, determined SIRG allocations available to the regional offices.[61] Determining regional allocations of grant money was done by using a formula that calculated the number of homes likely to have exposures exceeding the action level of 4 pCi/L.

IMPLEMENTATION ISSUES SURROUNDING IRAA

Several implementation issues surround IRAA, including: encouraging people to test and fix their homes through a nonregulatory apparatus; the best orientation for the public information campaign; continued debate regarding "safe" levels of radon exposure; and the availability of federal funding for state programs. Each will be discussed in turn.

Unlike AHERA, IRAA established no federal regulatory mandates for controlling radon exposure. Absent federal regulations, any regulations governing radon exposures became the responsibility of the states. Using SIRG funds as a carrot, Congress expected to entice states to take up the regulatory reins in the form of state licensing of radon professionals, requiring disclosure of radon levels during real estate transactions, passing mandatory school testing legislation, and adopting radon-resistant building codes.

States, however, have often been as reluctant as Congress to regulate radon. While most states have passed mandatory school testing legislation, fewer states have been willing to require schools with radon levels above 4 pCi/L to mitigate. Nor have states rushed to embrace radon-resistant building code requirements or mandatory real estate disclosure laws, although failure to disclose elevated radon levels during a real estate transaction may be cause for a court case.[62]

Unfortunately, the nonregulatory approach has made little headway in convincing people to test their homes for radon. Only about 9 percent of American homes have been tested for radon, even though about 70 percent of American homeowners are aware that radon represents a public health risk.[63] More troubling is the fact that only about 10 percent of the homes with elevated radon levels have been mitigated.[64]

States with radon disclosure requirements for real estate transactions appear to have higher rates of both testing and mitigation.[65] As of 1995, seventeen states had some type of disclosure requirement, with most of the states simply requiring that the seller inform the buyer of radon test results.[66] States that offer free or low-cost radon test kits have generally been able to increase the rate of home testing.[67]

This presents a challenge for maintaining a viable public information campaign. The EPA Radon Division has adopted a number of different approaches to encourage the public to voluntarily test their residences for radon. In 1989 the national Advertising Council and the EPA developed a radon public information campaign which attempted to persuade people to test their homes out of fear. Public service announcements labeled radon the "deadly intruder." As shown in Figure 3-1, print ads showed a chest X-ray and warned readers that "radon is deadly in this area."

Backlash from some health physicists, state officials, and members of the media community that the EPA was trying to scare people into testing their homes prompted the agency to adopt a light-hearted approach to communicating radon risk. The following year's public service announcements showed people on stilts and posed the question, "What are you doing that is so important you can't test your home for radon?" With this strategy, the EPA sought to create public awareness of radon with the hope that people would then test their homes. The implicit message in the ad was that testing for radon was probably more important than many other weekend activities. Later radon campaigns have fallen somewhere in the middle of these two approaches, but none have been dramatically successful in persuading people to test their homes.

Some scholars have criticized not only the EPA's vacillating position on risk communication, but also the EPA's attempt to reach everyone, rather than to focus on the areas of greatest risk. A long-standing critic of the EPA's radon program, Anthony Nero, commented, "In its zeal to spur millions of homeowners to act, EPA directed an alarmist—

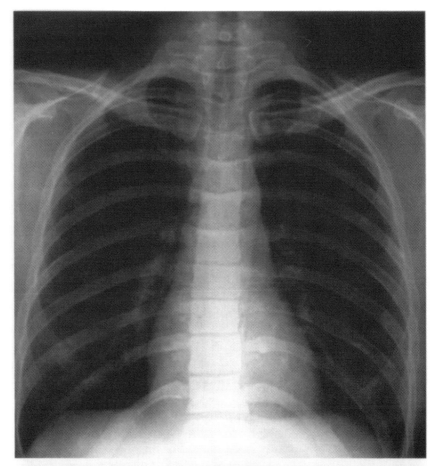

WARNING: RADON IS DEADLY IN THIS AREA.

Figure 3-1   EPA/Ad Council Radon Public Awareness Advertisement

Source: U.S. Environmental Protection Agency, Radon Division.

and often misleading or inaccurate—public information effort. The practical outcome has been a confused public, a frustrated EPA, and a large number of households that are still exposed to a very significant cancer risk."[68]

Research indicates that most people do not believe that radon presents a serious health risk.[69] Radon can't be seen, smelled, or touched. Since it doesn't arouse any of the senses, it is hard for the public to believe radon is a problem. Moreover, the consequences of radon exposure may not be manifest for two decades or more. Absent immediate health effects, visible evidence, or a culprit on which to blame the pollution, radon as a health risk is hard to be taken seriously, except among radiation scientists. Moreover, the costs of mitigating an existing home (ranging from $500 to $2,500) are borne by the home-owner.[70] Costs of lowering radon levels in the home may be low-priority items for many household budgets.

Another communication challenge for the agency involved choosing the appropriate testing protocol for the updated edition of the *Citizen's Guide to Radon*. The earlier version of the guide instructed homeowners to test in the lowest "livable" area of their residence. For many homes, this protocol suggested that people test their basements, whether they used them as a living space or not. Amid much debate among radon professionals, state radon program coordinators, reloca-tion companies, and health physicists, the EPA Radon Division changed the protocol to suggest testing in the lowest "lived-in" area.[71] The distinction was not insignificant, because many homes have higher radon levels in the basement than in the ground or upper-level floors.

Perhaps the most challenging communication effort was related to the dissemination of the EPA Map of Radon Zones, released in 1994. This map, created with the assistance of the U.S. Geological Survey, identified counties within states according to three levels. A county designated as Zone 1 has a predicted average indoor screening level for homes greater than 4 pCi/L; Zone 2 counties have a predicted average screening level between 2 and 4 pCi/L; and Zone 3 counties have a predicted average screening level less than 2 pCi/L. The in-tended audiences for the radon map were state and local governments and building code officials. While Sections 307 and 309 of IRAA directed EPA to list and identify areas of the United States with the potential for elevated indoor radon levels, the radon map was greeted with skepticism by some state officials and EPA regional staff. Concerns included designating a county based upon a paucity of available data (sometimes only a handful of test results were used to determine the zone); the preference of the EPA to use EPA–state survey data rather than data generated through other sources; and a fear that Zone 2 and Zone 3 counties would feel that they were "off the hook" and not obliged to adopt radon-resistant building codes.[72]

Yet another issue that plagues IRAA implementation is the contin-ued debate concerning the dose–response relationship.[73] Extrapolation from excess lung cancer deaths of uranium miners to American house-holds presents uncertainty about the real extent of risk. Especially troublesome is the assumption by the EPA that dose–response between

WHAT ARE YOU DOING THIS WEEKEND THAT'S SO IMPORTANT YOU CAN'T TEST YOUR HOME FOR RADON?

Figure 3-2   EPA/Ad Council Radon Public Awareness Advertisement, Second Year

Source: U.S. Environmental Protection Agency, Radon Division.

radon and lung cancer is linear (i.e., there is no threshold tolerance or safe level of radon exposure). The EPA set an action level of 4 picocuries per liter (pCi/L) as a technologically achievable level of radon exposure, but states in its guidance documents that no level of radon exposure is safe.

Compounding the issue of a threshold or "safe" radon level is the synergistic effect of cigarette smoking and radon exposure. The EPA estimates that current smokers average 20 times the risk of people who have never smoked and face about 70 percent of the total risk from radon. This led the EPA to conclude that while radon represents a danger to all people, ". . . any change in smoking patterns would have a dramatic impact on both the total and the radon-attributed lung cancer mortality rates."[74]

Debate about safe exposure levels of radon continues, however, with no consensus in the scientific community. Some scientists reject the linear dose–response assumption and argue that people can be exposed to radon levels over 4 pCi/L and not face increased health risk. After all, they argue, radon is present in the ambient air. Other scientists agree with the EPA assessment and support the 4 pCi/L guidance level and the zero threshold assumption.

The ongoing debate in the scientific community is then translated into some mixed messages in more popular media. The following quote from the *Berkeley Wellness Letter* published by the University of California is a case in point:

"How much radon would it take over what period of time to cause cancer, and how many people would it affect? In spite of years of research (19 more studies are currently underway) and millions of dollars spent, there's no answer to these questions . . . epidemiological studies concerning radon are good at detecting high risk, as in uranium mines, but not sensitive enough to detect low risks, such as may result from exposure in smoke-free homes."[75]

Thus radon, like other environmental carcinogens, suffers from scientific uncertainty about acceptable risk. However, unlike other carcinogens that may be regulated under other environmental laws, reducing radon exposure is primarily a voluntary activity. People may look at reports about scientific uncertainty as providing a reason to delay or avoid addressing elevated radon levels in their homes. This is especially true when the media attention to radon as a carcinogen has faded.

A final implementation issue rests with the availability of federal funding. IRAA was not reauthorized when it expired in 1992, although several radon bills were introduced in 1993, 1994, and 1995. Many of these bills attempted to establish a national regulatory presence in real estate disclosure requirements, building codes, or school testing. Absent new authorization, federal funds for state radon programs are tenuous, although state radon programs were funded under authority from the Toxic Substances Control Act in fiscal years 1993, 1994, 1995, and 1996.[76]

Still, federal funding for state radon programs has been decreasing. Initially, IRAA Section 306(j) authorized $10 million for three years (federal fiscal years 1989, 1990, and 1991) to get state radon programs operational. Roughly $8.1 million was available to states annually under the SIRG program during those three years.[77] That amount, however, has recently declined. Thirty-two states received smaller grants in 1993 than previous years.[78] The average radon grant for 1993 was $139,000, down from $151,000 in 1992. For fiscal year 1996, only $5.2 million is anticipated to be available to fund state radon programs.[79]

Perhaps more importantly, states with the highest exposure risks do not necessarily receive large SIRG grants. South Dakota, ranked highest of all states in terms of radon concentration per unit of livable space, received only $30,000 in 1993.[80] North Dakota and Nebraska, ranked second and third in terms of percentage of homes over the EPA guidance level of 4 pCi/L, received $100,000 and $40,000 grants, respectively, in 1993. In many cases, reduced grant awards are the result of states' inability to meet escalating match requirements.

In sum, a number of issues at the national level surround the continued implementation of IRAA, including the challenge of effectively communicating risk, determining best testing protocols, addressing scientific uncertainty, and continuing the program in the absence of IRAA reauthorization. However, state-level issues, as well as state perceptions of the federal–state radon efforts, are equally important. These are reported in the next section.

PERCEPTIONS OF STATE RADON OFFICIALS

In 1995, fifty-three surveys were sent to state officials identified by the EPA Radon Division as directing state radon programs. Forty-four were returned, for a response rate of 83 percent. In 1995 and 1996, twelve additional interviews were conducted in order to better understand the perspectives of state radon staff. Data from an earlier survey mailed to state radon program directors in 1994 will also be used as appropriate. In that study, thirty-nine surveys were received, for a response rate of 79 percent. In both cases, the response rate was reasonably high, and phone calls to state officials and to EPA radon project officers in several EPA regional offices suggest that there is no nonrespondent bias in the survey results.[81]

State radon programs operate with small staffs. Ninety-five percent of state officials responding to the survey function with five or fewer full-time equivalent personnel, and 43 percent of those have only one (or less than one) full-time equivalent personnel devoted to the radon program. Most state radon programs are located within state health departments, although a few are in environmental quality departments operating as an independent program or as part of an environmental health unit.

According to survey respondents, 75 percent of state radon programs have been established for more than five years but less than ten years. Most state programs were created when states received their first SIRG grants. Eighty-seven percent of state radon programs depend upon federal grants for at least 50 percent of operational expenses, and 45 percent of these programs rely on federal funding for most or all of their programmatic expenses. Since under current SIRG requirements states must contribute 50 percent of their own-source funds, this suggests a heavy reliance by state radon programs on in-kind money. In other words, many state radon programs use federal monies for ongoing expenses and use staff time or other "soft dollars" to meet the SIRG matching requirements. Only 9 percent of state radon program coordinators report that they receive little or no federal funds to operate their programs.

As matching requirements have increased and available federal funds have decreased, some states have opted out of the SIRG program. In 1996 Maryland, Texas, and Georgia indicated that they would not participate in the SIRG program.[82] For some states, radon programs are left to county governments. The State of Washington dropped their radon program in 1992, after providing minimal funding ($6,000) to support the radon consultation and referral services offered by the Spokane County Health District.[83] Yet other states have very few homes with elevated radon levels and are hard-pressed to find even soft money matches to continue their radon efforts. Only 0.01 percent and 0.05 percent of the homes in Louisiana and Hawaii, for example, are estimated to have elevated levels of radon.[84]

Factors Which Facilitate or Hinder Implementation

When asked what facilitates implementation, 55 percent of state radon program directors identified adequate federal funding as the most important factor. Adequate state funding, technical expertise of the staff, and support of their departments were equally chosen as the next most important factors. (See Table 3-5.) Factors which were ranked as relatively unimportant to implementing their state radon programs

TABLE 3-5   Factors Which Facilitate Implementation of the Radon Program (Percent of State Officials Ranking Factor as One of the Top Three)

Adequate federal funding	55
Adequate state funding	30
Technical expertise of state staff	30
Support of the department	30
Support of the EPA regional office	25
Adequate staffing	23
Support of local governments	20
State laws mandating testing, building codes, or real estate disclosure	18
Clear and consistent state program goals and requirements	11
Clear and consistent EPA program goals and requirements	9
Assistance of the American Lung Association and other groups	9
Available solutions to address adverse environmental health effects	4
Citizen involvement and support	0

n = 44

included citizen support (which was not identified by any state radon program director), clear and consistent EPA goals and requirements under the SIRG program, or the assistance of the American Lung Association or other "partners." Only 9 percent of the respondents felt that the support of other groups facilitated the implementation of IRAA.

Data in Table 3-6 illustrate that state radon officials perceive little state-level support for their program. Only 29 percent (compared to 66 percent of all environmental program directors) believe that officials in their departments are concerned about radon as a public health risk. Even fewer state radon program directors (11 percent) perceive support for their state radon program coming from state legislators, and 57 percent believe that state legislators are not very concerned about radon. Also, less than half of state radon program directors responding to the survey believe that their programs are improving (compared to 75 percent of all other program directors).

Interviews revealed a frequent belief among state radon officials that their programs are in jeopardy. As one official noted, "We're concerned about potential negative impacts on state health agency funding for radon because of the EPA block grants (performance partnerships) that may be targeted to another state agency, causing competition among departments and reducing or even eliminating our radon program." Another comment was quite similar, "I'd like to reduce the potential negative impact of 'hiding' radon grant support in block grants. If block grants come to our state, wave good-bye to the state

TABLE 3-6   Survey Questions About the Operation of State Radon Programs and State-Level Implementation Variables (Responses of State Radon Program Officials)

Survey Questions	% Agree	% Disagree	Other Programs % Agree*
Officials are concerned	29	43	66
Administrators are concerned	27	39	57
Program is effective	75	14	68
Program funding is adequate	48	34	34
Program is improving	41	25	75
Legislators are concerned	11	57	26
Citizens are concerned	43	5	45
Need a stronger state program	25	43	49
Need a stronger local program	65	16	51
Staff adequately trained	91	7	74

n = 44

*denotes the responses from 230 state directors for asbestos, coal, lead, drinking water, and wellhead protection programs (controlling for radon responses)

radon effort." (Performance partnership grants, approved by Congress as part of the EPA 1996 appropriations bill, may dramatically alter the implementation landscape by collapsing categorical environmental grants into one block grant for states.)

Another comment held the same sentiment, "The state radon program needs to be supervised by someone who can give it a high priority, or any priority, in the department." While 43 percent of state radon officials believe that the public is concerned about radon, many state officials do not believe this concern often translates into voluntary action to test or mitigate homes. When asked about citizen involvement in 1994, many state radon directors labeled citizens as "apathetic" about radon and the media as uninterested.

On the positive side, state radon directors overwhelmingly believe (91 percent) that their staff is adequately trained to run the radon program, and most officials believe that their program is effective (75 percent). As one official put it, "Our radon program runs very well as a community involvement program at the local level (due mostly to our efforts at the state level), but this happens with little middle and top-level management support. This is true even though over three-fourths of our citizens live in Zone 1 and Zone 2 counties." However, these programs are very small, as mentioned earlier, and many state officials mentioned staffing problems. "A dedicated full-time employee for the radon program would greatly help. We have had difficulties retaining part-time staff and training them."

EPA Radon Program and Working Relationships

Another dimension of IRAA implementation emerges when state officials express their opinions about the EPA radon program, as shown in Table 3-7. While more state radon staff are likely to view the EPA radon program as effective when compared to state staff in other environmental programs (40 percent to 16 percent, respectively), this is still not an overwhelming endorsement of EPA efforts. Nearly a third of state radon program directors do not believe the EPA radon program is effective. When asked to explain why they felt that way, several themes emerged.

TABLE 3-7   Survey Questions About the Operation of the EPA Radon Program and National-level Implementation Variables (Responses of State Radon Program Officials)

Survey Questions	% Agree	% Disagree	Other Programs % Agree*
EPA program is effective	40	30	16
EPA officials are concerned	74	12	60
EPA program is adequately funded	40	21	24
EPA staff have a high degree of technical expertise	60	14	21
Regional and headquarters staff view program similarly	42	35	22
Oversight needed to encourage program implementation	44	34	30

n = 44
*denotes the responses from 230 state directors for asbestos, coal, lead, drinking water, and wellhead protection programs (controlling for radon responses)

First, state radon officials perceive that the EPA radon proficiency programs have gone awry. The radon measurement proficiency program and the radon contractor proficiency program have recently been changed by increasing fees and qualification requirements. This causes problems for many states which have few people interested in pursuing a business in radon testing or mitigation. As the interest in radon has waned, so too has the radon business. In 1994, when increased fees for radon professionals were established, the number of organizations and individuals listed on the EPA's proficiency list fell by 17 percent.

"EPA is destroying an already dying radon industry. No one wants to do radon work anymore, yet EPA makes it more expensive to be a radon professional. [EPA should] make the radon proficiency programs more cost-effective for participants so that we can be assured of an adequate list of service providers in various areas of our state."

A second comment suggests that EPA staff could be better trained. As one radon official commented, "Improve the technical expertise at EPA headquarters. Most of the people in EPA that we deal with these days have a political science background."

Yet another common suggestion for improving the EPA radon program focuses on communication. One aspect of this focus was on the communication efforts to alert the public about the dangers of radon. Some state officials lamented the results of the national Advertising Council program with comments like, "less terror tactics, more information" and "EPA never should have bought the Ad Council program. The fallout from that stupidity is all around us."

More frequently, comments about communication dealt with improving communication between states and EPA headquarters. Some state officials believe that the EPA does not solicit their input in a timely fashion. For example, many state officials believe that the Radon Division staff in EPA headquarters consulted them too late in the evolution of the national radon map or in the development of the *Citizen's Guide* and other EPA radon documents.

On the other hand, a few state officials believed the EPA contacts them too much for their input, "The EPA needs to realize that the states are very busy with their own programs and we don't always have time to do what the EPA wants us to do. The amount of mail sent to the states is overwhelming."

Still, when compared with other environmental programs, perceptions of state officials about the EPA program are positive and state perceptions of working relationships are exceedingly positive. Ninety-five percent of state officials believe that EPA regional staff are supportive of the state radon program, and 90 percent believe they have sufficient flexibility to run their programs. (See Table 3-8.) Moreover, 88 percent agree that they have a positive working relationship with their EPA counterparts, and only 12 percent believe that state–EPA relationships have gotten worse, even though federal funding has decreased and program requirements have increased.

State radon officials are also likely to perceive adequate flexibility to run their programs (90 percent agree). In addition, 68 percent agree that the EPA fairly evaluates their program (compared to 56 percent of state officials in other environmental programs), and 65 percent of state radon program coordinators agree that reporting requirements

TABLE 3-8 Survey Questions About Federal–State Working Relationships (Responses of State Radon Program Officials)

Survey Questions	% Agree	% Disagree	Other Programs % Agree*
EPA regional staff supportive	95	5	80
EPA headquarters supportive	58	7	35
Positive working relationship	88	0	82
State–EPA relationships have gotten worse	12	66	13
States have sufficient flexibility	90	7	49
Evaluations by EPA are fair	68	5	56
Reporting requirements are reasonable	65	16	30
Program requirements are consistent	40	26	31
EPA clearly communicates program requirements	44	30	27
EPA stays in frequent contact with me	60	19	70

n = 44

*denotes the responses from 230 state directors for asbestos, coal, lead, drinking water, and wellhead protection programs (controlling for radon responses)

are reasonable (compared to 30 percent of the state officials in other programs). Finally, although only 44 percent of state radon officials agree that the EPA clearly communicates program goals and requirements, this is still somewhat higher than the number of respondents overall who agree (27 percent).

Similar to the drinking water, wellhead protection, and asbestos programs already reviewed, radon staff perceive less support from EPA headquarters personnel than EPA regional personnel (58 percent to 95 percent). However, this is twice as many state radon directors perceiving support from EPA headquarters than from their own state administrators or top-level officials (27 percent and 29 percent, respectively).

When asked about improving working relationships between the EPA and states, one state radon director suggested, "Make the relationship more partnership-oriented, instead of the feds treating states as second-class entities." Another state official noted the lack of communication, "Make some program managers at [EPA] headquarters more accountable for their actions and improve communication between

[EPA] headquarters and [EPA] regions, as well as between [EPA] head-quarters and states."

CONCLUSIONS ABOUT THE RADON PROGRAM

According to the dimensions of the working relationship typology, the state and federal actors in the radon program seem to be "pulling together," with high levels of mutual trust and involvement. EPA regional staff and state radon staff share the belief that elevated radon levels present a serious risk to the public; they also tend to feel neglected when compared to other environmental programs. Several state radon program directors interviewed have the attributes of policy champions—one director from a sparsely-populated western state has a radon "road show" that she presents to communities in all areas of the state.

State staff feel that they occupy tenuous positions—especially as state budgets are decreased and radon no longer captures the attention of the public. This coupling of shared consensus about policy goals with nervousness about the continued fiscal health of the program works to increase the cooperative spirit of intergovernmental relationships. High levels of information sharing are occurring between states, at least as perceived by EPA regional radon project officers and state radon program directors.

That is not to say that no improvements could be made to federal–state working relationships. From the perspective of the states, EPA headquarters personnel are more remote, less interested, and less helpful than EPA regional staff. Room for improving communication exists, but communication of policy goals has not been as confused or distorted as what occurred in the asbestos program. In the radon program, most of the criticisms surrounding EPA communication are to involve states earlier and more actively in the development of public outreach materials.

Extrinsic variables that influence implementation of the radon program include the nature of the problem (with the law relying on the public to voluntarily respond to health risks associated with radon exposures in the home). The demand for putting the radon program into place at the national level has waned, with the national dialog surrounding radon focused on the adequacy of the EPA's risk assessment and merits of the 4 pCi/L action level and testing protocols. The EPA, in turn, has found persuading people to test their homes for radon an increasingly hard sell. It is likely that most future radon mitigation will be the result of policy change at the state level (such as requiring disclosure during real estate transactions), rather than at the EPA.

CONCLUSIONS ABOUT RADON AND ASBESTOS PROGRAMS

The study of radon and asbestos has provided rich opportunities for comparing implementation constraints and considering whether state and federal officials are "pulling together" or "coming apart." In the case of asbestos, legislative and regulatory legacies continue to dog the implementation of AHERA. Congress demanded that the asbestos emergency in schools be quickly addressed; meanwhile, the EPA was first choosing to tell school officials to remove asbestos and then opting for a more practical approach—managing asbestos-containing materials in place. State and national politics clearly affect the ability of state asbestos coordinators to implement the program, as state legislators and members of Congress adopt a public position that champions protecting children at all costs, but a private position that underfunds the program and reduces asbestos staff.

The vacillating posture of the EPA over asbestos removal, coupled with the regional downsizing of asbestos staff, and the tepid response of states to seek EPA waivers for their approved programs is reflected in the responses of state asbestos officials. State asbestos officials are the least likely of officials in any program to agree that EPA officials are concerned or that federal oversight is needed to promote implementation (Table 3-3). In short, it appears that federal and state asbestos officials are less likely to pull together and more likely to come apart.

On the other hand, EPA and state radon officials appear to be pulling together. This seems a reasonable response to a program that is generally small and seldom captures the attention of the media, the public, state administrators, or legislators. State radon staff are much less likely to feel supported within their borders and therefore seek to garner support from their EPA regional colleagues. By the same token, federal and state radon staff are both in the same boat, headed in the same direction: inform citizens about radon and persuade the public that yes, indeed, radon may potentially present a serious health risk. The Watras story has faded from media memory and, with it, the ability of radon as an environmental contaminant to compete with other more provocative substances—like lead-based paint, alar, or even polychlorinated biphenyls (PCBs).

The four programs reviewed in Chapters Two and Three have looked at environmental programs for which the EPA has responsibility. The next chapter examines the surface mining program, operated under the Office of Surface Mining.

NOTES TO CHAPTER 3

1. Denise Scheberle, "Radon and Asbestos: A Study of Agenda Setting and Causal Stories," *Policy Studies Journal* 22 (Spring, 1994), 74–86.

2. For an excellent description of the history of governmental attention to asbestos, see Charlotte Twight, "From Claiming Credit to Avoiding Blame: The Evolution of Congressional Strategy for Asbestos Management," *Journal of Public Policy* 11, no. 2 (1991): 153–86.

3. For a discussion of history of medical and legal understanding of asbestos-related disease, see Barry Castleman, *Asbestos: Medical and Legal Aspects* (Clifton, N.J.: Prentice Hall, 1990).

4. U.S. Congress. House. "Failure to Regulate—Asbestos: a lethal legacy." Hearing before Committee on Government Operations, 98th Congr. 1st. sess. (June 28, 1983), p. 193.

5. Rajiv M. Rao, "End of the Line: Manville is No More," *Fortune*, (April 29, 1996): 42.

6. U.S. House of Representatives, Committee on Education and Labor, Subcommittee on Elementary, Secondary and Vocational Education. *Oversight Hearings on Asbestos Health Hazards to School Children*. Hearing, 96th Cong., 1st. Sess. (1979).

7. U.S. Environmental Protection Agency, Office of Public Affairs, *Asbestos Fact Book*, A-107/86-002 (Washington, D.C.: U.S. EPA, June 1986), p. 4.

8. Asbestos Hazard and Emergency Response Act, 15 U.S.C. 2641 et seq (1986).

9. U.S. Environmental Protection Agency, Office of Air and Radiation, *The Asbestos Informer*, EPA 340/1-90-020 (Washington, D.C.: U.S. EPA, December 1990), p. 11.

10. U.S. Environmental Protection Agency, Office of Toxic Substances, *100 Commonly Asked Questions about the New AHERA Asbestos-in-Schools Rule* (Washington, D.C.: U.S. EPA, May 1988), p. 59.

11. U.S. Congress. Senate. "Implementation of the Asbestos Hazard Emergency Response Act." Joint hearing before the subcommittees on hazardous wastes and toxic substances and superfund and environmental oversight. Committee on Environment and Public Works. S.Hrg. 100-575. 100th Congr., 2nd sess. (March 15, 1988).

12. U.S. Congress. "Asbestos Issues," S.Hrg. 101-835, 7.

13. U.S. Congress. House. "Asbestos Dangers: Presence in Schools and Incompetent Disposal." Hearing before Committee on Government Operations. 100 Congr., 1st sess. (August 3, 1987), 285.

14. The hearing can be found at the following cite: U.S. Congress, Senate, Committee on Environment and Public Works, Subcommittee on Superfund and Environmental Oversight, Hearing on the Implementation of the Asbestos

Hazard Emergency Response Act, 100th Congr., 2nd sess. (S.Hrg. 100-575, March 15, 1988); the report is U.S. Environmental Protection Agency, *EPA Study of Asbestos Containing Materials in Public Buildings* (Washington, D.C.: U.S. EPA, February 1988).

15. U.S. Environmental Protection Agency. "Asbestos Facts: Demolition and Renovation Regulations" (Washington, D.C.: U.S. EPA, March 1991), p. 2.

16. U.S. Environmental Protection Agency, *A Guide to the Asbestos NES-HAP*, EPA-340/1-90-015 (Washington, D.C.: U.S. EPA, November 1990).

17. Peter Cary, "The Asbestos Panic Attack: How the Feds Got Schools to Spend Billions on a Problem That Really Didn't Amount to Much," *U.S. News and World Report* 188 (February 20, 1995), 61–64.

18. U.S. Environmental Protection Agency, "Asbestos Fact Book," A-107/86-002 (Washington, D.C.: U.S. EPA, June 1986).

19. U.S. Environmental Protection Agency, *Guidance for Controlling Asbestos Containing Materials in Buildings*, EPA 560/5-85-024 (Washington, D.C.: U.S. EPA, June 1985).

20. Federal Register, Vol. 52, No. 210. 40 CFR Part 763: Asbestos- Containing Materials in Schools, Final Rule, Supplemental Information (October 30, 1987), 41832.

21. U.S. Environmental Protection Agency, *Managing Asbestos In Place: a Building Owner's Guide to Operation and Maintenance Programs for Asbestos Containing Materials*, TS-799 (Washington, D.C.: U.S. EPA, July 1990).

22. U.S. Environmental Protection Agency, "The Asbestos Informer," EPA 340/1-90-020, (Washington, D.C.: U.S. EPA, December 1990).

23. U.S. Environmental Protection Agency, Office of the Administrator, "Asbestos, Sound Science, and Public Perceptions: Why We Need a New Approach to Risk," address by William Reilly, 20Z-1006 (Washington, D.C.: U.S. EPA, June 1990), p. 4.

24. U.S. Congress. Senate. "Asbestos Issues." Hearing before the Subcommittee on Toxic Substances, Environmental Oversight, Research and Development, Committee on Environment and Public Works. S.Hrg. 101-835. 101st Congr. 2nd sess. (April 26, 1990), p. 50.

25. *Corrosion Proof Fittings v. EPA*, 947 F2d. 1201 (5th Cir. 1991).

26. B. T. Mossman, J. Bignon, M. Corn, A. Seaton, J. B. L. Gee, "Asbestos: Scientific Developments and Implications for Public Policy," *Science* 247 (January, 1990): 294–301; B. T. Mossman and J. B. L. Gee, "Asbestos-Related Diseases," *New England Journal of Medicine* 320 (1989): 1721–30.

27. See Lynn MacDonald and Jerod M. Loeb, "The Health Hazards of Asbestos Removal," *Journal of the American Medical Association* 267 (January 1, 1992), 52–54; Jan Bone, "Custodial Workers Face Asbestos Hazards," *Safety and Health* 146 (July 1992), 70–75.

28. U.S. General Accounting Office, *School Facilities: Condition of America's Schools*, GAO-HEHS-95-61 (Washington, D.C.: U.S. GAO, February 1995), p. 4.

29. U.S. General Accounting Office, *School Facilities: Condition of America's Schools*, p. 2.

30. U.S. General Accounting Office, *School Facilities: Condition of America's Schools*, p. 2.

31. Bailey, Glenn W. "Litigation Is destroying American Companies," *USA Today* (magazine) 122: 2584 (January 1994), 76.

32. U.S. Environmental Protection Agency, Office of the Administrator, *Asbestos, Sound Science and Public Perceptions* (Washington, D.C.: U.S. EPA, June 1990), p. 5.

33. U.S. Congress, "Asbestos Issues," 6.

34. Memorandum from John J. Neylan, Director, Policy and Grants Division, Office of Compliance Monitoring, U.S. EPA, dated June 13, 1994.

35. Fiscal year 1995 data was provided by an asbestos program coordinator in EPA Region 8.

36. This observation was made by an asbestos program coordinator in EPA Region 8.

37. U.S. Environmental Protection Agency, Office of Enforcement and Compliance Assurance, *FY 95 TSCA Cooperative Agreement Guidance*, unpublished and undated document, p. 9.

38. U.S. Environmental Protection Agency, Office of Enforcement and Compliance Assurance, *FY 95 TSCA Cooperative Agreement Guidance*, unpublished and undated document.

39. Based on a conversation with an AHERA inspector in EPA Region 2 and an AHERA enforcement specialist in EPA Region 5.

40. Telephone interview with Region 2 asbestos staff member in March 1996.

41. U.S. Environmental Protection Agency, Office of Radiation Programs, *EPA's Radon Program: Reducing the Risk of Indoor Radon* (Washington, D.C.: U.S. EPA, July 1991), p. ES-1.

42. Office of Radiation Programs, *EPA's Radon Program*, p. ES-1. For a discussion of relative risk, see U.S. Environmental Protection Agency, *Unfinished Business: A Comparative Assessment of Environmental Problems* (Washington, D.C.: U.S. EPA, 1987).

43. National Research Council, Committee on the Biological Effects of Ionizing Radiation, *Health Risks of Radon and Other Internally Deposited Alpha-Emitters: BEIR IV* (Washington, D.C.: National Academy Press, 1988).

44. Office of Radiation Programs, *EPA's Radon Program*, pp. 2–3.

45. Richard Guimond, W. Elliott, J. Fitzgerald, S. Windham, and P. Cumy, *Indoor Radiation Exposure Due to Radium-226 in Florida Phosphate Lands* (Washington, D.C.: U.S. EPA, July 1979).

46. Margo Oge, Acting Director of the Office of Radiation Programs, "Overview of the U.S. Environmental Protection Agency's Radon Action Program." Speech given to the International Symposium on Radon and Radon Reduction Technology, Philadelphia, Pennsylvania, April 1991.

47. Denise Scheberle, "Stalking the Deadly Intruder: Agenda-setting for Radon." Paper presented at the 1992 Annual Meeting of the Western Political Science Association, San Francisco, Calif., March 1992.

48. Thomas M. Gerusky, "The Pennsylvania Radon Story," *Journal of Environmental Health* 49 (January/February 1987): 197.

49. Allan Mazur, "Putting Radon on the Public's Risk Agenda," *Science, Technology and Human Values* 12 (Summer/Fall 1987) 84–98: 89.

50. Susan L. Rose, "Radon: Another Perspective," *Forum for Applied Research and Public Policy* 4 (Spring 1989): 12; Kathryn Harrison and George Hoberg, "Setting the Environmental Agenda in Canada and the United States: The Cases of Dioxin and Radon," *Canadian Journal of Political Science* 24:1 (March 1991): 3–27.

51. Gerusky, "The Pennsylvania Radon Story," p. 197.

52. Publ. L. 100-555, Sec. 301.

53. Publ. L. 100-551, Sec. 303.

54. Office of Air and Radiation, *1989 Summary of State Radon Programs*, p. 3.

55. U.S. General Accounting Office, *Air Pollution: Actions to Promote Radon Testing*, GAO/RCED-93-20 (Washington, D.C.: U.S. GAO, December 1992), p. 19. Delaware, Florida, New Hampshire, New Jersey, New York, and Utah conducted independent surveys; South Dakota and Oregon declined to participate in the state–EPA residential survey.

56. U.S. Environmental Protection Agency, Office of Policy, Planning and Evaluation, *Radon Program Review*, draft report (Washington, D.C.: U.S. EPA, May 1992), p. III-5.

57. U.S. Environmental Protection Agency, Radon Division, data provided from a memorandum dated March 1, 1993. The states, in rank order based upon radon concentrations in the livable spaces of homes, are South Dakota, Iowa, Pennsylvania, North Dakota, Montana, Nebraska, Colorado, and New Hampshire.

58. U.S. Environmental Protection Agency, Office of Indoor Air and Radiation, *Administrative Guidance for the State Indoor Radon Grants Program* (Washington, D.C.: U.S. EPA, December 1992), p. 2.

59. U. S. Environmental Protection Agency, Office of Indoor Air and Radiation, *Administrative Guidance for the State Indoor Radon Grant Programs* (Washington, D.C.: U.S. EPA, December 1992).

60. U.S. Environmental Protection Agency, Office of Air and Radiation, *1989 Summary of State Radon Programs*, EPA 520/1-91-015 (Washington, D.C.: U.S. EPA, September 1990).

61. Office of Air and Radiation, *Administrative Guidance for the State Indoor Radon Grants Program*, p. 2.

62. For example, a pending case in Pennsylvania charges Howard Hanna Real Estate Company and Prudential Preferred Realty with two counts of fraud and one count of negligent misrepresentation and violation of the state's consumer protection law, as reported in the article, "David Takes on Goliath in Real Estate Test Case," *Emanations: Newsletter of the Regional Radon Training Centers* 5, no. 4 (Manhattan, Kans: Kansas State University September 1995), p. 7.

63. U.S. General Accounting Office, *Air Pollution: Actions to Promote Radon Testing*, GAO/RCED-93-20 (Washington, D.C.: U. S. GAO, December 1992), p. 3.

64. U.S. Environmental Protection Agency, Office of Policy, Planning and Evaluation, *Radon Program Review*, draft document printed May 1992, p. III-15.

65. Office of Policy, Planning and Evaluation, *Radon Program Review*, p. III-15.

66. U.S. Environmental Protection Agency, Regional Radon Training Centers, *Emanations: Newsletter of the Regional Radon Training Centers* 5, no. 2 (Manhattan, Kans.: Kansas State University, April 1995): p. 6.

67. U.S. Environmental Protection Agency, Office of Air and Radiation, *Activities and Factors Contributing to Effective State Radon Programs*, Final Draft (Washington, D.C.: U.S. EPA, September 1994), p. 13.

68. Anthony V. Nero, Jr., "A National Strategy for Indoor Radon," *Issues in Science and Technology* (Fall 1992): 33–40, at 33. See also Leonard A. Cole, *Element of Risk: The Politics of Radon* (Washington, D.C.: AAAS Press, 1993).

69. Examples include Neil D. Weinstein, Mary Lou Klotz, and Peter M. Sandman, "Optimistic Biases in Public Perceptions of the Risk from Radon," *American Journal of Public Health* 78, no. 7 (July 1988): 796–800; and Peter M. Sandman, Neil D. Weinstein, and M. L. Klotz, "Public Response to the Risk from Geological Radon," *Journal of Communication* 37, no. 3 (Summer 1987): 93–108.

70. Office of Air and Radiation, *A Citizen's Guide to Radon*, p. 9.

71. Office of Air and Radiation, *A Citizen's Guide to Radon*, p. 5.

72. These concerns were identified through conversations with radon staff in two different EPA regions.

73. One example of criticism of the EPA's radon dose–response relationship is found in an article by Susan L. Rose, Radon Program Manager for the Department of Energy, titled, "Radon: Another Perspective," *Forum for Applied Research and Public Policy*, 4 (Spring 1989): 12–15. Rose argues that, ". . . direct knowledge of lung cancer from residential radon, *at any level*, does not exist and that for the average homeowner there may be no risk at all." For recent criticism, see Phillip H. Abelson, "Radon Today: The Role of Flimflam in Public Policy," *Regulation* 14:4 (Fall 1991): 95–100.

74. Office of Policy, Planning and Evaluation, *Radon Program Review*, p. III-7.

75. For example, see "Reassessing Radon Risk," *Berkeley Wellness Letter* 11, no. 5 (1995): 4–5, at 4.

76. Conversation with Radon Division staff in March 1995.

77. Many states began SIRG cooperative agreements in fiscal year 1990, thus funding was available through fiscal year 1992.

78. U.S. Environmental Protection Agency, Office of Indoor Air and Radiation. Internal memo listing state radon grant allocations.

79. U.S. Environmental Protection Agency, Region 5, internal memorandum dated March 6, 1996.

80. U.S. Environmental Protection Agency, Office of Indoor Air and Radiation, "State Indoor Radon Grants Policy Priorities for 1993." Unpublished document given to SIRG recipients.

81. The results of the first survey of state radon program directors were reported in "Pesticides and Radon: State Perceptions of EPA and Administrative Support," a paper presented at the Midwest Political Science Association meeting in April 1994.

82. U.S. Environmental Protection Agency, Region 5, Internal memorandum dated March 6, 1996.

83. Personal correspondence with the Spokane County Health District dated June 27, 1995.

84. U.S. Environmental Protection Agency, Radon Division, "Cumulative Ranking of States by Radon Concentration in the Livable Space," unpublished report dated July 1993.

4

Scratching the Surface: The Story of the Surface Mining Program

The story of the Surface Mining Control and Reclamation Act (P.L. 95-87) (SMCRA) implementation is worth telling, for it illustrates the importance of many facets of implementation—from the disposition of the federal overseers and changes in national political climate, to the various permutations of implementation performance observed at the state level, to the wide variations in the targeted regulatory population and the importance of statutory language. This chapter begins with a brief review of the partial preemption regulatory scheme and the history of surface mining policy formulation. Additional time is devoted to a discussion of primacy because the surface mining law is the most command–control oriented of the five programs reviewed in this book (for reasons which will be described later). Moreover, while the wellhead protection, drinking water, and asbestos programs largely look at changing the behaviors of public entities (communities, public water suppliers, or schools), the surface mining program seeks to address the behavior of private coal companies. Subsequent sections detail the key provisions of the law and the evolving OSM oversight role. The chapter concludes with a discussion of the perceptions that state surface mining officials have about the implementation process.

WRESTLING WITH ISSUES OF CONTROL: THE PRIMACY APPROACH

When SMCRA was signed into law by Jimmy Carter on August 3, 1977, undoubtedly jubilant members of Congress cheered. Legislation regulating the environmental effects of coal mining, the product of a tortuous decade-long congressional battle, had finally become a reality. For environmentalists, residents of coal mining areas, and many federal policy makers, SMCRA provided a much-needed national regulatory presence in a long-ignored environmental area. But, while the political skirmishes surrounding the adoption of this national policy were over, a new battle was about to begin. SMCRA, after twenty-five different bills and two presidential vetoes, was on paper; now it had to be put into practice in the coal fields.

The political struggles over coal would now take place on new battlefields. The policy had been formulated in a national arena; the implementation of SMCRA would take place in each coal-producing state. This shift of the locus for battle from a national to state arena was not by chance; it was by design. Like many environmental laws, congressional architects of SMCRA had chosen to use a partial-preemption approach for implementation of this regulatory policy. As discussed in Chapter One, the partial-preemption regulatory approach returns regulatory control to the states—but only after the states adopt enforcement programs that meet national standards, as evidenced by federal approval of each state's program.

The partial-preemption regulatory approach represents a middle ground in the implementation of a national regulatory policy. Unlike total preemption, complete with federal mandates requiring state performance according to federal prescription, partial-preemption allows states a certain flexibility in program design. States have the leeway to implement their laws and design their enforcement strategies, but the laws must be at least as stringent as the applicable federal statute.

Furthermore, states can opt not to go along. If state officials choose not to shoulder implementation responsibility for the regulatory program, the federal government remains the regulatory agent. And if approved state programs prove inadequate in enforcing national standards, the federal government reserves the right to "preempt" state authority. Thus, the states' acceptance of primary enforcement of a national regulatory program is not, in theory at least, an abdication of national control.

Once a state receives primacy, a tumultuous in-state implementation process begins. Several factors may cause state discomfort: First, state regulators now must practice a "hands-on" enforcement strategy, such as periodic inspections of businesses, which is intrinsically confrontational. Second, regulatory policy like SMCRA requires that a target group (coal miners) act according to a set of nationally-derived instructions, despite the costs or behavioral change required. Substantial compliance costs may squeeze the profit margins of regulated companies, prompting their active interest in state agency enforcement activity. This "interest" may be expressed through interactions with agency personnel, administrators, or state representatives.

Finally, state legislators and executive sovereigns may be inclined to listen to economically-important industries within state boundaries. They will most likely advocate a more relaxed enforcement strategy and be more sensitive to costs associated with regulatory compliance, according to the attendant political pressures exercised by the target group.

State bureaucrats frequently find themselves in uncomfortable adversarial relationships with members of the regulated industry. This discomfort may be alleviated by the assumption of an accommodating regulatory posture.[1] On the other hand, it may be increased by the presence of citizen or environmental groups pushing for rapid and strict implementation. Thus, the nature of regulatory policy under primacy creates an environment with mixed local pressures on state officials charged with implementation responsibilities.

Simultaneous with local pressures, however, are national pressures. Federal oversight of state programs may exert countervailing pressures on primacy states, since such states serve as implementors of national policy goals. State enforcement programs are constrained by policy decisions made at the federal level; states must conform to the operative framework established by the federal oversight agency. Crotty (1987) argues that one political effect of primacy may be to weaken the ability of the states to respond to the demands of their constituents (such as regulated coal firms), by replacing those local demands with demands from nationally based environmental and other groups.[2] These bottom-up and top-down pressures result in an "implementation squeeze" in which states are pressured on the one hand to adopt a more accommodating enforcement of regulatory policy and on the other to achieve national objectives established by the enabling legislation.

In short, federal regulatory programs embodying national goals but administered by state agencies almost inevitably create tensions between the two levels of government over the nature, timing, and scope of implementation. Understanding these pressures and their relative effects on implementing the surface mining program and on developing state–federal relationships is the goal of this chapter.

A PRIMER ON COAL MINING AND THE COAL INDUSTRY

Although it is common to talk about "scarce" natural resources, this term is not easily applied to U.S. coal. Coal is by far America's most abundant fossil fuel, with over 21 billion short tons of estimated recoverable coal reserves at active mines.[3] About 438 billion tons, referred to as demonstrated reserves, are potentially minable on an economic basis with existing technology. These reserves are estimated to be the largest in the world and are enough to supply America's energy demand for several hundred years.[4] Given this abundance, it is little wonder that salons returned to the saving graces of King Coal when supplies of other fossil fuels became precarious shortly before the passage of SMCRA in 1977.

Historically, coal has represented America's staple energy source. First mined commercially in 1748, coal production trends have reflected industrial progress, competition from other fuels, coal miners' strikes, economic conditions, wars, and health and safety regulations. Coal production, fueling industrial development, reached 200 million tons before 1900. Steadily growing since the 1970s, production of coal in 1994 reached a record 1,034 million short tons.[5]

America's coal production increases were accompanied by dramatic changes in the geographic distribution of coal mining and in the number and size of coal mines. Two factors characterize these changes, both of which have profound impact not only on the shaping of coal mining regulation, but also on the implementation process. The first factor is the exponential growth of coal production in the West; the second is the accompanying decline of small mining operations in the Appalachian coal mining region.

Coal mining in the West before 1970 represented a relatively minor contribution to overall U.S. coal production, as shown in Table 4-1. In 1965, for example, only 4 percent of America's coal was mined from western mines.[6] However, the hegemony enjoyed by eastern coal companies was coming to an end. By 1994 western coal comprised over 39 percent of the total annual U.S. coal production and 57 percent of the surface mine production.[7] Moreover, the western contribution is projected to continue to grow.[8]

Several factors explain the rapid rise of western coal production. Perhaps the most significant relates to the timely joining of energy

TABLE 4-1 Coal Production by Coal Region for Selected Years in Million Short Tons (Percent of Total U.S. Coal Production)*

	1965	1975	1994
Appalachian Region	371 (72%)	396 (61%)	445 (43%)
Interior Region	120 (23%)	162 (25%)	180 (17%)
Western Region	20 (4%)	89 (14%)	408 (39%)
Total	512	648	1,034

*numbers and percentages are rounded.
Source: U.S. Department of Energy, Energy Information Administration, *Coal Production 1988* (November 1989); U.S. Department of Energy, Energy Information Administration, *Coal Data: A Reference* (May 1989); U.S. Department of Energy, Energy Information Administration, *Coal Industry Annual 1994* (October 1995). Computation is the author's.

demand and environmental policy. In response to political directives in the wake of the Arab oil embargo to increase domestic energy use, coal became the energy source of choice for the generation of electricity. Power plants became the major consumers of U.S. coal, accounting for more than eight out of every ten tons of coal produced.[9] This increased demand for coal by U.S. power plants was affected by the passage of the Clean Air Act in 1970 which, among other provisions, required power plants to reduce sulfur emissions.[10] Most western coal has a low sulfur content, which provides a cost-efficient alternative to installing pollution-control systems or scrubber technologies for power companies. (The passage of the Clean Air Act Amendments in 1990 further tightened sulfur dioxide emissions limits on older power plants, beginning in 1995.)

Increased western coal production had profound effects on the composition of mining firms and on the relative productivity of coal firms nationwide. Many small eastern coal operations, faced with the arduous task of competing with the tremendous economies of scale of western coal, simply disappeared. Before the expansion of western mining, these operators could hold on to narrow profit margins and move in and out of the coal mining business. In 1967 there were over 7,000 mines, most of them in Appalachia. By 1987 less than 4,000 mines existed, and the 3,000 plus mines which discontinued operation were almost exclusively in the Appalachian Region.

Increasing the challenge for small Appalachian coal operators to remain viable is the introduction of new but expensive technologies for mining coal. The most notable of these methods is longwall mining. The next paragraphs discuss coal mining techniques.

Coal is mined in different ways, based on regional variations in the terrain and in the coalbed size. Many people typically think of coal as being mined underground, as indeed it is. Coalbeds located more than 200 feet underneath the surface are usually mined by one of several underground mining methods. The traditional "room and pillar" mining is still widely practiced. With this technique, a series of rooms are cut into the coalbed and coal is extracted. Pillars of coal are left to support the mine roof. As mining advances to new "rooms," an undersurface grid pattern is formed. The open rooms are left behind, supported by the pillars.

A more recent underground mining technique is longwall mining, a form of high-extraction underground mining incorporating planned subsidence. In longwall mining, a machine moves back and forth across the face of the underground coal seam. Self-advancing hydraulic jacks support the underground roof as the coal face is sheared by the machine. As mining advances into the coalbed, the jacks follow—allowing the roof above the previously mined area to fall (hence, the term "planned subsidence"). A longwall panel is larger than the "room and pillar" mined area, averaging 800 feet wide and up to two miles in length.[11] Longwall mining is generally more productive than more conventional underground methods because the operation is continuous, larger, and requires fewer workers.[12] Underground mining is principally conducted in the Appalachian Region, although some underground mining occurs in the Interior and Western Regions.

Surface mining, sometimes referred to as strip mining, is employed when coal is located within 200 feet of the land surface. Surface mining is basically a large-scale earth-moving operation in which the soil above the coal, or overburden, is scraped away and the underlying coal is removed. The efficiency of a surface mine is determined in part by the overburden ratio, or the amount of overburden excavated per ton of coal recovered. The lower the ratio, the more productive the mine. Most low-ratio mining operations are in the West. Coal-recovery rates at these large open-pit surface mines, such as the most productive American mines in the Powder River Basin area of Wyoming, often exceed 90 percent.

Regardless of mining method, coal mining can have profound consequences on the environmental quality of postmined land, as well as on associated surface water and ground water areas. Many supporters of federal regulation of coal mining shared a mutual concern for inadequate or nonexistent reclamation, which was not only aesthetically troublesome but also dangerous. Erosional instability caused the collapse of a coal waste dam in Logan County, West Virginia, in 1972, killing 125 people. This disaster brought the specter of unregulated "rape and run" coal mining practices to the homes of many Americans.[13] While inadequate reclamation of postmined lands continues to dominate discussions of potential environmental damage due to coal mining, other environmental issues are also of concern.

Other major environmental impacts associated with underground mining are the subsidence of overlying and adjacent land, the loss of surface water and groundwater, and discharge of acid mine drainage. Subsidence is particularly troublesome when high extraction techniques are used because it is rapid, inevitable, and covers large areas. Environmental concerns associated with surface mines include soil erosion, reestablishment of wildlife and native vegetation, and depletion and/or contamination of groundwater supplies. Reestablishment of vegetation is especially difficult in the arid West.

To summarize, the U.S. coal industry is etching an ever-increasing presence in America's energy mosaic, despite the concern of some about the effects of over-regulating coal mining operations. As illustrated in Table 4-1, coal production has increased steadily since the passage of SMCRA, and as of this writing has shown no signs of slowing down.

However, the continued health of the coal industry has not guaranteed success for all individual coal operators. Indeed, the number of coal mines in operation since the passage of SMCRA has been cut nearly in half as small eastern coal miners lost their competitive edge to monolithic western coal concerns and larger local eastern corporations. Thus, the advent of surface mining regulation occurred just as western coal was being positioned to challenge the dominance of Appalachian coal mines. The ability of western coal miners, especially in Wyoming, to operate massive coal mines by taking advantage of low overburden ratios and generous coalbed deposits would dictate the shape of regulatory enforcement in both regions, as discussed later in this chapter.

FORMULATING FEDERAL SURFACE MINING POLICY

A culmination of over a decade of political maneuvering, seven separate bills, and two presidential vetoes, the federal mining law ultimately represented an uneasy merger of two political camps: (1) persons inside and outside of government who pushed for increased domestic coal production, and (2) environmental and grassroots citizen groups who sought to curtail the ecological degradation caused by surface and underground mining.

Inside the federal bureaucracy, a chorus of voices sang the "gloom and doom" song of the potential impacts of federal legislation on coal production. In congressional testimony after the second presidential veto in 1975, administrators from the Federal Energy Administration, the Department of the Interior and the Department of Commerce, among others, predicted the demise of smaller coal companies and the attendant rise of America's dependence on foreign oil. The most vociferous position was taken by Federal Energy Administration Administrator Frank Zarb, in justifying President Ford's veto:

> The facts and figures . . . demonstrate that the responsible, if perhaps not the politically popular, course has been taken. . . . We have estimated that from 40 to 162 million tons of annual coal production would be lost during the first full year of implementation. . . . We are talking about locking away billions of tons of coal and we consider our estimates to be conservative.[14]

Other testimony pointed to the loss of mining jobs: "Not only would American consumers pay more (for energy) . . . many thousands would lose their jobs . . . we have concluded that from 9,000 to 36,000 jobs would in fact be lost."[15]

The most condemning administrative argument against a federal surface mining law was the impact it would have on national security vis-à-vis coal's ability to replace imported oil, as suggested by this testimony: "The loss of even 40 million tons of coal per year could increase imports by more than 450,000 barrels [of oil] per day . . . with additional costs of $1.9 to $7.8 billion a year for energy. Because of the gravity of our energy situation . . . this nation cannot afford to reduce the availability of our one abundant energy resource unless we have another to replace it. Coal is the only major domestic resource upon which we can rely as a secure source of energy in the coming decades."[16]

Mining interests were divided as to whether or not to support SMCRA. Large western coal firms tacitly supported federal surface mining legislation: first, because legislation would end the uncertainty of the "rules of the game" of coal production; second, because these firms invariably would mine coal on public lands, they needed the security of one set of mining regulations; finally, because the legislation did not seriously encroach upon company profit margins.

Moreover, western coal operators preferred to position themselves to shape the character of subsequent regulations rather than lose the opportunity at hand by blocking the passage of SMCRA.[17] By nominally supporting what appeared to be an inevitable federal presence in coal regulation, these large coal firms were able to direct their political resources toward ensuring that the final law would be flexible enough to accommodate their interests, which included the allowance of site-specific mining variations, mining on alluvial valley floors, and less stringent restrictions on the length of mining permits.

Many coal firms in the East, however, were vehemently opposed to SMCRA.[18] Eastern operators were fearful that the bill's provisions for requiring that mined land be returned to its approximate original contour would make mining eastern coal virtually impossible. Smaller operators in Appalachia were especially vociferous in their opposition because compliance costs posed significant economic hardships for these marginally profitable mines.

It was no accident that SMCRA coincided with the triumph of the environmental movement. National environmental groups like the National Wildlife Federation, the Sierra Club, the Environmental Defense Fund, and Friends of the Earth joined forces with a growing number of state-based citizen groups such as the Citizens for Better Reclamation in Virginia and the Northern Great Plains Resource Council in Montana and Wyoming to lobby for federal regulation of surface mining. Buoyed by national media attention to vast acres of unreclaimed land, the eventual passage of federal legislation seemed certain.[19]

Organized labor initially supported federal environmental controls on surface mining. Contrary to the administration's predictions, members of the United Mine Workers felt the passage of SMCRA would secure current employment and even provide more jobs. Since SMCRA was directed toward surface mining operations (and the UMW membership was composed of less than 10 percent surface miners), it had the potential to solidify the position of labor-intensive deep coal mines.[20] Still reeling from the effects of the Mine Health and Safety Law (1969), underground mining interests supported SMCRA as a political trade-off for their recently-incurred economic costs in complying with federal mine safety standards.

Furthermore, SMCRA potentially would remove the small operators from Appalachia, many of whom were able to avoid operating with unionized employees. Finally, the reclamation effort was recognized for its potential to provide "new" jobs for UMW membership. However, as SMCRA evolved to include regulation of the "surface effects" of underground mining, the UMW's formal position changed to oppose the law, although local groups continued to support federal intervention in surface mining.[21]

In addition to these political battles, yet another key political issue was raised in an attempt to thwart federal legislation: the contention by coal states and the coal industry that state regulations were adequate and, therefore, federal regulations would be an unnecessary encumbrance to proper state regulatory operations. (In fact, many states had not addressed surface mining problems. The majority of coal states passed legislation after national attention was directed toward surface mining: thirty-two out of thirty-eight states implemented state regulatory programs between 1970 and 1975 while federal legislation was being most strongly debated.)[22]

However, even though most coal-producing states had regulatory programs in place by 1975, there were widely disparate degrees of program effectiveness and state enforcement.[23] It was this perceived lack of uniformity, coupled with the problem of interstate competition, that eventually determined the need for federal legislation. As described in a U.S. Senate Committee Report: "The primary problem alleged with individual states regulating mining for coal is that a uniform set of regulations is lacking. This . . . arrangement allows the states to regulate mining activities according to the[ir] unique conditions. However, when one state passes stringent rules and enforces these rules when a neighboring state does not, it creates a condition of unfair competition for mine operators . . . ."[24]

Thus, by any measure, passing an acceptable federal coal mining law designed to protect the environment was fraught with complex political alliances and obstacles. But what effect did this contentious and protracted development of federal surface mining legislation have on the implementation process? In many ways, it guaranteed that implementation would be as tortured a process as policy formulation had been.

Each time Congress went back to the legislative "drawing board," it emerged with bills that, while granting some additional variances to the coal industry, were more precise in regulatory requirements. This increasingly detailed articulation of legislative intent resulted in a longer list of major provisions and performance standards for both the state and federal regulatory agencies. Furthermore, recurring delays in the enactment of a federal surface mining bill produced more— rather than less—stringent requirements for the coal industry. In short, Public Law 95–87 offered little flexibility for regulators in developing a regulatory program to implement the act or for the targeted industry in complying with its provisions.

Some detailed provisions embodied conflicting requirements, such as Section 516, which requires operators to "prevent subsidence causing material damage to the extent technologically and economically feasible . . . except in those instances where mining technology used requires planned subsidence in a controlled manner . . . provided that nothing in this section shall be construed to prohibit the standard method of room and pillar mining."[25]

This section is mystifying; it simultaneously allows and prevents subsidence, and leaves ambiguous the terms "planned subsidence" and "material damage." This section also illustrates the deference given to underground mining of coal vis-à-vis surface mining.

Second, congressional and administrative debates directed SMCRA toward dual national goals: coal production and environmental protection. In Section 101(b), SMCRA states it is "essential to the national interest to insure the existence of an expanding and economically healthy" underground coal industry.[26] Therefore, only the *surface* effects of underground coal mining are regulated under SMCRA.

Yet another effect apparent from the development of federal coal mining legislation is that it opened wide the arena of federal–state mistrust. Ongoing debates regarding which level of government to entrust with primary regulatory authority, federal or state, and then how much authority to allow, were major parts of congressional deliberations. Ultimately, SMCRA delegated responsibility to states—but only after significantly constraining state regulatory power.[27]

The legislative testimony indicates that Congress considered environmental performance standards too important to be rendered meaningless through lax state enforcement (which had prompted federal regulation in the first place). Thus, while SMCRA tacitly recognizes the need for "site-specific" implementation, the statute offers little opportunity for regulatory flexibility. The fact that Congress stated the state–federal relationship in great statutory detail also precludes federal regulators from deviating too far from a narrowly prescribed oversight role.

Finally, the passage of SMCRA left a chasm within the targeted industry—not only between East and West coal concerns, but also between underground and surface operations. Political realities dictated the sacrifice of marginal Appalachian coal companies, which lacked both the expertise and production levels to readily absorb compliance costs. At the same time, it provided protection for large eastern underground and western surface operations, both of which could accommodate compliance costs.

Congress attempted to maintain the viability of the small Appalachian coal miner by establishing a two-acre exemption, by which mining operations that disturbed less than two acres would not be required to comply with SMCRA's requirements. However, this opened wide the opportunity for unethical coal operators to circumvent SMCRA by mining the same seam of coal from multiple sites (all under two acres) or by establishing shell corporations of separate mining companies which would share common equipment, personnel, and offices. (The two-acre exemption was repealed in 1987.)[28]

Thus the struggle to enact a surface mining bill set the stage for continued conflict during implementation, as states sought regulatory control and various components of the coal industry pursued mutually-exclusive agendas. Statutory language, however, can be moderated by the way the federal agency approaches its oversight role. The next sections, therefore, examine the major elements of the surface mining law and OSM's response to SMCRA.

KEY PROVISIONS OF SMCRA

SMCRA is a complex law embodying both detailed instructions for regulating the coal industry and allowances for state flexibility. The statute created the OSM within the Department of the Interior and charged the Secretary of the Interior with the responsibility of carrying out the act directly and through promulgating regulations.

SMCRA has two major components. Title IV establishes a program to reclaim lands that were mined prior to August 3, 1977 (the date of the act) and abandoned without reclamation. The Title IV abandoned mine land (AML) program is funded by a tax on current producers of coal.[29] At least 50 percent of the tax monies collected within any state are returned to that state, provided it has a federally-approved AML program.[30] Because states are likely to receive several million dollars, AML funds provide an enticement for states to seek and maintain primacy. State reclamation grants under the AML program totaled over $180 million in 1995, and nearly $2.5 billion has been distributed to states since 1979.[31]

Coal mining is currently regulated under Title V, which allows for state assumption of regulatory duties upon federal approval. To receive approval, state programs must be "no less stringent" than federal provisions.[32] Regulatory requirements for coal mining operations begin with premining activity. Coal operators are required to submit detailed mining plans that are used by state regulators to identify potential environmental problems before a permit to mine is issued. Permits are issued for five years, subject to renewal. In addition to detailed permitting provisions, SMCRA also requires that reclamation bonds be posted by coal firms before mining begins. These bonds ensure that mine sites will be fully reclaimed, even if operators fail to undertake reclamation activity.[33]

Once a mine is operating, the state enforcement system contains four interlocking components: performance standards, inspections, enforcement actions, and penalties. SMCRA sets detailed performance standards for surface mining and the surface effects of underground mining.[34] These include requirements that the land be restored to its approximate original contour (referred to as AOC), that it be revegetated, that acid mine drainage be prevented, that subsided lands be restored, that "prime farmland" be restored to productivity, that hydrological disturbance be minimized, and that erosion be controlled. Other provisions include a requirement that reclamation proceed "as contemporaneously as practicable" and that highwalls (exposed vertical rockfaces) be limited in height during mining and ultimately eliminated.

Not all areas can be surface mined. SMCRA prohibits mining in national parks, federal lands within national forests, areas within 100 feet of a public road or cemetery, and within 300 feet of a public building or occupied dwelling, unless waived by the owner. These prohibitions may be relaxed in cases where a coal operator can establish "valid existing rights."[35] Finally, states can declare areas where successful reclamation is unlikely, or areas with particular historical or environmental value, as "off-limits" to mining operations.

While Congress required the OSM to establish a regulatory program for surface mining of coal on federal lands, primacy states may enter into cooperative agreements to assume the permitting, inspection, and enforcement responsibilities. By the end of 1995, cooperative agreements were established with twelve states.[36]

State inspections are conducted to ensure compliance with the performance standards and other SMCRA provisions.[37] Every mine must be inspected monthly, and at least one inspection each calendar quarter must be a full inspection. Inspections must occur on an irregular basis without advance notice to the operator.[38] Observed violations must be cited. Usually the coal operator is given a notice of violation (NOV), which specifies the methods for abatement and sets a reasonable time limit (ninety days or less) for correcting the violation.

Operators who do not abate the violation within the NOV time frame must receive a Failure to Abate Cessation Order (FTACO). However, if a violation is serious enough to constitute imminent danger to public health and safety, or can reasonably be expected to cause significant environmental harm, then a cessation order (CO) must be issued immediately and the operator must cease mining activity until the violation is addressed.

Two elements of the enforcement system make SMCRA prone to a highly command and control approach. First, inspectors must take action on every violation they observe, regardless of its perceived environmental impact. SMCRA provides for no exceptions; inspectors cannot legally substitute written or verbal warnings for formal enforcement actions (NOVs or COs). Second, NOVs must be issued immediately on-site. These two requirements place the onus of enforcement squarely on the shoulders of field inspectors, which was just what Congress intended. As explained by the congressional authors, "By mandating primary enforcement authority to field inspectors, this bill recognizes that inspectors are in the best position to recognize and control compliance problems."[39]

Civil penalties are also part of the state's enforcement fabric. COs and FTACOs have mandatory monetary penalties; state inspectors may attach monetary penalties with NOVS at their discretion. Typically, fines are established on the basis of four criteria: seriousness, negligence, violation history of the coal company, and the company's good faith abatement effort. Once fined, the operator may pay the penalty or request an informal hearing. During the hearing, the operator and the inspector make presentations to state agency administrators, and a decision is made to abate the violation or enforce the penalty. If the operator is not satisfied with the decision, a formal administrative hearing is held. The resulting decision can then be appealed to the courts.

SMCRA also authorizes criminal penalties for willful violations and, in cases where a pattern of abuse is evident, mining permits may be suspended or revoked. Criminal penalties apply to company executives as well as corporate officers and directors. Chronic violators, if convicted, may be individually fined up to $10,000 or imprisoned for up to one year.

Congress recognized that SMCRA's regulatory provisions under the permanent program would prove to be an arduous task for primacy states alone and, therefore, relied on citizen participation for enforcement. Citizens can request that state or federal regulatory authorities conduct inspections, and citizens have the right to accompany regulatory personnel on-site. Permits, permit revisions, and proposed reclamation bond releases are all subject to public comment and must be publicly advertised for citizen review. Citizens may seek legal redress by suing either federal or state regulatory authorities for failure to enforce SMCRA; they may also sue coal operators for permit or regulatory violations. Finally, citizens may petition states to designate certain areas as unsuitable for mining.

Given the myriad of requirements incumbent upon primacy states, Congress provided a financial incentive in the form of state grants. In addition to the monies available through the Abandoned Mines Land (AML) Fund, states receive operating grants for the Title V regulatory program. Federal funds are matched at the 50 percent level. However, states receive up to 100 percent of the costs of operating the regulatory program on federal lands within their borders.

The combination of Title V, AML, and federal lands funding can be substantial. For example, Kentucky has received $170 million in cumulative regulatory grants since it received primacy through 1995. Wyoming has received $21 million in regulatory grant assistance since it received primacy, but received nearly that much ($19 million) in AML funds in 1995 alone.[40]

OVERSIGHT ROLE OF THE OSM

The OSM serves two functions as federal overseer: it evaluates primacy state performance in carrying out its approved program; the OSM also provides backup enforcement against violating operators in the event that the state fails to enforce SMCRA provisions.[41] Currently, oversight responsibilities have been delegated to eleven OSM field offices and nine area offices located within the three coal-producing regions. OSM field offices conduct complete inspections of randomly-selected coal mines; respond to citizen complaints by conducting on-site inspections; issue ten-day notices (TDNs) to state agencies when a violation is observed during an inspection; and issue NOVs to coal operators when a state does not respond to TDNs and cite the violation. (The OSM's approach to TDNs has changed; see the last section of the chapter.) OSM inspectors also must issue cessation orders (COs) directly to a

coal operator when they observe a violation that may create an imminent danger to the health or safety of the public or when a violation
will cause significant damage to the environment. Finally, the OSM
field office staff annually evaluates each primacy state's inspection and
enforcement program.

TDNs are designed to reflect the congressional deference given
to state regulatory programs. Unless federal inspectors feel that an
operator's violation represents "imminent harm" and requires an immediate CO, states are given the first opportunity to interact with the
coal operator. To start the process, a federal inspector who observes a
violation during an oversight inspection issues a ten-day notice (TDN)
to the state agency. Only after a TDN expires and the state has failed
to respond can OSM inspectors issue a NOV to the coal operator.[42]

Direct enforcement by the OSM has been challenged by both primacy states and individual coal operators as extending beyond the
boundaries of SMCRA, but has been upheld in several court decisions.[43]
Critics of the TDN system have also charged that coal operators are
placed in the middle of federal–state disputes and, thus, are unduly
punished because the two regulatory agencies disagree on the nature
of violations. However, the OSM seldom issues a NOV directly to a
coal mining operation. Of the 134 TDNs issued in 1987, only forty-two
(or just over one-fourth) ultimately resulted in NOVs. Almost half of
those occurred in the state of Kentucky, which has long been recognized
for its enforcement problems.[44] Further, federally-issued NOVs were
given in only eight primacy states, although all states but Montana
received at least one TDN.

In sum, OSM oversight is closely wedded to all phases of the state
regulatory program and represents an especially close scrutiny of the
primacy state's inspection and enforcement program. But the realities
of oversight depend upon the nature of the organization and agency
culture, as evidenced by its subsequent policy orientation. The next
section examines changes in the role orientations of OSM administrators for their implications on implementation effectiveness and federal–
state working relationships.

EVOLUTION OF OSM OVERSIGHT

A review of the history of SMCRA since its enactment suggests that
there have been four "implementation phases" which can be associated
with different styles of federal oversight: regulatory enthusiasm (1977–
1980); regulatory retrenchment (1981–1984); regulatory realignment
(1985–1994); and shared commitment (1995 through current).[45]

The OSM's first task as a fledgling oversight agency was to ensure
the development of adequate state programs through its own initial

regulations. In this, the OSM chose to adopt an ambitious and vigorous posture toward implementing oversight. This regulatory enthusiasm reflected not only a desire to immediately curtail environmental abuses, but also a general distrust of state regulatory ability to control the coal industry. OSM began its regulatory program with the dual goals of minimizing state discretion and ensuring programmatic consistency among primacy states.

The components of this strategy are evident in the regulations which were promulgated by the first OSM task force. For example, reclamation standards developed by the OSM typically employed design and performance criteria.[46] One intensely debated design criteria was OSM's requirement of sedimentation ponds to control acid mine drainage. Sedimentation ponds were required at all mine sites and interim regulations stipulated specific construction design criteria. Although the coal industry challenged some of these early standards, the permanent program rules contained many more design criteria than those of any existing state program.

Another example of the enforced compliance strategy embodied in the initial rule-making process was the narrowing of state discretion, or the "state window." The state window permitted states to employ alternative regulatory standards and procedures upon OSM approval. Although originally conceived as a way of accommodating legitimate state interest in regulatory flexibility, the final OSM "state window" provision was viewed by states as effectively precluding their authority and counterproductive to a partial-preemption regulatory partnership.[47]

Finally, OSM inspectors were recruited for their commitment to a strict "going by the book" enforcement strategy.[48] Top OSM managers wished to put coal operators on notice that the letter of the law would be enforced. Headquarters staff, not field office personnel, developed inspection and enforcement guidelines that directed federal inspectors to "ticket" every observed violation.[49]

The detailed regulations coupled with the regulatory enthusiasm of the OSM were destined to stir the wrath not only of most coal firms, but also of most primacy states. By 1979 coal mining states and mining interests had captured the attention of Congress, where a bill was introduced (and passed the Senate, but not the House) to sharply curtail the rule-making and enforcement authority of the OSM.[50] Thus the OSM began to come under scrutiny not for being too lax in its enforcement effort, but for being overzealous in its pursuit of regulatory goals.

The second phase of regulatory retrenchment began, and the honeymoon period of regulatory enthusiasm ended, with the new Reagan administration. In order to undo what administrative critics of OSM termed its "regulatory excesses," the administration radically altered the organizational mission, structure, and purpose of OSM. Perhaps the most ominous signal that the implementation of SMCRA would pursue a different tactic was the appointment of three proindustry institutional leaders: Secretary of the Interior, James Watt; Director of OSM, James Harris; and Assistant Director of OSM, J. Steven Griles. Under this leadership, the implementation tools of OSM were gutted and the "style" of enforcement moved from vigorous to accommodating oversight.

This regulatory reversal was predicated on three notions: First, the OSM regulatory pendulum had swung too far toward environmental concerns, failing to recognize the act's mandate to balance environmental protection with the nation's need for coal production. Second, the OSM in its earlier regulatory zeal had overstepped its legislated authority, to the detriment of legitimate state regulatory discretion. Third, many of the OSM's regulations violated the tenets of Executive Order 12291, which required the elimination of unnecessary or overly burdensome regulations.

OSM Director Harris argued that "the measure of a good regulation is its effectiveness, not its stringency. Some definitions of stringency connote punishment. The proper mission of the OSM is to regulate the coal industry, not punish it."[51] Accordingly, all OSM regulations were reviewed for their inclusion of "unnecessary design criteria" and impracticability to "actual field situations."[52] Agency review of its regulatory program was swift: within two years, 91 percent of OSM regulations were rewritten and the nearly sixty revisions to original rules were approved by 1983.[53]

The strongest rationale for a new OSM mission came from the agency's relationship with the states. OSM administrators argued that the federal government had "grown out of proportion," becoming "a ponderous burden on the states," and promised to restore regulatory balance. Citing that state primacy was SMCRA's main objective, OSM Director James Harris criticized the agency's "heavy-handed" approach in its regulatory scheme and state program approval process.[54]

Two tactics were employed to effectively increase reliance on state rather than federal regulatory activity: First, OSM staffing levels were decreased. In 1980 OSM employed 891 full-time equivalent personnel (FTE); by 1982 FTE had been reduced to 742, a decrease of 20 percent. Furthermore, almost all of the decrease was due to the elimination of federal oversight inspectors (from 210 in 1980 to 69 in 1983).[55]

A second tactic aimed at restoring regulatory responsibility to the states was a major reorganization of the agency. All five regional field offices and twenty out of forty-two established OSM state offices were eliminated. In the West, the former Region V office was dissolved and its regulatory duties split among three field offices: the Casper Field Office, Albuquerque Field Office, and the Western Technical Center.[56]

The legacy of this period and its profound influence on the implementation strategy of SMCRA are described in Table 4-2. All quantitative measures of oversight performance declined dramatically. Federal inspections went from 29,639 in 1981 to 5,088 in 1985. NOVs also declined, from a high of 3,094 in 1981 to 872 four years later.

TABLE 4-2   Evolution of OSM Oversight for Selected Years

	1981	1985	1989	1994	1995
Number of inspections	29,639	5,088	4,241	3,882	3,722
Notices of violation	3,094	872	677	114	140
Cessation orders	863	110	10	60	60
Regulatory grants	9.3	36.0	41.7	51.3	51.5
AML grants					
(in millions of dollars)	97.8	113.2	99.6	205.8	162.5
OSM staff	772	822	1,264	952	664

Source: U.S. Department of the Interior, Office of Surface Mining, Annual Reports for 1981, 1985, 1989, 1994, and 1995; press release dated November 1, 1995.

Yet another indicator of OSM's changing regulatory posture was its inability or unwillingness to employ alternative enforcement techniques, such as the imposition of civil penalties. By legislative provision and the Parker Order, the OSM was required to collect civil penalties from coal companies not in compliance with the regulations.[57] By 1986, over $181 million in civil penalties had been assessed by the OSM; only $14.4 million, or roughly eight percent, had been collected. Moreover, testimony at congressional hearings suggested that penalties had not been assessed for all observed violations; the status of thousands of outstanding violations may require additional penalties, the amount of which was conjecture at the time of the hearing.[58]

In the mid-1980s, several factors indicated that the OSM was readjusting its enforcement orientation. New leadership in the Department of the Interior, as well as the OSM, had reduced the proindustry tenor of the OSM.[59] James Harris resigned in 1984 and was replaced by Jed D. Christensen in 1995. Among other issues, Christensen sought to improve OSM management, address delinquent penalty collections, and maintain consistency in enforcement to protect the environment.

For example, the agency's objective, as stated in the 1989 budget justification report, is "to assure that mining's economic benefits are not achieved at a cost of long term environmental degradation."[60] This appears to be more closely in conformance to the initial posture of the OSM, but with less attention paid to citing every violation.

Technical innovations have also been made. Chief among these innovations is the installation in 1989 of the Applicant Violator System (AVS). This computerized system is designed to identify coal firms across the country which have outstanding violations and subsequently prevent them from receiving mining permits in other locations. The system, which was required by court order, may have the potential to track violators and increase the collection of civil penalties. Perhaps the most potent element of the AVS rests with the ability to stop new mining permits for companies that have failed to reclaim previous mine sites.[61]

Other signs, however, indicate that OSM administrators of the 1990s are not ready to embrace the missionary-like zeal of their predecessors and, in fact, there is still some confusion at the top of the organization as to what posture to ultimately adopt. For one thing, OSM administrators do not stay long enough for an especially strong philosophy to permeate the organization. During the 1980s, the average tenure of the OSM director has been less than two years—hardly long enough to inculcate a particular policy philosophy.[62]

While the official OSM oversight policy has vacillated, many of the same OSM inspectors have remained on the job. This has created apparent confusion within the agency, especially between the field office and OSM headquarters staff. Interviews with OSM officials outside of Washington, D.C., suggest that they have not recovered from the internal dissension created in the early 1980s. One OSM field director complained: "We were muzzled early by [James] Watt. The leadership in the agency has been so bad. We don't have a mission; the OSM has no goals. Ask anyone—no one [in the agency] could tell you what it is [agency mission]."[63]

In short, the enforcement style of the OSM has, in pendulum-like fashion, moved from a style of enforced compliance and limited state discretion during the agency's early years to an accommodative posture minimizing federal intervention in the 1980s. The OSM posture has wandered between these two positions from the late 1980s through most of the 1990s. However, perhaps the most dramatic change in oversight philosophy since the inception of the agency nearly two decades ago began in 1996, when the OSM revealed its strategy of "shared commitment."

GETTING AWAY FROM THE "GOTCHA" SYNDROME

It now appears that the OSM has embraced a new philosophy of oversight that permeates the oversight duties and official orientation of the agency toward primacy states. The 1995 annual report released in March 1996 sports the slogan, "Protecting the environment: a shared commitment." OSM Director Robert J. Uram refers to the agency as the "new" Office of Surface Mining, and suggests that the OSM has "reengineered oversight from a process-driven to a results-oriented system."[64]

Further reflecting this new orientation is the agency's "remolding" of the contentious Ten-Day Notice process to "truly respect state judgments" and to "end intrusive federal second-guessing" of state inspectors.[65]

The new oversight policy is the product of an OSM–state oversight team which began a dialog on state–federal interactions in 1994. The new policy began with interim approval for the 1996 evaluation year (July 1, 1995); the OSM Directive REG-8 was released for comment on January 31, 1996, and took effect in July 1996.[66] Among the major changes in oversight approach are the development of performance agreements with states that allow states the opportunity to be evaluated for "on-the-ground" results.

Figure 4-1 illustrates the new OSM oversight approach. This flowchart implies that primacy state programs should be afforded greater opportunities for positive evaluations, as evidenced by the three directives to "report it" (meaning report a positive evaluation for the primacy state). For example, if the OSM evaluator believes that while the state did not achieve the targets established in the performance agreement and failed to address off-site impacts, but subsequently took action to address the problem, the state's performance should be reported as adequate. Only upon reaching the bottom of the flowchart should OSM corrective action be taken. Thus, the OSM would most likely exercise its TDN and NOV authority only in situations that are not corrected by the state and that have the potential to affect reclamation success, impact health or safety, or cause off-site damage—certainly a far cry from the initial agency posture to cite every violation.

What is not yet resolved, however, is how to determine when situations call for OSM backup enforcement. For example, when a citizen complains to the OSM about a coal mining operation, does the OSM field office disregard that complaint or refer it to the state without follow-up? OSM Director Uram has called the need for federal enforcement "strong and compelling," and argued that "many coalfield citizens tell us that OSM's presence in the coalfields is one of the most important benefits they get from the surface mining law . . . the agency's official vision statement provides that OSM will act independently to protect the public interest. . . ."[67] Thus, the new philosophy of federal–state shared commitment and results-oriented oversight is not without limits.

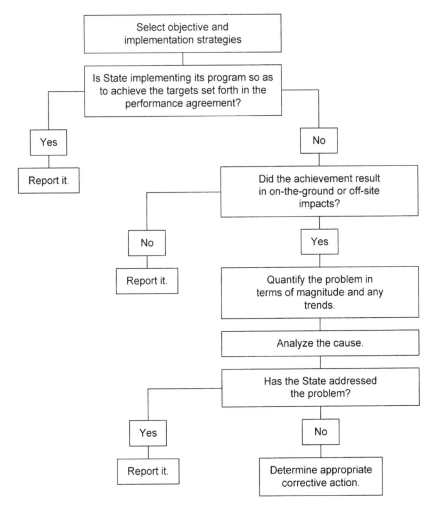

Figure 4-1   Flowchart for Evaluating State Performance to Be Used by OSM Field Office Personnel (effective in 1996)

Source: U.S. Department of the Interior, Office of Surface Mining, *Reg 8 Directive: Oversight of Regulatory Programs* (Washington, D.C.: Office of Surface Mining, January 30, 1996), p. 7.

Gone forever, at least in the eyes of the oversight team, is the perceived propensity of OSM inspectors to engage in detailed oversight of state inspection staff. In the past, according to OSM western regional office officials, OSM field office inspectors spent too much time trying to find fault with state inspections. Good oversight was measured by the number of "gotchas"—or the number of times the OSM staff could catch an omission of the state inspection or enforcement effort. This "gotcha" syndrome of OSM field offices was recognized as a particular sore spot by the oversight team. It is not yet clear, however, how OSM field office staff will feel about this new direction. It is also not yet clear how confident state officials are that the new direction will improve federal–state working relationships. Thus, the chapter now turns to the perceptions of state officials regarding working relationships and SMCRA implementation.

STATE OFFICIALS' PERCEPTIONS OF SMCRA IMPLEMENTATION

Surveys were sent to state surface mining officials in the twenty-four coal-producing states in July 1995. Of twenty-eight surveys sent (some states list multiple officials), twenty-four were returned for a response rate of 86 percent.[68]

State surface mining regulatory programs are older programs than the asbestos, radon, or wellhead protection programs discussed in earlier chapters. According to the respondents, half of the programs are over twenty-five years old, and range from fourteen to fifty-four years. Similarly, state surface mining programs tend to be larger than the other programs reviewed, with between fifteen and 120 full-time equivalent personnel involved in SMCRA implementation.

Factors That Facilitate or Hinder Implementation

When asked to identify factors that contribute to implementation success, most state surface mining program officials point to adequate staffing levels, and clear and consistent state program goals and requirements. (See Table 4-3.) Also recognized as important are the technical expertise of the state staff and adequate state and federal funding. Absent from the list of the top three are the support of the OSM field office or clear and consistent OSM program goals and requirements.

When compared to the other environmental programs, state officials responsible for SMCRA generally perceive higher levels of political attention to their program. Respondents are likely to believe that state administrators, legislators, and citizens are concerned about the surface mining program (86 percent, 67 percent, and 62 percent, respectively). Moreover, they all agree that their program is effective (compared to only 66 percent of the respondents in other programs) and that there are fewer environmental problems associated with coal mining than there were five years ago. (See Table 4-4.)

The political attention that state officials perceive as directed toward their program does not necessarily improve implementation

TABLE 4-3 Factors Which Facilitate Implementation of the Surface Mining Program (Percent of State Officials Ranking Factor as One of the Top Three)

Adequate staffing	52
Clear and consistent state program goals and requirements	48
Adequate state funding	43
Technical expertise of state staff	43
Adequate federal funding	38
State laws mandating environmental protection	19
Support of the department	14
Clear and consistent OSM program goals and requirements	5
Citizen involvement and support	5
Support of the OSM field office	0
Support of local governments	0
Available solutions to address adverse environmental health effects	0

n = 24

TABLE 4-4 Survey Questions About the Operation of State Surface Mining Programs and State-Level Implementation Variables (Responses of State Surface Mining Officials)

Survey Questions	% Agree	% Disagree	Other Programs % Agree*
Officials are concerned	71	10	58
Administrators are concerned	86	5	47
Program is effective	100	0	66
Program funding is adequate	70	15	34
Program is improving	75	10	67
Legislators are concerned	67	15	20
Citizens are concerned	62	10	43
Need a stronger state program	63	11	43
Environmental problems are more serious	0	100	na
Strong enforcement depends upon citing violations	21	60	na

n = 24
*denotes the responses from 230 state directors for asbestos, radon, lead, drinking water, and wellhead protection programs (controlling for coal responses)

performance. As discussed in the next chapter and in Chapter Six, political attention may serve to constrain the regulatory choices made by inspection personnel, as evidenced by this comment: "One of the major problems in administering a reclamation program is the lack of uniformity of mission between state regulators who are charged with obtaining good reclamation and elected officials who desire only to get re-elected."

The political attention directed to the program is compounded in the Appalachian Region, where state officials express concern about the demise of the small coal operator. Small mining operations put out of business create stress in the communities where the state officials live. As one official noted, "Our coal communities are always facing high unemployment rates—the unemployment rate for the state is less than six percent, but the seven coal-mining counties have unemployment rates three to four times as high." Thus, state surface mining officials in the East perceive the political influence of large coal operations, but also recognize the pressure placed in local areas when small coal mines close.

Also evident from the survey data and from interviews with state personnel is the fact that state inspectors are more likely to embrace a more accommodative role orientation toward coal operators. One state inspector observed that their state agency embraces "compliance through education" and that it does little good to cite a violation or assess a fine if the operator was unaware of the regulation or if the violation is minor (i.e., does not harm the environment). Indeed, only 21 percent of the state respondents agree that strong enforcement is linked to citing violations, and 60 percent disagree that such a connection exists.

In sum, when state-level implementation variables are considered, state officials have positive perceptions about the way they operate the regulatory program, the accomplishments of the program, and the ability of their staff to continue to implement SMCRA under primacy. They are much more likely to agree (when compared to state officials in other environmental programs) that their program is adequately funded and supported by state legislators and top-level administrators. However, they are less confident of the OSM's efforts, as illustrated by the responses shown in Table 4-5.

Perceptions About the OSM Program and Working Relationships

State regulatory officials have quite different perceptions about the OSM program than they do their own program, as shown in Table 4-5.

TABLE 4-5 Survey Questions About the Operation of the OSM Program and National-Level Implementation Variables (Responses of State Surface Mining Officials)

Survey Questions	% Agree	% Disagree	Other Programs % Agree*
OSM program is effective	11	39	22
OSM officials are concerned	65	5	63
OSM program is adequately funded	55	10	24
OSM staff have a high degree of technical expertise	25	20	40
Regional and headquarters staff view program similarly	20	60	25
Oversight needed to encourage program implementation	19	67	36

n = 24

*denotes the responses from 230 state directors for asbestos, radon, lead, drinking water, and wellhead protection programs (controlling for coal responses)

Only 11 percent of state officials believe that the OSM program is effective, and only one-fourth believe that OSM staff have a high degree of technical expertise. When asked about the oversight role of the OSM, many state officials expressed criticism. One official suggested that the OSM should "eliminate the second-guessing of state actions," while another commented that the agency is "too intrusive and mistrusting of states. . . . OSM believes a bold allegation from a citizen before they believe a state [official]."

Other state officials noted what they perceived to be a tendency of the OSM field office staff to look for small violations—evidence of the "gotcha" syndrome: "The OSM [staff] is too rigid in their enforcement procedures. They do it by the book whether or not it makes sense in a particular situation." Perhaps the most eloquent comment regarding OSM oversight was offered by a coal program supervisor in a western state who said, "Instead of assuming that state programs would not be as strong without federal oversight, I believe that most state programs would remain strong and be more efficient without an OSM presence. In many instances, the oversight role of the OSM has ebbed and flowed based on factors outside of state efforts. Meanwhile, we keep doing what we've been doing for fourteen years—running a sound program and protecting the environment."

State officials in the surface mining program are not likely to agree that oversight is needed to encourage implementation. Indeed, over two-thirds of state officials strongly disagree with the necessity of OSM oversight, a level over twice as high as in other state environmental programs.

When asked about working relationships, about half of state program officials believe their working relationships with the OSM are positive. (See Table 4-6.) This is much lower than the perceptions of state officials in other programs (57 percent to 88 percent, respectively). Similarly, state surface mining officials are much less likely than state officials in other programs to agree that the OSM supports their program (43 percent to 89 percent). Of the state officials who do not believe working relationships are positive, the comments most frequently point to what state officials perceive to be a micromanagement of their program by field office staff.

"We do not receive support from our OSM field office. They continually attempt to disparage and frustrate our efforts. They refuse to acknowledge that we are both working toward the same goal. They continually choose to substitute their judgment for ours. OSM dictates how the program is to be run, frequently changes directives with no notice, and constantly finds fault with minor details of our program."

These comments from state officials reflect a common theme among

TABLE 4-6 Survey Questions About Federal–State Working Relationships (Responses of State Surface Mining Officials)

Survey Questions	% Agree	% Disagree	Other Programs % Agree*
OSM field office staff supportive	43	29	89
OSM headquarters supportive	52	5	40
Positive working relationship	57	14	88
State–OSM relationships have gotten worse	15	65	14
States have sufficient flexibility	24	43	60
Evaluations by OSM are fair	29	43	62
Reporting requirements are reasonable	14	71	39
Program requirements are consistent	35	50	33
OSM clearly communicates program requirements	35	45	31
OSM stays in frequent contact with me	76	20	67

n=24
*denotes the responses from 230 state directors for asbestos, radon, lead, drinking water, and wellhead protection programs (controlling for coal responses)

state program directors: "OSM focuses on dotting the 'i's' and crossing the 't's' and does not focus on whether the environment is ultimately protected," and "The true measure of our program should be the extent to which we mitigate environmental harm, not how many violations we cite, how many reports are on time, how many signs are upright, and whether or not every map is stamped by a registered engineer."

Also evident from the survey data and interviews are the perceptions that reporting requirements of the OSM under cooperative agreements tend to be overly burdensome. Nearly three-fourths of the state officials (71 percent) believe that the reporting requirements are unreasonable. Moreover, state officials are less likely to perceive that the OSM evaluates state programs fairly or that they have sufficient flexibility in operating their programs (29 percent and 24 percent, respectively).

In sum, it appears as if intergovernmental relationships negatively affect the operation of state surface mining programs, at least from the perspective of many of the state coal officials. Contentious working relationships are viewed as hindering implementation success, and many state officials believe that their state programs would be better run without federal involvement. However, this belief may be a bit disingenuous because many state inspectors believe that political relationships between coal companies and top state officials are strong and may also constrain strong enforcement of regulatory requirements. This is especially true in states which produce a lot of coal and rely heavily on the economic contribution of major coal enterprises.

CONCLUSIONS

Constraints to SMCRA implementation are not found in the lack of financial resources to operate the program, but are more likely to be found in the politicization of the regulatory program within the state and in disagreements between state and federal officials. Thus it appears that little, if any, "pulling together" is occurring between state and federal staff charged with implementing the surface mining program. When considered in light of the working relationship typology, the history of this federal–state relationship seems to be the ideal type for the "coming apart and contentious" quadrant, with ample levels of what state staff believe to be the wrong kind of federal involvement in their program and very low levels of mutual trust and respect.

As noted earlier, however, the OSM has recently undertaken major changes in the way it conducts oversight of primacy states with its philosophy of "shared commitment," and it appears that the agency has moved against the "gotcha" syndrome present in federal–state working relationships and toward a more open and consensual regulatory approach.

The conceptual framework of extrinsic and intrinsic factors that influence implementation seems useful in evaluating this program, as virtually every element in the framework has added its own challenge to implementing SMCRA. The OSM remains an agency in transition and one that continues to be battered by national political forces. As evidenced by SMCRA's legislative history, Congress has been eager to be on both sides of the issue: protecting the environment and supporting coal production, while simultaneously supporting states' rights and strong enforcement.

The legislative language is as interesting for what was left out as for what was eventually retained in SMCRA. For example, underground mining of coal was protected (SMCRA regulates only the surface effects of coal mining), and hard rock mining of copper, gold, or other metals was totally excluded from the law. Regulatory requirements have been challenged for being overly prescriptive and not allowing sufficient state discretion. Meanwhile, potent political forces capture the ear of the salons in Congress and in state capitals with continued challenges to existing SMCRA provisions and OSM regulations. (One need only review the OSM annual reports to get a sense of the litigation that surrounds implementation.)

The evolving OSM oversight philosophies, frequent changes in structure, and new leadership in the agency and in the administration have further complicated SMCRA implementation. The legacy of organizational upheaval spanning the nearly twenty-year history of the agency will likely continue to affect the ability of agency headquarters and field office staff to move collectively toward the same goal. Reductions in force amounting to nearly 28 percent of the OSM's personnel will likely not do much to instill a sense of mission and high morale. However, OSM officials point to stronger enforcement techniques (such as the Applicant Violator System) and a renewed commitment to establishing better working relationships with state implementors as reasons for optimism about the surface mining program.

NOTES TO CHAPTER 4

1. Eugene Bardach and Robert A. Kagan argue that regulators should adopt a more accommodating regulatory posture in their book, *Going by the Book: The Problem of Regulatory Unreasonableness* (Philadelphia, Penn.: Temple University Press, 1982).

2. Patricia McGee Crotty, "The New Federalism Game: Primacy Implementation of Environmental Policy," *Publius* 17, no. 3 (1987): 53–67.

3. U.S. Department of Energy, Energy Information Administration, *Coal Industry Annual: 1994*, DOE/EIA-0584 (Washington, D.C.: Energy Information Administration, October 1995): p. 2. A short ton is a unit of weight equal to 2,000 pounds.

4. U.S. Department of Energy, Energy Information Administration, *Coal Data: A Reference* (Washington, D.C.: Energy Information Administration, 1989): 7.

5. Energy Information Administration, *Coal Industry Data: 1994*, p. *xi*.

6. U.S. Department of Energy, Energy Information Administration, *Coal Data: A Reference* (Washington, D.C.: Energy Information Administration, 1989): p. 15.

7. Energy Information Administration, *Coal Industry Annual: 1994*, p. 1.

8. U.S. Department of the Interior, Office of Surface Mining, *1989 Annual Report* (Washington, D.C.: U.S. Department of the Interior, 1990): p. 6.

9. Energy Information Administration, *Coal Data: A Reference*, p. 22.

10. For an excellent discussion of the potential regional impacts of the Clean Air Act for the coal industry, see Bruce A. Ackerman and William T. Hassler, *Clean Coal, Dirty Air* (New Haven, Conn.: Yale University Press, 1980).

11. U.S. Department of Energy, Energy Information Administration, *Longwall Mining*, DOE/EIA-TR-0588 (Washington, D.C.: U.S. Govt. Printing Office, March 1995), p. 3.

12. Energy Information Administration, *Longwall Mining*, p. *vii*.

13. U.S. Congress. House Committee on Interior and Insular Affairs, Subcommittee on Energy and the Environment, "Tenth Anniversary of SMCRA of 1977," Serial No. 100-26 (August 3, 1987), p. 2.

14. U.S. Congress, House Committee on Interior and Insular Affairs, hearing before the Subcommittee on Energy and the Environment, *Surface Mining Veto Justification Briefing*, 94th Congr., 1st sess. (94-23, June 3, 1975), p. 15.

15. House Committee on Interior and Insular Affairs, *Veto Justification*, p. 17.

16. House Committee on Interior and Insular Affairs, *Veto Justification*, pp. 14–15.

17. See Richard Harris, *Coal Firms Under the New Social Regulation* (Durham, North Carolina: Duke University Press, 1985) for a discussion of how coal firms would be affected by federal regulations.

18. For a discussion of the position of Appalachian coal companies, see Neal Shover, Donald A. Clelland, and John Lynxwiler, *Enforcement or Negotiation: Constructing a Regulatory Bureaucracy* (Albany, New York: SUNY Press, 1986).

19. Environmentalists initially focused attention on Appalachian coal mining. An earlier report on surface mining, issued in 1967 (and before the concern over foreign oil dominated administrative thought) by the Department of Interior Secretary Stewart Udall, made policy makers aware of the dire ecological results of coal mining in Appalachia and provided ample political fodder for environmental organizations. Attention was subsequently directed to western mining, as environmentalists urged Congress to avoid a "second Appalachia."

20. The concern over union jobs in Appalachia prompted an alliance between grassroots citizen groups and local chapters of the UMW. For example, the Virginia Citizens for Better Reclamation efforts were formally endorsed by the Virginia UMW Association, and several members of that group were UMW members. (U.S. Congress, Senate Committee on Energy and National Resources, *Surface Mining Reclamation and Control Act of 1977*, 95th Congr., 2nd sess. (95–32, 1977), pp. 557–58.

21. *Washington Post*, "UMW Shifts Stand on Strip Mining," September 30, 1976.

22. U.S. Congress, Senate Committee on Energy and Natural Resources, *State Surface Mining Laws: A Comparison with the Proposed Federal Legislation and Background Information*, report by the Congressional Research Service (95-25, June 1977), p. 14.

23. For a discussion of the inadequacy of state programs as perceived by congressional architects of SMCRA, see U.S. Congress, Senate Committee on Energy and Natural Resources, Subcommittee on Public Lands and Resources, *Surface Mining Control and Reclamation Act*, 95th Congr., 2nd sess., March 1–3, 1977. For a general discussion, see Morris Udall, "The Enactment of the Surface Mining Control and Reclamation Act of 1977 in Retrospect," *West Virginia Law Review*, 81:4 (1977).

24. U.S. Congress. Senate Committee on Energy and Natural Resources, *State Surface Mining Laws: A Survey and Comparison with the Proposed Federal Legislation and Background Information*, Congressional Research Service Report, 95th Congr., 1st sess. (1977): p. 20.

25. Quoted in K. W. James Rochow, "The Far Side of Paradox: State Regulation of the Environmental Effects of Coal Mining," *West Virginia Law Review* 81 (1979): 585.

26. SMCRA PL 95-87 Sec. 101(b). [30 U.S.C. 1201]: 1.

27. On this point, see Hamlet J. Barry III, "The Surface Mining Control and Reclamation Act of 1977 and the Office of Surface Mining: Moving Target or Immovable Object?" *Rocky Mountain Mineral Law Institute* 27 (1982): 169–337.

28. U.S. Department of the Interior, Office of Surface Mining, *1987–1988 Annual Report* (Washington, D.C.: U.S. Department of the Interior, 1989).

29. Taxes on active coal production are levied at the following rates: 35 cents per ton of surface-mined coal; 15 cents per ton of underground-mined coal, and 10 cents per ton of lignite coal.

30. The Abandoned Mine Reclamation Act of 1990 (P.L. 101-508) extended fee collection authority for the OSM through September 30, 1995. The Energy Policy Act (P.L. 102-468) subsequently extended fee collection authority until September 30, 2004.

31. U.S. Department of the Interior, Office of Surface Mining, *1995 Annual Report* (Washington, D.C.: OSM, 1996), pp. 10 and 29.

32. SMCRA. [U.S.C. 1251], Sec. 501 (b).

33. The reclamation bond provision is found at 30 U.S.C. 1259, Sec. 509 (a). The amount of reclamation bonds required has often been judged to be insufficient to fully reclaim the land; see U.S. General Accounting Office, *Surface Mining: Cost and Availability of Reclamation Bonds*, PEMD-88-17 (Washington, D.C.: U.S. General Accounting Office, April 1988).

34. SMCRA, [30 U.S.C. 1265 and 1266].

35. SMCRA, Sec. 522(e)(1).

36. Office of Surface Mining, *A Shared Commitment: 1995 Annual Report*, p. 20.

37. SMCRA [30 U.S.C. 1267], Sec. 517 and 518.

38. U.S. General Accounting Office, *Surface Mining: Interior Department and States Could Improve Inspection Programs*, GAO/RCED-87-40 (Washington, D.C.: U.S. General Accounting Office, December 1986), p. 9.

39. U.S. Congress, Senate Committee on Interior and Insular Affairs, *Legislative Proposals Concerning Surface Mining of Coal*, 92nd Congr., 1st sess. (1971), p. 129.

40. Office of Surface Mining, *A Shared Commitment: 1995 Annual Report*, p. 28.

41. States, theoretically at least, must run a regulatory program in accordance with SMCRA provisions. A state which fails to do so may face program revocation, and the OSM reassumes regulatory control. Loss of primacy also means loss of AML funds, as well as loss of regulatory control. But, in practice, the OSM has been reluctant to take over state programs, only reassuming regulatory authority in Tennessee after that state's legislature repealed its state surface mining law, and temporarily assuming the inspection and enforcement (I/E) program in Oklahoma. Typically, the OSM relies on less drastic oversight measures.

42. In 1988, in response to state criticism, the OSM lengthened state response time from ten to up to twenty days, plus mailing time, according to an OSM official.

43. See National Coal Association v. Christensen, Civ. No. 87-2076 (DDC July 27, 1987); Clinchfield Coal Co. v. Department of the Interior, 802 F.2d 102, 17 ELR 20240 (4th Cir. 1986); Annaco, Inc. v. Interior Dept. 27 Envt. Rep. Cas. (BNA) (1140 E.D.Ky. 1987).

44. James M. McElfish, Jr., "The Surface Mining Control and Reclamation Act and Environmental Groups," in *Moving the Earth: Cooperative Federalism and Implementation of the Surface Mining Act*, ed. Uday Desai (Westport, Conn.: Greenwood Press, 1993), pp. 67–86.

45. Although this section is based upon the author's review of OSM annual reports and other information, the reader is encouraged to read Donald C. Menzel, "Creating a Regulatory Agency: Profile of the Office of Surface Mining," in *Moving the Earth: Cooperative Federalism and Implementation of the Surface Mining Act*, ed. Uday Desai (Westport, Conn.: Greenwood Press, 1993), pp. 31–45, for a more comprehensive discussion of the topic.

46. Performance standards require a regulated industry to meet certain requirements, but allow the industry discretion in achieving the standard. Design standards, in contrast, require that the industry also employ specific technologies in meeting the performance standards.

47. Many scholars have noted the changing orientation of the OSM; see, for example, Donald C. Menzel, "Redirecting the Implementation of a Law: The Reagan Administration and Coal Surface Mining Regulation," *Public Administration Review* 43, no. 3 (1983): 411–20.

48. Conversation with an OSM inspector in the Big Stone Gap Field Office in June 1991.

49. Donald C. Menzel, "Creating a Regulatory Agency: Profile of the Office of Surface Mining," in *Moving the Earth: Cooperative Federalism and Implementation of the Surface Mining Act*, ed. Uday Desai (Westport, Conn.: Greenwood Press, 1993), pp. 31–45: 34.

50. Donald C. Menzel, "Creating a Regulatory Agency: Profile of the Office of Surface Mining," p. 35.

51. U.S. Department of the Interior, Office of Surface Mining, *Annual Report for Fiscal Year 1981* (Washington, D.C.: OSM, 1982), p. 4.

52. U.S. Department of the Interior, Office of Surface Mining, *Annual Report for Fiscal Year 1983* (Washington, D.C.: Office of Surface Mining, 1984), p. 3.

53. U.S. Department of the Interior, Office of Surface Mining, *Annual Report for Fiscal Year 1982* (Washington, D.C.: Office of Surface Mining, 1983), p. 3; and *Annual Report for Fiscal Year 1983* (Washington, D.C.: Office of Surface Mining), p. 3.

54. Office of Surface Mining, *Annual Report for Fiscal Year 1981*, p. 2.

55. Office of Surface Mining, *Annual Report for Fiscal Year 1983* (Washington, D.C.: U.S. General Accounting Office, 1984).

56. U.S. Department of the Interior, Office of Surface Mining, *Annual Report for Fiscal Year 1982* (Washington, D.C.: Office of Surface Mining, 1983), p. 51.

57. The "Parker–Gash Order" issued in December 1982, required OSM to assess and collect civil penalties against coal mine operators who failed to abate strip mining violations when notified. It also required the OSM to remain current with respect to a timely assessment of its penalties and not to issue new permits to individual or corporate violators. This order implicitly applied to all primacy states.

58. U.S. Congress, House Committee on Government Operations, *Surface Mining Law: A Promise Yet to Be Fulfilled*, 100th Congr., 2nd sess. (H.R. No. 183, 1987).

59. James Watt resigned in 1983; James Harris resigned in 1984.

60. U.S. Department of the Interior, Office of Surface Mining, *Budget Justification Report for 1989*, unpublished document (1989), p. 2.

61. Michael Lipske, "Cracking Down on Mining Pollution," *National Wildlife* 33, no. 4 (1995): 20–24, at 24.

62. Based upon a review of annual reports for the Office of Surface Mining from 1981 to 1987.

63. Personal interviews with OSM field officers on April 19, 1989, and on April 6, 1990.

64. Office of Surface Mining, *A Shared Commitment: 1995 Annual Report*, p. 3.

65. Office of Surface Mining, *A Shared Commitment: 1995 Annual Report*, p. 3.

66. Office of Surface Mining, "Surface Mining Director Proposes New Oversight Policy," press release dated November 1, 1994; Office of Surface Mining, "New Surface Mine Oversight Directive Focuses on Results," press release dated January 31, 1996.

67. U.S. Department of the Interior, Office of Surface Mining, "Federal–State Shared Commitment to Reclamation Remains Strong Despite Lack of Consensus on Federal Enforcement" (Press released dated March 14, 1996).

68. The surveys were sent during the time when state officials were aware of the new OSM oversight policy changes, and also near the time when new performance agreements were being written. Note, however, that the new OSM philosophy was not fully in place until 1996.

5

Implementing Public Programs: The Federal Regional Office Perspective

The previous chapters offered a look at five very different environmental programs, first by providing an overview of program implementation and constraints, and then by exploring the perceptions of state officials involved in the various programs. What remains, in order to more fully examine environmental policy implementation, is to explore the perceptions of Office of Surface Mining (OSM) field office and Environmental Protection Agency (EPA) regional staff associated with these programs. While some scholars have examined the importance of federal administrative regional offices in implementing policy, most scholars have considered the national implementing agency as a single unit.[1]

The thesis of this book is that regional officers are important implementation actors, and thus merit closer attention. This chapter focuses on implementation from the vantage point of federal regional staff. Doing this should help to develop the unique perspective of people placed in charge of direct oversight of state programmatic operations, the people who are most likely to "pull together" with state officials to make environmental programs work.[2]

Because federal regional offices have typically been neglected in policy implementation studies, the chapter begins with a brief overview of the structure of the EPA regional offices and the OSM field offices. Subsequent sections examine the role orientations of the staff located in these offices and report the results of the survey and interview data collected in this study. Some of the results are counterintuitive and may surprise the reader.

LOCATION, STRUCTURE, AND REINVENTION OF EPA REGIONAL OFFICES

Ten EPA regional offices serve fifty states, the District of Columbia, and U.S. territories including Guam, Puerto Rico, and the Virgin Islands. (See Figure 5-1.) Geographic ranges and number of states to

159

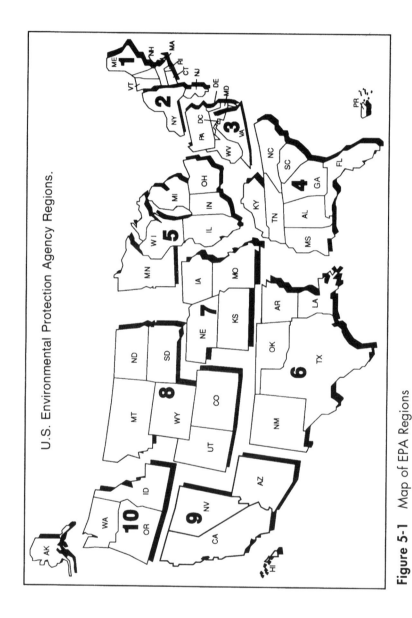

U.S. Environmental Protection Agency Regions.

Figure 5-1 Map of EPA Regions

Source: U.S. Department of the Interior, U.S. Geological Survey, *The Geology of Radon* (Washington, D.C.: U.S. Government Printing Office, 1992).

oversee varies considerably among regional offices. Region 8, for example, oversees environmental programs in six states, while Region 2 oversees environmental programs in two: New York and New Jersey.[3]

Traditionally, EPA regional offices were organized around media-related programs, including divisions for air, hazardous waste, superfund, and water. Begun in 1995, EPA headquarters and the EPA regional offices are in the process of reorganization as part of the national reinventing government initiative of the Clinton Administration. Although the extent of reorganization varies among regional offices, most regional reorganizations share some common characteristics.

First, enforcement activities under several environmental laws will be consolidated into one division. Second, many regional offices are attempting to manage environmental programs more holistically, with more attention directed toward ecosystem protection, rather than toward specific media. Third, regions are downsizing and, in the process, reducing the number of middle-level managers. Fourth, regions are embracing a more collaborative working style, with more emphasis on working as teams and on empowering key stakeholders in environmental programs.

According to the *Reinvention Implementation Plan* for EPA Region 5, such change is necessary because the "effectiveness and the relevancy of the federal government's efforts to protect the environment and improve the quality of life for its citizens are being questioned," and the agency's "key partners in environmental protection, the States, the Tribes, and local governments, are critical of our methods and dissatisfied with our delivery of services, and are calling for fundamental change in our respective roles and responsibilities."[4]

The reinvention process of EPA regions has not been underway long enough to tell what effect it will have on the perceptions of regional project officers and other EPA regional staff members working directly with states on program implementation. However, it is important to keep in mind, because reinvention, reduction in staff, and flatter organizational structures seem to address some of the concerns voiced by state environmental officials in the previous chapters.

REORGANIZING, REFOCUSING, AND REINVENTING OSM FIELD OFFICES

Until the summer of 1995, thirteen OSM field offices oversaw the operations of twenty-four coal mining states with primacy under the Surface Mining Control and Reclamation Act (SMCRA). On May 1, 1995, a new organizational structure became operational, consistent with the goals of the National Performance Review.[5]

Figure 5-2   Map of OSM offices

Source: U.S. Department of the Interior, Office of Surface Mining, *1995 Annual Report* (Washington, D.C.: Office of Surface Mining, 1996), p. 10.

The newly reorganized OSM has three regional coordinating centers located in each of the three coal-producing regions (Pittsburgh, Pennsylvania; Alton, Illinois; and Denver, Colorado). OSM closed two small field offices located in Springfield, Illinois, and Kansas City, Missouri, and abolished the eastern and western support centers located in Pittsburgh and Denver. As of 1996, the OSM consisted of eleven field offices, three coordinating centers, and nine area offices. (The area offices report directly to the field offices, which in turn report to the OSM deputy director.) Eleven states without primacy, called federal program states, are under direct OSM regulatory authority. However, only two federal program states, Tennessee and Washington, have active coal mining operations.[6] OSM area offices are located in those states. See Figure 5-2 for the location of regionally located OSM offices.

Like the EPA reinvention effort, the OSM's reorganization is designed to reflect philosophical changes in the agency. One such change is the attempt to decentralize decision-making authority to the field offices. According to the OSM Annual Report, reorganization was underway to "empower employees in the field to make decisions and accept more responsibility."[7] The agency also seeks similar goals in its reinvention, including improving customer satisfaction, promoting involvement and teamwork, and creating a flatter, more flexible organization.

In addition to the reorganization activities noted, in August 1995, 265 of the OSM's 920 employees received separation notices, with 182 civil service positions ultimately lost in November 1995, representing a reduction in force of 28 percent.[8] It is likely that this reduction, occurring in both field offices and OSM headquarters, will affect SMCRA implementation, as noted by OSM director Robert J. Uram. "These lamentable staff separations are the direct result of those damaging budget cuts [by Congress]. There is no question that these reductions will inevitably impair OSM's ability to carry out its basic function under the surface mining law."[9]

A VIEW FROM THE MIDDLE

In some senses, the staff in EPA regional offices or in OSM field and area offices represent the "guys in the middle." Staff in regional offices are often placed in difficult implementation positions, because they simultaneously have to please both their fellow federal colleagues in the national office and their counterparts in state environmental programs. For headquarters personnel, regional staff must demonstrate that the states over which they have oversight are performing admirably—or at least well enough to continue being funded or retain delegated authority. For state officials, regional staff must help communicate and clarify EPA or OSM policy, programmatic requirements, or new initiatives, while at the same time exacting some measure of performance from state programs and serving as resources for state program coordinators.

From a managerial perspective, this is difficult to do. Though regional personnel may offer the enticement of some federal monies by which to run a state program, they do not make hiring or firing decisions within the state; they have little or no control over state political forces. Additionally, regional staff have their own resource problems—limited personnel, time, and funds for supervision. Finally, if regional staff make unpopular decisions regarding state programs, they risk alienation from the state officials whose cooperation is sorely needed to implement the environmental program.

Stillman (1996) distinguishes between the activities of headquarters and regional bureaucrats according to the types of outputs produced.

In his description of the federal bureaucracy, Stillman notes that head-quarters personnel translate political mandates into operational public programs, while middle management personnel in regional offices engage in system maintenance and program management and supervision.[10] Headquarters personnel have the unenviable task of transforming often overly ambitious legislative goals into workable programs within federal agencies. Regional personnel must direct their collective attention to maintaining the viability of their programs and at the same time encourage robust state programs.

Regional office staff must see to it that the system of implementing a particular program runs as designed by employing managerial, communication, or technical skills as well as fiscal and personnel resources. Thus, to remember the trip metaphor introduced in Chapter One, head-quarters staff may help determine the rules of the trip, but regional staff exercise greater control inside the car, making certain that the travelers cooperate and assume collective responsibility for a safe trip.

It is possible to apply this difference in role orientations and responsibilities to the programs reviewed in this study. EPA staff involved in radon, asbestos, drinking water, and wellhead protection, and OSM staff involved in coal mining regulation outside of Washington, D.C., play roles equally as important in policy implementation as those of headquarters staff. Differences are many, but include some of the following:

First, regional staff are the primary contacts for state officials. They work directly with states to develop eligible activities to be funded under federal–state cooperative agreements; they receive state quarterly performance reports if federal funds support the state program; and, in many cases, they become involved in state-level activities. The nature of this involvement varies, depending upon the type of program: OSM field inspectors, for example, conduct oversight inspections in primacy states; EPA staff under the AHERA program only conduct inspections in states without waivers (states without an EPA-approved program); EPA wellhead protection staff may provide technical assistance for wellhead delineations or support for wellhead protection programs in local community public meetings. Regardless of the type of interaction, this relationship often means that regional and field office staff have more communication with their state program counterparts than with their colleagues back in Washington, D.C.

Second, regional staff are often the receivers of new policy, rather than the initiators of policy change. As mentioned before, rule-making activities to implement new or established programs occur within agency headquarters, as do any activities that result in new program guidance or other implementation documents. This is not to say that regional staff are totally isolated from the process, but that their role is often secondary to that of headquarters program staff. While the input of regional staff is solicited and may shape new directions for a particular program, the final decisions usually come from the top (headquarters).

Often the solicitation of regional staff input by headquarters is limited by available communication tools. The principle interactive communication tool used between most regional personnel reviewed in this study and headquarters staff is the conference call. This is an adequate, but not ideal, way to communicate ideas, information, and concerns. Through this connection, and sometimes through other methods such as face-to-face annual meetings, regional staff learn of new directions proposed by the headquarters staff.

Finally, in most of the cases reviewed, general funding decisions are made by headquarters staff and then translated into specific state allocations by regional personnel. For example, in the radon program, each of the ten EPA regional offices is given an allocation for State Indoor Radon Grant (SIRG) programs. Regional allocations are based upon a formula that includes the number of people likely to be exposed to elevated levels of radon, measured at 4 picocuries per liter (pCi/L) and above, and a state's allocation in the previous year. Within that allocation, each regional office decides how much federal funding individual states receive. In a practical sense, this is usually an incremental adjustment up or down from the previous year's grant award for any state.

Regional discretion for awarding state grants, then, is broad within the scope of the regional allocation. However, it is limited in terms of significantly increasing the amount of money available to any regional office. Regional staff may find it difficult to persuade headquarters staff to dramatically increase the allotment of state grant monies, because a funding increase in one region means a subsequent decrease in another regional office. Thus, individual regions may try to champion the needs of states within their geographic jurisdiction in order to increase the amount of available grant money.

For example, in 1992 EPA regional offices which serve states with low populations but significantly higher levels of indoor radon argued for a change in the way state radon allocations were determined. Staff in these EPA regional offices felt that these "pockets" of high radon risk deserved more attention (and more funding) than would be accounted for under the existing allocation formula, which made no distinction between homes with radon levels above 4 pCi/L and those with 10 or more pCi/L.[11]

In short, it is reasonable to suspect that EPA regional or OSM field office staff may feel quite differently from EPA headquarters staff about state environmental programs. Regional staff maintain closer contact with state officials, have more opportunities to observe on-the-ground implementation efforts, and often make the final decisions for funding state programs within the parameters established by the national offices. Moreover, regional staff frequently serve as the receivers of top-down communication, which must then be relayed to state officials.

As mentioned earlier, most implementation studies fail to separate the regional (or front-line implementors) from the headquarters (policy initiating) staff. The implicit assumption is that personnel from regional and headquarters offices agree on the best way to implement environmental programs and evaluate state progress. The next section highlights the opinions of some EPA and OSM staff located outside of Washington, D.C.

EPA REGIONAL AND OSM FIELD OFFICE
PERCEPTIONS ABOUT IMPLEMENTATION

Surveys were sent to EPA and OSM regional staff in 1995 in order to better understand implementation constraints and working relationships from these unique perspectives.[12] Of 101 surveys sent, sixty-three responses were received for a response rate of 62 percent. Surveys were sent to regional staff with direct responsibility for program implementation who were, therefore, likely to have frequent interaction with state environmental officials. Additionally, twenty-five interviews were conducted with EPA regional and OSM field office personnel in order to more fully explore their views about the programs. The survey results appear in Tables 5-1 through 5-5. Major findings are discussed in turn.

EPA Regional and OSM Field Office Staff Perceptions
about State Environmental Programs

Following the implementation framework presented in Chapter One, federal regional staff were asked their opinions about factors which influence the implementation of their environmental programs. The results are reported first by perceptions of state-level variables, then by perceptions of federal-level implementation variables, and finally by perceptions about the quality of working relationships among national, regional, and state personnel.

Responses were mixed about characteristics of state agency capacity, depending upon which characteristic was considered. When asked whether state officials were committed to implementing the program, 47 percent of OSM field office staff and 69 percent of EPA regional office staff agree that they are (Table 5-1). Only about half of the respondents (56 percent) believe that state programs are running effectively. Moreover, regional staff are even less likely to believe that state

TABLE 5-1   Perceptions of EPA and OSM Staff About State Agency Capacity Variables

	OSM staff % agree	EPA staff % agree	Total % agree
State staff are committed to running the program	47	69	63
State administrators are very supportive	35	30	32
State programs are working effectively overall	59	54	56
State programs are adequately funded	77	22	41
State programs are stronger now than three years ago	71	59	63
State staff are adequately trained to run the program	76	75	75
	n = 17	n = 46	n = 63

administrators are supportive of the state environmental program (only 32 percent agree).

When asked about funding levels, another element of state agency capacity, OSM field office staff were likely to believe that state coal mining enforcement operations were adequately funded (77 percent agree). Indeed, regulatory grant funding for states which have primacy under SMCRA represents considerably more money than under every program but the drinking water program. Through 1994, the OSM awarded $623 million to run primacy states, with average annual appropriations to states ranging from $103,000 in Kansas to $12 million in Kentucky.[13] Coal mining enforcement programs were more constrained by other implementation variables, most notably the political climate in coal mining states, as discussed in Chapter Four and later in this section.

EPA regional staff, on the other hand, were likely to perceive inadequate funding for state programs (22 percent agree). This perception is especially true for the wellhead protection program, where no EPA regional staff member interviewed agreed that funding was sufficient for the states to operate the program. As one regional project officer suggested, "It should be no surprise—there is never enough funding for ground water or wellhead protection programs. Without adequate funding, especially to states and communities for wellhead protection, there is little incentive for financially strapped state and local governments to pursue these pollution prevention efforts."

Similarly, not one EPA regional asbestos staff member strongly agreed that the state asbestos program was effective or properly funded. Beleaguered asbestos staff felt that both the state and the federal asbestos programs were under political fire. (See Chapter Three.) Funding for both state and federal asbestos programs was woefully inadequate, from the perspective of these staff members.

Concerns about states' ability to fund their programs were also evident in the drinking water program when EPA regional officials stated that, "Federal funding is completely inadequate for the job to be done." While grants under the drinking water program range from $200,000 to over $3 million and are larger than every other program reviewed except surface mining, many EPA regional staff believe that funding is not enough for states to monitor public water suppliers or for public water suppliers to appropriately test and treat drinking water supplies. One EPA official made this comment, "While federal funding granted to states has been increasing, it has not kept pace with the new requirements and expectations of states."

Staff from the radon and asbestos programs suggested that the requirements for state matching funds sometimes sidetracked implementation. An EPA regional asbestos coordinator commented, "Asbestos is not a high state priority and matching requirements [for federal grants] result in states choosing not to want federal funding for AHERA enforcement, but [instead] funding their small asbestos programs from [state] fees for asbestos certification and licensing."

In the radon program, several regional project officers lamented the effect of the match. "The match required of states is too high and limits success of the radon program," or "The 50 percent match limits states' ability to accept funds, although in the current political climate some states are refusing federal funds when no match is required. Fiscal year 1996 funding is very uncertain and may eliminate or severely limit some states' ability to address radon."

OSM field office and EPA regional staff (75 percent) agreed that state officials implementing the program had adequate skills and training. From the EPA regional perspective, then, any limitations in running the program were caused more by fiscal constraints than from inadequate knowledge or capabilities of state staff.

When evaluating state-level political support for state environmental programs, EPA regional staff and OSM field office staff believe that state legislators are not very supportive of these environmental programs. (See Table 5-2.) Only 13 percent of the regional staff overall agreed that state legislators support the program. In most instances, lack of state legislative support translates to lack of legislative attention. In the case of the radon program, lack of legislative support results in the inability of states to get real estate disclosure requirements enacted;

TABLE 5-2 Perceptions of EPA and OSM Staff About State-Level Political Variables

	OSM staff % agree	EPA staff % agree	Total % agree
State legislators are very supportive of the program	12	13	13
Citizens are very supportive of the program	53	35	40
We need a stronger state program, one that decreases the role of the OSM/EPA	29	48	43
	% strongly agree		
Without federal oversight, states would not be as serious about implementing the program	71	15	24
	n = 17	n = 46	n = 63

for the wellhead protection program, the inability to pass state laws mandating source water protection is due in large part to the lack of legislative interest in the wellhead program.

In other cases, the lack of legislative support was viewed as the unwillingness of state legislators to enforce regulatory requirements. Although state political actors are very interested in the environmental program, they are most interested in the way the program is enforced. Perhaps in no other program is the state political climate perceived to be as powerful a constraint on state program implementation as in the coal mining program. Nearly all OSM field office personnel pointed to what they view as the reluctance of state administrators to strongly enforce SMCRA, as indicated by comments like these: "The only problem with implementation is politics as far as I'm concerned. Getting compliance with the law by the active mining sites is hard in states where 'coal is king.' However, the abandoned mine land side of the state program I oversee is superb," or simply, "Certain mines have in-state political connections," or "Undue influence from state legislators prevents full enforcement of coal mining regulations and promotes favoritism by state inspectors."

An OSM official from a field office in the eastern United States observed, "Our state agencies see themselves as existing to help the coal industry, at all costs—not to make fair regulatory decisions that protect the good mining operators and weed out the uncaring operators." Another OSM field official noted that implementation challenges rested with "getting top state officials to acknowledge that they have problems such as inadequate bonding systems, acid mine drainage, and subsidence, and then resolving them."

In short, whether due to suffering from a lack of legislative attention or more due to interference and pressure from some state legislators, administrators, and other executive personnel, few OSM or EPA regional staff find a supportive state political climate for implementing state environmental programs.

Likewise, EPA regional staff also do not perceive a lot of citizen support for the maintenance of several environmental programs. This seemed especially true of the radon program. As one EPA radon official commented, "The two main implementation challenges are funding and citizen apathy. Citizens seem particularly apathetic about the health risk of radon; even those who test for radon seldom fix their homes if elevated levels are discovered. Increased funding for state programs could fuel increased public outreach and education."

Not surprisingly, given the common perception of lackluster citizen involvement and low levels of state political support for the environmental program, less than half of the regional personnel in either agency believe that the state program should be strengthened at the expense of the federal program (29 percent of the staff at the OSM; 48 percent of the staff at the EPA). (See Table 5-2.) Of course, many regional staff do not support the idea of diminutive federal programs, partly because this may affect their work positions. But they also feel it may affect the integrity of the program because state program officials would not be as eager to attend to their implementation duties.

How much the federal role is needed depends upon the program reviewed. OSM field office staff strongly agreed (71 percent, with 82 percent agreeing) that without federal oversight, states would not be as serious about implementing their coal mining enforcement program (Table 5-2). On the other hand, no EPA regional staff from the asbestos or the wellhead protection programs, and only a handful (15 and 14 percent) of the radon and drinking water staff, strongly agreed that states would be less serious about program implementation without a federal presence. (Overall, 60 percent of EPA staff disagreed or were neutral that state officials would not implement the program as vigorously without federal oversight.)

Whether or not programmatic oversight occurs consistently, however, is debatable according to several regional staff. As one project officer commented, "States should be more accountable. Grants should be tied to performance. Though our states don't meet the agreed-upon objectives of the program which the grant funds, no punitive measures (decrease in funding) ever take place."

Others pointed to the adversarial nature of the federal–state relationship: "We need to acknowledge that we are striving to achieve the same goals and develop closer working relations to ensure their achievement. Oversight naturally fosters adversarial relations," and "Tensions are a fact of life when you are in an evaluation or oversight position."

In sum, state-level variables affect implementation differently according to OSM field office and EPA regional staff. For OSM staff, state political climates are the largest impediments to effective programs, while funding is not a very important issue. Consequently, a stronger federal presence is needed, according to many OSM field staff. For EPA regional staff, the lack of state funding affects the implementation of both the small, nonregulatory programs (wellhead protection and radon) and the regulatory programs (asbestos and drinking water). Little state political support is perceived for maintaining the wellhead protection, asbestos, and radon programs. EPA regional and OSM field office personnel do perceive some state-level variables consistently: the training of the state staff is adequate and state environmental programs are improving.

Perceptions of Regional Staff about the National Program

If EPA and OSM regional officials are concerned about the lack of state legislative and administrative support for their programs, they tend to be nearly as unforgiving about the nature of federal efforts (Table 5-3). Only about half of the regional personnel interviewed or responding to the survey believe that the federal implementation efforts have been effective (50 percent of OSM staff and 46 percent of the EPA staff).

Moreover, the majority of EPA regional staff do not believe that they have adequate funding to run their programs. Only 17 percent of the EPA staff feel that they have enough money to operate. In contrast, OSM field office personnel were much more likely to perceive adequate funding for their program (62 percent), although they were no more likely to agree that their program was effective (50 percent) (Table 5-3).[14]

By the same percentage as how they feel about state legislative support for state programs (13 percent), EPA and OSM regional officials are not likely to perceive support from Congress. Nor are overwhelming majorities of OSM field office or EPA regional office staff likely to agree that the national office is committed to their environmental program (50 percent for the OSM; 65 percent for the EPA).

However, most OSM and EPA staff feel that they are adequately trained to implement the environmental program to which they are assigned (81 percent and 67 percent, respectively), though they are much less confident in their headquarters colleagues' abilities (44 per-

TABLE 5-3   Perceptions of EPA and OSM Staff about Their Agency's Implementation Efforts

	OSM staff % agree	EPA staff % agree	Total % agree
Federal implementation efforts have been effective	50	46	47
Our staff is very committed to implementing the program	94	80	84
Headquarters staff are very committed to the program	50	65	61
The program is adequately funded	62	17	29
Our staff is adequately trained to run the program	81	67	72
Headquarters staff are adequately trained	44	33	35
Congress is very committed to implementing the program	12	13	13
	n = 17	n = 46	n = 63

cent of OSM staff and 33 percent of EPA staff). When asked why headquarters staff are less prepared, the responses varied, but many officials interviewed believed that the staff at headquarters have less substantive training. As one regional radon project officer suggested, "How can someone with a public administration degree know anything about radiation?"

Other staff commented that the EPA headquarters tended to serve as a revolving door for people wanting better jobs. These staffers would spend limited amounts of time in one area in the hopes of rotating out of the program into a new, more highly rated position. Still others pointed to the comparative longevity of many field office personnel. One OSM field office staff member commented that his enforcement staff had an average tenure of 10 years, compared to directors who come and go as political appointees or other headquarters personnel who remain with the agency for only a few years.

In short, staff in federal regional offices are likely to view their programs as ineffective, and many EPA staff are likely to perceive inadequate funding for their programs. Moreover, while regional staff believe that they are committed to running an effective program, they are not as likely to see program commitment from their headquarters counterparts. Finally, regional staff tend to perceive higher levels of training to successfully implement the program in the regions and field offices rather than in headquarters.

PROGRAM EFFECTIVENESS AND THE "EYE OF THE BEHOLDER"

The issue of program effectiveness can be explored more fully by examining both state and regional staff perceptions. Some variations in responses about effectiveness exist, depending upon the program, as shown in the bottom half of Table 5-4. For example, not one interviewee or survey respondent working in the EPA regional office in the wellhead protection program agreed that the EPA wellhead program was effective. (They were, however, almost as likely to see state programs as ineffective.) EPA regional radon staff, by contrast, were most likely to agree that their programs were operating effectively (77 percent). Overall, though, federal regional staff were less likely to agree that federal programs were running effectively than they were to agree that state programs were effective.

In contrast, when state officials look at their own programs, they tend to view them more positively, as shown in the top half of Table 5-4. Between 45 and 100 percent of state program officials agree that their program is operating effectively. The lowest percentage of state staff agreeing that their program is effective is in the wellhead

---

TABLE 5-4   Comparison of State Staff and Federal Regional Staff Perceptions about Program Effectiveness

1. *State staff perceptions by program*		
Program Type	*State Implementation*	*EPA/OSM implementation*
	(percent agreeing that program is effective)	
Asbestos	81	28
Coal	100	11
Drinking Water	84	2
Radon	75	40
Wellhead Protection	45	26
n = 230		

2. *Federal regional staff perceptions by program*		
Program Type	*State Implementation*	*EPA/OSM implementation*
	(percent agreeing that program is effective)	
Asbestos	33	33
Coal	59	50
Drinking Water	71	57
Radon	70	77
Wellhead Protection	14	0
n = 63		

protection program, with 45 percent. In the case of the coal program, every state director believes the program is operating in the way it should.

On the other hand, state officials have negative perceptions about the federal program. In every program, state officials are less likely to agree that federal efforts are effective. The most dramatic differences in perceptions are found in the coal and drinking water programs, but the belief that state programs are more effective than federal programs is consistent among the program types. Only 2 percent of state drinking water directors believe that the EPA runs an effective program, followed by state directors in the coal program (with 11 percent). While state asbestos, wellhead protection, and radon program coordinators are more likely to agree that the federal program is effective, in no case is the response over 40 percent.

Table 5-4 thus suggests an interesting dynamic relating to state and federal regional staff perceptions about program effectiveness. Regional staff are less likely to perceive effectiveness in the national programs than state staff are in their state programs. Moreover, these differences in perceptions are often by large margins. For example, 81 percent of the state asbestos staff agree that their program is effective, while 33 percent of EPA regional staff agree that the national asbestos program is effective; 100 percent of state coal program directors agree, while 50 percent of OSM field office staff do; 45 percent of state wellhead program staff agree that the state program is effective, but no regional wellhead staff member believes that the national program is operating effectively. Only in the radon program do both state officials and regional staff perceive their programs as operating effectively (75 percent of state officials; 77 percent of regional radon staff).

In short, both federal regional staff and state staff perceive the operation of the state programs to be better than that of the national programs. This is a surprising result. One would expect that a respondent to a survey would always feel that his/her program is the most effective; the assumption was that regional staff would perceive the national program to be more effective while the state staff would perceive the state program to be more effective. Instead, only a fraction of state officials believe that the national program is operating the way it should, and OSM/EPA staff are equally or more likely to see state programs as more effective than their own.

What accounts for this result? Why do state officials appear more confident about state programs than the EPA and OSM staff are of the national programs? Several explanations are possible. State programmatic efforts simply could be more effective than federal efforts, and both federal and state staff see that this is the case. This would suggest that there are significant problems at the EPA and at the OSM in program implementation.

Another explanation rests with perceptions about funding, and has some support from the data in Table 5-5. Table 5-5 compares perceptions that state program officials and EPA regional or OSM field office staff have about the adequacy of funding for state and regional programmatic activities. What is interesting is that state officials in all five environmental programs are more likely to agree that the state program receives adequate funds than they are to agree that the regional program receives adequate funding. This result is somewhat counterintuitive, especially given the heavy dependence that most of these programs have on federal monies. One would expect that state officials would see inadequate funding for their programs (which, except for the coal program, they do), but not necessarily see that their regional counterparts are even worse off than they are.

TABLE 5-5 Comparison of State Staff and Federal Regional Staff Perceptions about Adequate Funding

| | State Staff | | Regional Staff | |
| | (percent agreeing that funding is adequate) | | | |
Program	For States	For Regions	For States	For Regions
Asbestos	54	25	17	0
Coal	70	55	77	63
Drinking Water	29	12	29	43
Radon	48	40	46	31
Wellhead Protection	15	7	0	0
	n = 230		n = 63	

EPA regional and OSM field office staff also are more likely to agree that state programs are relatively better funded than their own (except for the drinking water program). In two programs, asbestos and wellhead protection, no EPA regional official agrees that adequate funds were provided to operate her/his program, and 71 percent disagree. Thus, it is reasonable to conclude that the federal programs are less effective than the state programs, from the perspective of state and federal regional officials, because they are less likely to be adequately funded.

Yet another explanation for the variation in perspectives about program effectiveness is that both the state officials and the EPA regional and OSM field office staff are evaluating the effectiveness of headquarters operations. Thus, when federal regional staff and state staff assess the overall operation of the federal agency in implementing the program, they are less likely to agree that those efforts are effective because they are directing their attention to headquarters operations. In order to explore this possibility, it is useful to turn to federal regional staff perceptions about working relationships with state and with headquarters personnel and role orientations within the agency.

GETTING ON THE SAME WAVELENGTH: PERCEPTIONS ABOUT WORKING RELATIONSHIPS

Exploring the perceptions that federal regional staff have about their relationships with the national office provides some support for the suggestion that regional staff view the operation of headquarters less favorably. When asked about their relationship with OSM headquarters, OSM field staff offered several comments, including ones of concern about the perceived lack of direction for the enforcement program on the part of headquarters staff. One OSM inspector chastised his own agency, saying, "The OSM has been in a state of turmoil and confusion since its inception."[15]

Also identified as constraints on establishing working relationships within the agency were potential budget cuts under consideration by Congress for the OSM in fiscal year 1996 and possible personnel reductions. "Every employee in the agency is carrying a heavy stress load because of the uncertainty of their job. This is absolutely not necessary and wastes tax dollars and employee time."

OSM field and EPA regional personnel, like their state counterparts, perceive a reduced level of commitment to the program on the part of headquarters staff. (See Table 5-3.) While 94 percent of the OSM field personnel believe that their staff is committed to implementing the program, only 50 percent of them believe that headquarters staff is committed to the program. Similar, but less dramatic, sentiments are held by EPA regional staff (80 percent agree that they are committed to the program, but only 65 percent agree that headquarters staff are).

Perhaps the most telling data are the perceptions of EPA and OSM regional personnel regarding the role orientations of regional and headquarters staff. Supposedly, if the EPA or the OSM can be considered as one implementation unit with shared goals, then all personnel within a program ought to view that program in the same way. Instead, 80 percent of EPA and OSM staff believe that headquarters officials do not share their perceptions about state programs (Table 5-6).

Most of these perceptions identify a lack of familiarity by headquarters staff with what goes on in state programs. One EPA project officer further distinguished herself from EPA headquarters by labeling only

TABLE 5-6 Perceptions of EPA and OSM Staff about Intraagency and Intergovernmental Relationships

	OSM staff % agree	EPA staff % agree	Total % agree
Headquarters and regional staff have the same views about state programs	18	20	20
State staff are supportive of the federal program	25	52	46
States have enough flexibility to run their program	81	57	64
OSM/EPA evaluates the state program fairly	75	65	69
OSM/EPA clearly communicates program goals and requirements	69	43	52
OSM/EPA reporting requirements are overly burdensome	18	26	24
State–federal relationships have gotten worse in the past year or so	12	13	13
	n = 17	n = 46	n = 63

headquarters staff as "federal" in this comment: "Federal EPA staff
need to get out in the field and work directly with state partners and
the regulated community to solve problems. Holding endless meetings
and requiring tons of paperwork will not solve environmental
problems."

Another regional staff member noted, "Stronger commitment to
the program by headquarters (upper management) is needed. That,
and less shifting of staff in headquarters who are supposed to be
running the national program." One regional official was more direct,
"Get headquarters staff off regional [officials'] backs. EPA headquarters
[staff] do not understand the realities of local governments, meeting
regulatory requirements, or what their directives mean at ground zero."
A wellhead protection project officer commented, "If the agency had
more people with field experience in Washington, [D.C.], then more
'real world' decisions would be made in headquarters."

In addition to the notion that OSM and EPA headquarters staff
should get their feet wet by experiencing on-the-ground implementation, regional staff also noted the political nature of headquarters staff
responsibilities, not the least of which is responding to Congress and
to the Office of Management and Budget. As mentioned earlier, only 13

percent of OSM and EPA staff members believe that Congress supports EPA's efforts in implementing their program (Table 5-3). This lack of congressional support, in turn, politicizes the efforts of headquarters. "EPA headquarters staff do not understand the problems of [EPA] regions or the states. Their agenda is often politically motivated, without regard for the input of regional or state personnel."

Finally, EPA regional staff note that much of the "bean-counting" efforts of the agency in an attempt to monitor state success originates in headquarters. While many EPA regional staff members criticized the reporting requirements for states as being overly oriented toward quantitative approaches, this criticism was most apparent in the drinking water program. Forty-three percent of EPA regional drinking water staff (compared to only 12 percent of the OSM staff, 14 percent of the wellhead protection staff, and none of the asbestos staff) believe that state–federal working relationships have gotten worse in the past few years—mostly because of the monitoring and reporting requirements on public water supply systems.

Especially troublesome, from the perspective of these staff members, were inconsistent program requirements and overly burdensome reporting requirements. Nearly 60 percent of the drinking water staff agree that the reporting requirements place undue burdens on states, compared to only 18 percent of the OSM staff and 26 percent of the EPA staff overall (Table 5-6). As one regional staff member put it, "Given the way EPA promulgates and implements delegated programs, the states do a fine job in responding to changes in programs. EPA does not do a very good job of getting programs up and running."

The end result of this mismatch in approach to the states by headquarters and regional staff is that regional–state relationships, particularly in nonregulatory programs, are often closer than the relationships between federal colleagues. As one EPA regional project officer commented, "There's a difference in relationships between EPA headquarters, regions, and states. The relationship between regions and states is stronger than between EPA regional offices and headquarters because we work together to make things happen."

Sometimes this close link between regional and state personnel working in an environmental program fosters some resentment when EPA headquarters staff make decisions about involving local governments or national associations. In the radon program, several personnel in different regional offices commented on the EPA's involvement with national associations such as the National Association of Counties or the National League of Cities. Some feel that this involvement came at a cost to state programs as monies otherwise available under state grants were given to national partners. This respondent noted: "We should streamline efforts at the EPA headquarters offices and reduce the number of cooperative partners at the national level while increasing them at the state level."

Regional staff also may disagree with headquarters staff about programmatic goals. For example, some regional staff wondered about the direction of the EPA radon program. "EPA has focused on public outreach regarding radon for many years and the public has been slow to act. That money may be better used to just provide radon testing services in high-risk areas." Similarly, the 1996 proposal to redirect EPA efforts under the Safe Drinking Water Act worried several regional staff members, because they saw it as jeopardizing state wellhead protection programs. "[EPA] regions were left 'out of the loop' while this redirection effort went forward. I just don't think they know how it will affect states in my region."

One comment seems to capture the sentiment of many regional personnel: "There's more than just geographical distance that makes headquarters [staff] seem remote. There's a philosophical difference. I trust my state, and see my role as one of a partnership. Sometimes I think headquarters [staff] are so concerned about their own accountability, they forget that states have come a long way, and basically want the same thing we do."

CONCLUSIONS

In sum, most EPA regional staff perceive themselves as "buffers" in the system, simultaneously responsible for maintaining state performance to achieve national goals while also assisting state program directors in running their programs. Most regional project officers perceive their position as more collaborative and less confrontational toward state directors. More generally, the proximity regional officers have to state officials puts them on the "same wavelength" with states, while simultaneously making the headquarters staff seem more remote and less in touch with state agency activities.

On the other hand, OSM field office staff are more likely to feel that political allegiances between coal companies and state administrators or legislators constrain state coal mining enforcement programs. Political pressures, however, emanate from above and below to change the nature of federal coal mining enforcement activities. As OSM field offices conduct oversight of state programs, they feel abandoned by their headquarters counterparts, especially to the extent that they want to run an aggressive federal oversight effort. These field office staff may feel betrayed; after all, they are following the original "gotcha" philosophy that emanated from the top of the organization. Moreover, citizen complaints regarding surface mining are likely to be received at the OSM regional locations, not at headquarters. Thus, OSM field officers also feel that they are not on the same wavelength as their headquarters colleagues, but for different reasons than the EPA regional staff.

Finally, continued pressure to implement the national programs by exacting performance from the states while also working on improving relationships and increasing outputs has taken a toll on many regional staff members. Frustration, low levels of morale, and a lack of esprit de corps within the agency exists in several regional and field offices, at least according to the staff interviewed.

Current reinvention and reorganization efforts underway in both agencies may indeed serve to increase morale and reduce frustration. However, it is also important to seek higher levels of empathy and understanding for the particular role of regional staff in implementation and the constraints these staff members face in their daily activities. While specific recommendations are not the focus of this study, the mismatch in perceptions (with only one in five regional staff members believing that headquarters staff share their views about implementation) suggests that more dialog within the agencies is warranted if these agencies as a whole are going to "pull together."

NOTES TO CHAPTER 5

1. Some notable exceptions to this include: Patricia McGee Crotty, "Assessing the Role of Federal Administrative Regions," *Public Administration Review* (March/April 1988), pp. 642–48; William T. Gormley, Jr., "Food Fights: Regulatory Enforcement in a Federal System," *Public Administration Review* 52:5 (May/June 1992), pp. 271–80; Neal Shover, Donald A. Clelland, and John Lynxwiler, *Enforcement or Negotiation: Constructing a Regulatory Bureaucracy* (Albany, New York: SUNY Press, 1986).

2. The perspectives and role orientations of the staff in the national offices of the OSM and the EPA are also important to policy implementation. However, the research was designed to focus on working relationships between state and federal policy implementors, and therefore did not systematically collect primary data from the national offices.

3. EPA Regional Offices are listed numerically from one to ten, using either arabic or Roman numerals.

4. U.S. Environmental Protection Agency, EPA Region 5, *Reinvention Implementation Plan* (Chicago, Ill.: EPA Region 5, March 1995): p. 1.

5. U.S. Department of the Interior, Office of Surface Mining, *Protecting the Natural Environment: A Shared Commitment, 1995 Annual Report* (Washington, D.C.: U.S. Department of the Interior, 1996): p. 9.

6. U.S. Department of the Interior, Office of Surface Mining, *1994 Annual Report* (Washington, D.C.: Office of Surface Mining, 1994), p. 12.

7. U.S. Department of the Interior, Office of Surface Mining, *1994 Annual Report* (Washington, D.C.: Office of Surface Mining, 1994), p. 8.

8. Office of Surface Mining, "182 OSM Employees Lose Jobs in RIF," press release dated November 1, 1995.

9. Office of Surface Mining, "182 OSM Employees Lose Jobs in RIF," press released dated November 1, 1995.

10. Richard J. Stillman II, *The American Bureaucracy: The Cord of Modern Government* (Chicago, Ill.: Nelson-Hall, 1996), p. 224.

11. Based on conversations with EPA regional radon staff.

12. The surveys were sent prior to the budget cuts and the reduction in force announcement made by the OSM in August 1995. It is the author's belief that impending budget cuts would increase the feelings of regional staff that they lack adequate funding and personnel to run the program, but not alter regional staff perceptions regarding other implementation components.

13. Office of Surface Mining, *1994 Annual Report*, p. 13.

14. The OSM field office staff were surveyed prior to the announcement of the reduction in force on November 1, 1995.

15. This quote appears in earlier research, "In the Eye of the Beholder: State and Federal Perceptions about the Surface Mining Control and Reclamation Act Enforcement," in Uday Desai, ed., *Moving the Earth: Cooperative Federalism and Implementation of the Surface Mining Act* (Westport, Conn.: Greenwood Press, 1993), pp. 197–214, at 210.

6

Pulling Together, Coming Apart, or Somewhere In-Between?

Are state and federal officials in regional and headquarters offices cooperatively "pulling together" to make environmental programs work, or are these relationships "coming apart" because these actors are responding to different political cues or have different expectations for performance and views about how performance should be evaluated? This study suggests that both "pulling together" and "coming apart" are occurring among the five environmental programs, although the balance differs significantly by the type of program reviewed.

This chapter begins with a way of distinguishing federal regional from federal headquarters personnel, and how such distinctions contribute to an understanding of federal–state working relationships. The next section presents a list of common observations among state program directors and regional program officials. The last section revisits the working relationship typology and policy implementation framework developed in Chapter One, and offers some suggestions for moving toward working relationships that "pull together."

CONSIDERING THE WHOLE RELATIONSHIP:
FEDERAL HEADQUARTERS, FEDERAL REGIONAL,
AND STATE OFFICIALS

Miles' law that suggests that "where you stand depends upon where you sit" is clearly operating among federal and state personnel. If the data from Chapter Five suggest anything, it is that relationships between federal headquarters and federal regional personnel are not necessarily cozy and comfortable, nor do federal actors from these positions view program implementation in the same way. Similarly, state officials have very different relationships with federal headquarters staff than they do with federal regional staff. Thus, relationships must be understood as part of a tripartite dynamic—with interactions occurring between state, federal regional, and federal headquarters officials.

One way of viewing the tripartite nature of federal–state relation-ships within programs is suggested in Figure 6-1. For most national environmental programs, federal–state relationships are comprised of three interactions: interactions between state and federal regional per-sonnel; interactions between state and federal headquarters personnel; and interactions between federal regional and headquarters personnel. The context around these interactions may be structured by varying levels of state and national political attention. Thus, the model is com-prised of five parts: the three governmental units involved in policy implementation, and the national and state political arenas.

In turn, each of these interactions can be described on a continuum which ranges from confrontational to very weak, weak, moderate, or strong. Stronger relationships are brought about by the attention that is paid to them by the actors in each bureaucratic unit. In general, the more frequent the personal contact; the more positive the communica-tion; and the more headquarters, regional, and state staff are "on the same wavelength," the stronger the relationship.

Interactions among these three actors is also influenced by the political environment. State environmental programs operate in politi-cal arenas that provide opportunities for very low to very high levels of political attention in the state program. Most often, this is interpreted as the nature of relationships that exist between state program per-sonnel and top-level agency officials, state administrators, and state legislators. This connection between state political actors and state implementors of environmental programs is noted in the lower right-hand corner of the figure.

Similarly, federal headquarters staff are influenced in their interac-tions with both regional and state officials by the level of national political attention directed to the program for which they have responsi-bility, as shown in the upper left part of the model. If Congress, the courts, or the administration is putting the collective feet of the agency to the fire in order to accomplish legislative goals, the attention of headquarters officials is first directed outside of the organization (and to the external actor or actors) and then focused on interactions with state and regional personnel.

The political context surrounding this tripartite group produces two possible effects. First, high levels of state or national political attention may work to make relationships stronger as pressure is put on both federal and state agencies to "do something" about the problem. Second, high levels of state or national political attention may work in the opposite direction: political attention directed toward policy implementation may fragment working relationships as different actors (national headquarters officials or state officials) respond to external

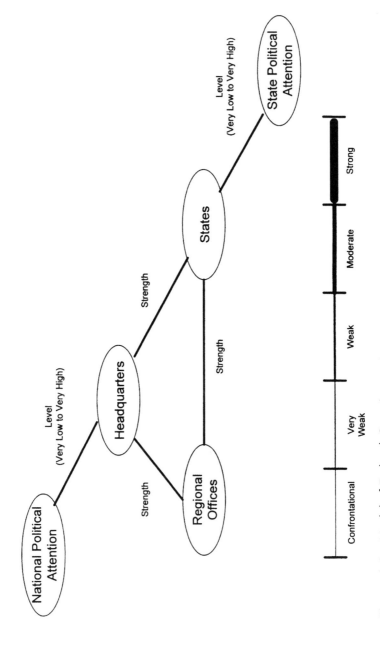

Figure 6-1 Model of Federal–State Interactions

demands. Both the drinking water and the surface mining programs operate in political environments that tend to frustrate cooperative interactions.

By the same token, when administrators and legislators are not very interested in a particular environmental program, the relationships between state and federal actors may grow stronger. This is not unlike the "picket fence" conceptualization of intergovernmental relationships, which suggests that federal, state, and local bureaucrats working in specialized programs develop close relationships because of the expertise that is required to operate the program.[1] Lack of state political attention to these specialized functional programs opens the window for increased federal–state staff activity, as federal and state actors become less concerned about the political examination of their programs. The radon program is a case in point.

However, while the "picket fence" model of federalism suggests that the bureaucrats tend to amass political power, this interaction model makes no such prediction. Indeed, it may be that state and federal officials in a specialized program like wellhead protection become allies simply to survive bureaucratic competition from more visible environmental programs.

In sum, the message of Figure 6-1 is simple: one must be sensitive to interactions that occur among all three actors involved in making a program work. To fail to consider the headquarters staff is to neglect the importance of national implementation constraints in the political arena, as well as to perhaps miss the physical and psychological distance that exists between headquarters personnel and other intergovernmental policy actors. To forget the regional staff—or worse yet, to lump them together with headquarters personnel—is to miss an opportunity to get a view from the middle of the process, from people who have the ear of both federal headquarters and the states. Finally, states as ultimate policy implementors react to federal headquarters program requirements, shifts in operation, and guidance. States interact with regional personnel in matters of oversight, grant administration, and program performance. States interact with and respond to the cues of both headquarters and regional personnel, so both units should be included in any systematic review of public programs.

An additional lesson from the model is that political arenas in which policy is implemented, which includes not only the national arena, but also the politics within each state, change the nature of the interactions that occur among each of the three units. Proximity to the Congress and the administration, combined with the distance from many states, works against strong federal headquarters and state interactions; regional offices are more likely to appreciate the nature of state political forces.

The challenge now becomes how to strengthen interactions, moving from weak to strong in the model, without decreasing legitimate oversight roles of the national actors. In other words, are there areas within federal–state relationships that could be improved while simultaneously increasing implementation performance? Is win–win possible—where working relationships AND policy outcomes are both improved? Before answering that question, it is appropriate to review the data from the study that suggests what state officials and regional staff want from working relationships.

REGIONAL AND STATE "WISH LISTS" FOR IMPROVING WORKING RELATIONSHIPS

Even in instances where working relationships are positive, state officials identify common elements of concern. Many of the same suggestions for implementation improvement emerge in all five programs, to greater and lesser degrees. Similarly, federal regional staff have common perceptions about program implementation and their own wish lists for change. Each of these viewpoints will be considered in turn.

What State Program Directors Want: Some Conclusions

Two general observations can be made from the interview and survey data of the program directors in these five environmental programs. First, cooperative intergovernmental relations seem, for the most part, to describe the relationship between EPA regional and state officials, signifying that state directors agree with the rowboat metaphor described in Chapter One, at least as it pertains to federal regional personnel. Most state officials agree that the EPA regional staff are supportive of their programs, and less than half of the respondents want to remove the national involvement in state programs.

However, if state environmental directors had a "wish list" for improving working relationships, several items would appear. As suggested in Table 6-1, state directors want more flexibility in program development, as well as more flexibility in tailoring federal funds to state priorities. A common trend identified in the implementation case studies presented in the previous chapters is for the EPA or OSM to increase demands for state performance under cooperative agreements without commensurate increases in federal funding. Thus, states resent what they believe to be an overly prescriptive federal orientation toward state programs, especially in light of stable or decreasing grant awards.

TABLE 6-1   Summary of Common Perceptions Among State Environmental
Program Staff

States perceive:
- need for national program and federal funding
- tendency of federal headquarters to micromanage programs, both in evaluation requirements and program requirements
- poor communication of national program goals and requirements
- support from EPA regional project officers
- little support of OSM field office staff
- little support from OSM or EPA headquarters staff

States want:
- adequately funded mandates (no increase in requirements without commensurate increase in funding)
- more flexibility in operating their programs, including funding flexibility
- less reliance on quantitative evaluation measures of state performance ("bean counting")
- clarification and anticipation of national goals
- headquarters staff availability
- increased understanding of on-the-ground enforcement
- ability to set own priorities for the program

On the other hand, state officials and regional project officers are wary of the effect that performance partnership grants may have on funding for their program. The move toward a block grant approach to funding state environmental programs puts low-priority programs in precarious positions. The ultimate in funding flexibility, then, is not necessarily what officials working in specific programs want. Flexibility in reporting requirements and flexibility in programmatic activities are desired by state personnel, but not when accompanied by the ability of top-level state administrators to make funding choices among programs.

Coupled with state concerns about the national EPA/OSM predilection to increasingly prescribe program requirements without commensurately increasing funding (or the possibility of increasing competition for funding within the state) is the concern that national goals for the programs are not clearly communicated. Poor goal clarification by EPA or OSM headquarters complicates state programs. When this happens, federal agencies become both *inflexible* regarding grant requirements and *vague* about the larger picture of desired policy outcomes.

As summarized by one state program director: ". . . the EPA stands on political quicksand, responding to the shifting mood in Washington.

Goals shift, and we wonder what the next 'priority du jour' will be. That wreaks havoc on our ability to plan a successful program."

Implicit in state directors' concerns about federal "bean counting" and inflexible requirements is a larger issue of trust. State directors feel adequately prepared to meet many of the implementation challenges inherent in their programs; however, they often feel that the institutions of the EPA or OSM have little or no regard for state programmatic innovation or similar dedication to the fundamental goals of the policy.

Another observation that can be made from the data is that state program directors tend to view EPA regional staff more positively than staff at EPA headquarters. One reason offered for a lower evaluation of headquarters relationships was a lack of communication. State directors are sometimes frustrated by what they view as inadequate communication from the EPA headquarters staff, but many remain in close communication with their regional counterparts. Several state directors expressed concern about EPA headquarters staff's inability or unwillingness to establish relatively simple communication connections with state personnel—even to the extent of returning phone calls. Many more state officials pointed to other communication problems, including untimely notification of major policy changes, short time periods for feedback and comments on pending changes, and insufficient attention paid by headquarters staff to state-level suggestions.

A second reason for lower evaluations of headquarters interactions by state officials was what they viewed as the inability of headquarters staff to appreciate the difficulties of achieving on-the-ground performance. State program directors note that federal headquarters staff seldom come to their offices to view their programs. This lack of first-hand information creates a kind of psychic distance between state and federal headquarters officials. From the perspectives of many state staff, this encourages rulemaking and other activities to occur without linkages to what is happening in communities where the program is being implemented.

This study suggests that while some of the national efforts to redirect environmental policy are aligned nicely with state officials' concerns, other initiatives are not. The movement toward increasing state flexibility and devolving environmental programs to the states correlates with state officials' concerns about reporting requirements. States being seen as "customers" of the federal agencies and recent efforts to improve these federal–state relationships as part of the National Performance Review seem warranted. The recent Reg 8 directive of the OSM to focus on state-specific results rather than nationally derived performance requirements also appears to be headed in the right direction, as does the National Environmental Performance Partnership system developed by the State/EPA Capacity Steering Committee.

Performance partnership grants or increasing the involvement of local governments or national associations, on the other hand, may not improve federal–state relationships, especially if state program officials feel that their program's funding is vulnerable. And no initiative can replace the simple but effective efforts of state and federal officials to keep in contact and to appreciate the conditions under which each one operates.

What Regional Officials Want: Some Conclusions

Chapter Five described in detail what the staff operating environmental programs in EPA regional or OSM field offices want to happen to facilitate policy implementation and improve working relationships. A brief summary appears in Table 6-2.

TABLE 6-2 Summary of Common Perceptions Among Federal Regional Environmental Program Staff

EPA Regional and OSM Field Office staff perceive:
- less effective federal programs than state programs
- political constraints on state program directors
- need for cooperative relationships between regions and states
- political constraints on headquarters staff
- capable state staff
- inadequate funding

EPA Regional and OSM Field Office staff want:
- recognition of their expertise by headquarters
- consistent messages about program requirements from headquarters staff
- greater input into policy decisions
- greater political support for their program
- an appreciation by headquarters staff of their perspective

Regional and field office personnel generally believe they are in that most maligned of positions: between a "rock and a hard place." Agency regional staff feel they have tough job assignments. Their burden is guaranteeing programmatic performance—but they often shoulder the responsibility for on-the-ground results with inadequate funding and lack of perceived empathy from the national office, and without a strong political base of support for their work from state or national actors.

A second observation is a corollary to the first one. That is, given the difficulty of their tasks, regional staff commonly express the desire for their headquarters colleagues to spend some time with them, to personally talk to state officials, to encounter the challenges of being the federal "conduit" for policy implementation. Many regional staff in these programs often feel they are the "Rodney Dangerfields" of federal–state working relationships—they get no respect from headquarters staff or from state officials. To return to Miles' Law, regional staff often express the desire that headquarters personnel come and sit where they do for some time.

This perception leads to a surprising finding reported in Chapter Five. That is, regional personnel have less confidence in their own programs than they do in the state programs. Moreover, they share a related belief with state officials that the national program is less effective than is the state program. Certainly, this observation challenges the "we versus them" problem so frequently pointed to in studies of regulatory federalism. In these cases, the "we" is as likely to comprise federal regional and state personnel as it is to comprise federal regional and federal headquarters personnel.

Implicit in these findings is the rather sad conclusion that many regional staff members are discouraged with their job assignments. While looking at agency morale was not the purpose of this study, it is troubling that state officials and regional personnel share rather dismal views of the operation of the national program. It may also be that headquarters personnel feel equally dejected. However, interview and survey comments suggest the need for developing greater levels of support for regional personnel.

What regional staff put on their "wish list" for improved working relationships and policy implementation (besides increased funding) are a desire to be recognized by headquarters staff for their substantive expertise, to be more a part of the front end of the implementation process, and to increase the awareness of headquarters staff of on-the-ground implementation obstacles. In short, regional staff seek many of the same things state officials do: recognition for the unique constraints on their work, the opportunity for more input in policy decisions, higher levels of trust on the part of headquarters staff, and more consistency in work requirements. State staff and federal regional staff wish lists, then, contain several suggestions about how to move to more cooperative and positive interactions. To return to the trip metaphor describing policy implementation and working relationships in Chapter One, travelers in the same car are happier when everyone agrees on the route, gets to participate in decisions about the rate of travel, and has at least some say in the conditions inside the car during the trip (use of the air conditioning, music, etc.).

If the travelers represent the typical players involved in the implementation of environmental policy, the ideal situation is to have strong relationships existing among federal regional, federal headquarters, and state personnel. The way to achieve solid relationships may be to address at least some of the wishes of federal regional and state officials. Moreover, many of the actions wished for by federal regional and state staff on these wish lists can be translated nicely into the working relationship typology developed in Chapter One. The next section revisits the typology and categorizes the five environmental programs.

REVISITING THE WORKING RELATIONSHIP TYPOLOGY

Chapter One presented a way of characterizing federal–state working relationships based on two dimensions: levels of trust and levels of involvement. The typology is reproduced here as Figure 6-2. This time, however, the five programs are categorized based upon the primary research and the results reported in Chapters Two, Three, and Four.

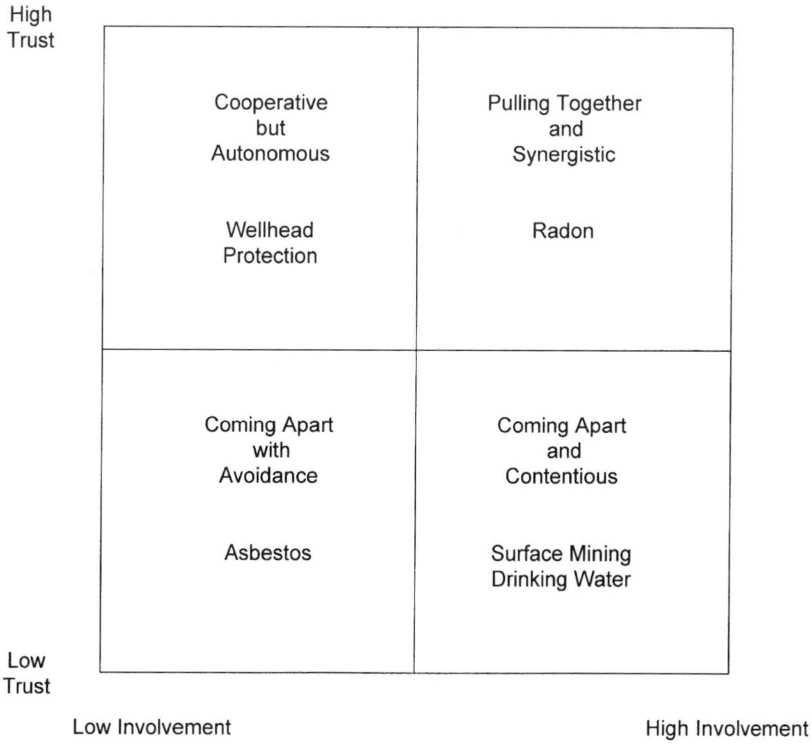

High
Trust

Cooperative but Autonomous	Pulling Together and Synergistic
Wellhead Protection	Radon
Coming Apart with Avoidance	Coming Apart and Contentious
Asbestos	Surface Mining Drinking Water

Low
Trust

Low Involvement   High Involvement

Figure 6-2 A Typology of Federal and State Relationships Revisited

As shown in Figure 6-2, only one of the five programs reviewed, the radon program, is "pulling together" and synergistic, with relatively higher levels of appropriate involvement and mutual trust when compared to the other programs. As described in Chapter Three and Chapter Five, state radon officials are more likely to perceive that the federal radon program is effective than are state officials in other programs. Similarly, intergovernmental harmony exists among federal regional radon and state radon staff due in part to the positive attitudes each of these participants brings to the table. In part, this harmony represents a strategic decision on the part of the EPA staff and state officials to protect a vulnerable program. Still, working relationships in the radon program, while not perfect, appear to be more positive and collegial than in any other program.

Federal and state working relationships in the wellhead protection program are also cooperative, but not synergistic and "pulling together." While wellhead protection staff from both federal and state agencies exhibit mutual trust, they lack opportunities for sufficient levels of involvement due primarily to funding constraints. Thus, state officials operating wellhead programs may seek, but cannot access, the same levels of support and interaction with their federal counterparts as are found in the radon program. Similarly, federal regional wellhead protection staff may find their own resources too limited to be effective change agents in states.

The drinking water program and the surface coal mining program are both characterized as "coming apart." However, these programs are located in the same box for slightly different reasons. State drinking water officials mistrust the federal EPA headquarters staff's ability to set appropriate standards for drinking water contaminants, establish monitoring programs or focus on the most serious risks to public health. Moreover, they perceive that the EPA is beholden to attentive congressional overseers and not necessarily attentive to them. In the minds of state drinking water officials, then, the EPA's drinking water program is ineffective as suggested by a meager two percent of the state staff who agree that the EPA runs a successful program (See Table 5-4).

State coal mining officials also mistrust their federal counterparts, but this time, the mistrust is directed toward the OSM field office staff more than the OSM headquarters personnel. Here, the primary obstacle defeating positive working relationships is the oversight posture assumed by OSM inspection and enforcement personnel toward state inspectors. As data from Chapter Four suggest, state officials are weary of what they perceive to be micromanagement of their programs, or being called to the carpet for minor infractions in the program operations. On the other hand, many OSM field staff believe that they must closely supervise the state program in order to achieve on-the-ground results, largely because of the inordinate political influence wielded by the coal industry.

Finally, federal and state working relationships in the asbestos program are also characterized as "coming apart." In this case, however, federal and state officials interact infrequently. Thus, instead of the contention which is evident in the drinking water and coal mining programs (and is the product of high levels of federal involvement), state asbestos programs operate with limited visibility and virtual anonymity. Federal regional asbestos operations are being scaled back and redefined—the inspection staff has been reduced in nearly every EPA regional office. Meanwhile, state officials run a program that is loved by no one and is constantly subject to ridicule for forcing schools into unneeded and even dangerous expenditures.

The typology seems to be useful. By using the dimensions of mutual trust and levels of involvement, the typology was able to characterize the five environmental programs. The message regarding working relationships from this study is that synergistic, "pulling together" relationships are rare and exist only when mutual trust and respect is coupled with high levels of the right kind of federal involvement in state programs. The next section offers suggestions for moving from one of the three sub-optimal categories into working relationships that pull together.

SUGGESTIONS FOR GETTING TO "PULLING TOGETHER" RELATIONSHIPS

Figure 6-3 offers tools for policy makers and program officials to work cooperatively. In other words, ways in which participants start to "pull together." Depending on where the program is located in the typology, participants need to increase levels of trust, levels of the right kind of involvement, or both.

Suggestions for increasing involvement include encouraging personal contacts, opening and using multiple communication channels, regularly sharing information and new knowledge, promoting organizational and interagency learning, communicating in a timely manner with opportunities for all participants to have feedback, and keeping participants in the loop.

Some of these suggestions recognize that regional offices of federal bureaucracies are more than just mouthpieces for headquarters' initiatives. Some amount of translation and interpretation occurs within the message intraagency before it is delivered to state implementors. Strategic relationships develop and are maintained between federal regional staff and state program officials. For example, it is not uncommon for regional staff to seek the opinions of state officials about new

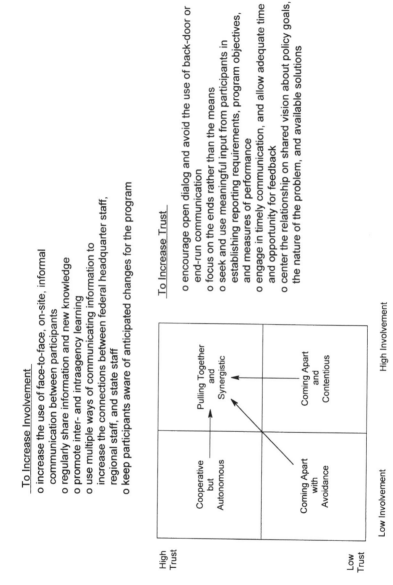

To Increase Involvement

o increase the use of face-to-face, on-site, informal communication between participants

o regularly share information and new knowledge

o promote inter- and intraagency learning

o use multiple ways of communicating information to increase the connections between federal headquarter staff, regional staff, and state staff

o keep participants aware of anticipated changes for the program

To Increase Trust

o encourage open dialog and avoid the use of back-door or end-run communication

o focus on the ends rather than the means

o seek and use meaningful input from participants in establishing reporting requirements, program objectives, and measures of performance

o engage in timely communication, and allow adequate time and opportunity for feedback

o center the relationship on shared vision about policy goals, the nature of the problem, and available solutions

High Trust

Cooperative but Autonomous

Pulling Together and Synergistic

Coming Apart with Avoidance

Coming Apart and Contentious

Low Trust

Low Involvement

High Involvement

Figure 6-3 Getting to Relationships That "Pull Together"

policy initiatives, public information tools, or similar outputs from agency headquarters and to include those state comments with their own.

Meanwhile, EPA or OSM headquarters staff are also communicating with state officials. Sometimes communication is two-way and direct, such as when state officials are invited by headquarters staff to comment during a rule-making procedure. State officials are also contacted to participate in program reviews, appear before congressional oversight committees, or to help develop new regulations. More often, the communication is one-way and indirect, with headquarters alerting regional offices of new requirements and the regional offices, in turn, passing that information on to the states.

When this happens, national-level implementors lose the opportunity for meaningful feedback. Richard Stillman views feedback processes as an integral part of maximizing bureaucratic outputs.[2] Feedback helps participants get involved in assessing the program. Accurate assessment, in turn, maximizes the outputs of agencies when it is immediate, supportive, and clear, and when it contains adequate information for program improvement.[3]

Clearer understanding of the different perspectives of state, regional, and headquarters implementors is more likely when participants can meet in person. Comments from both state and regional staff often pointed to the need to have their vantage point understood by other participants—not necessarily to have other participants adopt that position, but more to understand why people feel the way they do about a particular element of the program.

Increasing trust is not easily accomplished, if only because of the oversight role orientations and responsibilities of federal headquarters and regional staff. Suggestions for increasing levels of trust within federal–state working relationships include encouraging open dialog and avoiding the use of back-door or end-run communication tactics; focusing on the ends and not the means; establishing mechanisms for meaningful input by all participants; centering the relationship on shared visions about policy goals, problem dimensions, and available solutions; and increasing the connections within the tripartite relationship.

Many of these suggestions focus on the inherent strengths of intergovernmental relationships. For example, participants typically agree on the wisdom of the policy goal, which is, after all, the hoped-for "ends" of public policy. To the extent that micromanaging can be avoided on the part of the federal government overseers while all participants focus on the desired future state, trust can be increased. Similarly, state officials, in turn, may need to increase their receptiveness to the legitimate national interests in running effective on-the-ground environmental programs.

CONCLUDING THOUGHTS ABOUT ENVIRONMENTAL POLICY IMPLEMENTATION

The conceptual framework in Chapter One suggested that extrinsic and intrinsic factors affect the ability of state agencies to implement public policy. Extrinsic factors—political arrangements, role orientations of the federal oversight agency, the nature of the problem, resource allocation, statutory and regulatory language, judicial interpretations, and the demand for change—facilitated or hindered state implementation performance in varying degrees in all five programs reviewed. Intrinsic factors such as working relationships, agency capacity, and the nature of the target group in the state were equally as important.

Take, for example, political arrangements. In the asbestos program, the political fallout from school districts removing asbestos (rather than managing it in place) has, in part, resulted in reduced federal funding for asbestos, angry and litigious publics, and little oversight of state programs by EPA regional staff. For the surface mining program, political histories of state and federal conflicts, combined with political pressure from coal companies at the state level, explain more of the implementation story than lack of available state staff or funding.

On the other hand, state politicians are simply not very interested in funding the wellhead protection or radon programs. Radon in homes is an individual concern; few people care about mitigating existing housing stock. Radon in schools, on the other hand, may become the same political hot potato as asbestos, and the warning by school districts not to "make the same mistake with radon as was made with asbestos" does not go unheeded.

Looking at the nature of the environmental problem is also useful. Delineation of wellhead protection areas, for example, requires sophisticated methodologies that may not be readily available in many local communities. Promulgating "safe" levels of drinking water contaminants presents a regulatory nightmare for the EPA; understanding whether reclamation is successful or groundwater can be recharged may take decades in western states, where coal mining operations remove gigantic amounts of soil.

Lack of resources hampers the development of some state programs. Wellhead protection programs operate in most states with a handful of people; some states devote less than one full-time equivalent personnel to implementing the program. Adequate funding in the much larger drinking water program is less a problem at the state level than it is for public water suppliers in small communities.

Lack of agency capacity, in terms of available state staff in the program, may be partially overcome by the enthusiasm and dedication of policy champions. The radon program, while minuscule in terms of staff in many states, operated more effectively than what might be anticipated because of the motivation of one or two key people.

Intergovernmental relationships are important in all of the programs and have occupied much of the space in this book. If anything, reviewing five different programs has illustrated the need for more scholarly attention to be paid to this component of environmental policy implementation, especially to address the nature of working relationships, levels of trust, and interactions among participants.

It is also important to look at the relationships that exist between state and local staff responsible for implementation results. Increasingly, local governments are involved in environmental programs, as is evident in the drinking water, wellhead protection, radon, and asbestos programs.

The 1986 amendments to the Safe Drinking Water Act, which required the promulgation of national standards for eighty-three new contaminants, not only impeded the implementation of the current program but threw the agency into turmoil and the states into a fervor. Political revolts led by the battle cry of "unfunded mandates" were undertaken by local governments, which viewed the costs associated with compliance to be enormous, even overwhelming, for small public water suppliers. Clearly, statutory language is affecting the implementation of the drinking water program.

Role orientations of agency staff are important, as illustrated especially in the coal mining program. The different approaches to citing violations taken by OSM field office personnel and many state inspectors contributes to the more confrontational state–federal working relationship.

Finally, although the focus of this study was not to judge whether or not programs were successful, it does appear that agency outputs are different from policy outcomes. Activities undertaken by state agencies may or may not result in the achievement of desired policy goals. As mentioned earlier in the chapter, a number of state and regional staff members commented that some of the program requirements were "make-work" activities, which detracted from the ultimate goal of making the living environment a safer place. By the same token, policy outcomes are happening without the direct intervention of implementors—such as instances where schools are acting to eliminate asbestos exposures.

In sum, the implementation factors presented in the framework in Chapter One seem to make sense, at least when looking at these environmental programs. More study of the perceptions of intergovernmental actors involved in environmental policy implementation is needed. Studies of policy implementation that fail to consider federal–state interactions paint too simple a picture of what is a very complex web of relationships. Interactions between people matter; mutual respect is important. There is little evidence that changing orientations at the top of the intergovernmental chain produce more effective approaches in state implementation, nor is there evidence that state directors desire OSM- or EPA-dictated priorities. State program directors seem willing to pursue their own goals for the program, as expressed by one director:

"We can't wait for the EPA or the Office of Management and Budget (OMB) to decide what to do and how to do it. I've got high levels [of radon] in my state and I'm going to do what I can with the resources I have."

This study is only a beginning. Additional regulatory and nonregulatory programs should be studied in order to be more confident that the data in this study reflect a common orientation of state directors and regional EPA staff. Additionally, systematic study of national office staff is needed to better understand federal perceptions of state programs and individual role orientations.

Finally, demands for integration of environmental programs and for ecosystem management make understanding working relationships even more crucial. Strategies for coping with changes in agency culture, role orientations, and new organizational commitments will be paramount as we enter a new environmental decade. Agencies are in the midst of nonincremental changes in implementing environmental programs. The challenge is to continue to walk the vision of environmental and public health protection with other participants and stakeholders in environmental programs, with increased sensitivity to the important role that each participant plays in the implementation story.

NOTES TO CHAPTER 6

1. For a discussion of various models of federalism, see David C. Nice and Patricia Fredericksen, *The Politics of Intergovernmental Relations*, 2nd ed. (Chicago, Ill.: Nelson-Hall, 1995), pp. 4–15.

2. Richard J. Stillman, *The American Bureaucracy: The Core of Modern Government*, 2nd ed. (Chicago, Ill.: Nelson-Hall, 1996), p. 269.

3. Stillman, *American Bureaucracy*, p. 269.

Appendix

Research for this project was conducted in the summer of 1995, although in some instances throughout the book previous research conducted in 1990, 1993, and 1994 has been included where appropriate.

In 1995, 285 surveys were sent to state officials identified by the EPA as having primary responsibility for implementing the asbestos, drinking water, lead, radon, and wellhead protection programs, and by the OSM as having primary responsibility for implementing the surface mining program. A follow-up mailing was initiated to increase response rates in July and August. The 230 surveys returned gave an overall response rate of 80 percent. While state officials in the lead abatement program were surveyed, and the results are part of the 230 responses reported, the program was not reviewed as part of a book chapter due to space and time constraints.

Additionally, federal personnel in EPA regional and OSM field offices were surveyed during the same time. I sent 101 surveys to people identified as project officers in the various programs or, by using the mailing lists, to EPA branch chiefs in charge of the programs. The OSM phone book was used to send surveys to the persons with oversight responsibility (inspection and enforcement). The response rate for federal regional personnel was 62 percent.

After the surveys were sent, eighty-five telephone interviews were conducted with state and federal officials in the five environmental programs.

Index